Praise for *With Chatwin*

"A fresh, vivid portrait . . . full of subtle, revealing insights."
  —Edmund White, *Times Literary Supplement*

"If you want the authentic flavor of the man, you could not do better than read this excellent, absorbing, affectionate, unillusioned, vivid, and affecting memoir."
  —Craig Raine, *Financial Times*

"*With Chatwin* is [Clapp's] adoring memoir of this mercurial figure. . . . She accurately describes Chatwin's style as 'both spare and flamboyant,' with a kind of absent, icy brilliance reminiscent of his admired Rimbaud."
  —William Ferguson, *The New York Times Book Review*

"Entertaining. . . . *With Chatwin* lays out some of the quirks, vivacities and enthusiasms that made up Chatwin's charisma. . . . [Clapp] provides some deft analysis of how his books play off his various obsessions. . . . *With Chatwin* testifies to personality as a work of art, and to the surprising tenacity of a 'vivid presence.'"
  —*The Washington Post Book World*

"A remarkably fair-minded account of Chatwin's life. . . . Clapp has struck just the right note, marrying memoir, biography, and literary criticism. . . . She fleshes out the inner world of this secretive, curiously outward-looking man."
  —Thomas Curwen, *Los Angeles Times*

"Clapp paints an indelible portrait of a writer who approached life as performance art. . . . Spilling over with life, Clapp's Chatwin seems a man destined to meet the rigors of old age with a bark of anarchic laughter."

    —*People*

"Clapp describes Chatwin at the height of his good looks . . . and in his skeletal last months. She is indulgent to his preciousness, his deceptions, the purple passages that veined his character; is illuminating on the evolution of his books; and bristles with reticent affection for her wayward subject. . . . I am glad to have read Susannah Clapp's . . . solid and endearing portrait."

    —*Bookforum*

"A beautiful memoir."

    —Ian Buruma, *The Spectator*

"An elegant and subtle memoir."

    —Adam Begley, *The New York Observer*

"Clapp . . . offers a delightful remembrance of the celebrated travel writer and novelist, drawing on her own experiences and on those of his closest friends. . . . A must-read for all his fans."

    —*Kirkus Reviews*

"Clapp examines all six [of Chatwin's books] thoroughly, with a creative insight nourished by having known Chatwin personally. . . . What emerges is 'Bruce being brilliant and Bruce being batty'—and that makes for wonderful reading."

    —*Library Journal*

PENGUIN BOOKS

WITH CHATWIN

Susannah Clapp worked as an editor and reader at Jonathan Cape. She helped found the *London Review of Books*, where she was assistant editor for several years, and is currently theater critic for BBC Radio 3's *Nightwaves*. She lives in London.

WITH CHATWIN

Portrait of a Writer

SUSANNAH CLAPP

PENGUIN BOOKS

PENGUIN BOOKS
Published by the Penguin Group
Penguin Putnam Inc., 375 Hudson Street,
New York, New York 10014, U.S.A.
Penguin Books Ltd, 27 Wrights Lane,
London W8 5TZ, England
Penguin Books Australia Ltd, Ringwood,
Victoria, Australia
Penguin Books Canada Ltd, 10 Alcorn Avenue,
Toronto, Ontario, Canada M4V 3B2
Penguin Books (N.Z.) Ltd, 182–190 Wairau Road,
Auckland 10, New Zealand
Penguin India, 210 Chiranjiv Tower, 43 Nehru Place,
New Delhi 11009, India

Penguin Books Ltd, Registered Offices:
Harmondsworth, Middlesex, England

First published in Great Britain by Jonathan Cape, 1997
First published in the United States of America
by Alfred A. Knopf, Inc. 1997
Reprinted by arrangement with Alfred A. Knopf, Inc.
Published in Penguin Books 1999

10   9   8   7   6   5   4   3   2

Copyright © Susannah Clapp, 1997
All rights reserved

Owing to limitations of space, all acknowledgments for permission
to reprint previously published material may be found on page 241.

ISBN 0-679041033-3 (hc.)
ISBN 0 14 02.7645 9   (pbk.)
LC 97–73722

Printed in the United States of America
Set in Bembo
Designed by Misha Beletsky

for my mother, Marion King

CONTENTS

PREFACE   ix

❧ 1 CHATWINESQUE   3

❧ 2 EDITING *IN PATAGONIA*   25

❧ 3 SCHOOL   50

❧ 4 ART WORLD   73

❧ 5 OBJECTS   89

❧ 6 EDINBURGH   114

❧ 7 EXOTICA   136

❧ 8 ON THE MAGAZINE   164

❧ 9 TWINS   179

❧ 10 NOMADS   197

❧ 11 THE END   216

ACKNOWLEDGMENTS   239

PREFACE

Bruce Chatwin was a traveller, a teller of tales and a connoisseur of the extraordinary. He was also one of those few writers who are acclaimed before they are dead. When he died in January 1989, Chatwin was forty-eight and had completed six books. The first of these, *In Patagonia*, had made him known; the fourth, *The Songlines*, had turned him into a best-seller. His writing had been the subject of Ph.D.'s, and been turned into a comic strip called "Swamp Thing." And it had given rise to an adjective: at about the time that the term "Thatcherite" entered the English language, so did the word "Chatwinesque."

People were drawn to Chatwin because of what he was as well as what he wrote. He was fêted for his looks as well as his books, for his talk as well as his prose—though there were always those who thought him insufficiently frowning to be an author. He was famous for being a vivid presence. And he was famous for being absent: for being out of the country, out of his books. In time, he also became famous for being famous. Some readers wanted to be him. An Oxford therapist reports that several of her patients have cited his work as a source of support. After writing an obituary of his friend, the actor Peter Eyre was besieged by letters and telephone calls from a Chatwin admirer who proclaimed himself to have come hot-foot from shooting wolves in Iraq. And on

the island of Spetses in the Peloponnese a man calling himself Bruce Chatwin found that his glamour was an efficient
bait for a large number of young women. Among them was
a Dutch girl, who went back to Holland after her spell of
summer love. There she saw in a newspaper that the author
of *The Songlines* was signing copies of his books nearby and
went to greet her old flame. The real Bruce was then challenged—taxed with not being himself.

The traveller was in turn an art expert, an archaeologist
and a journalist, an enthusiast for objects and an abandoner
of them. It was one of Chatwin's charms to be several apparently contradictory things and to reconcile them in his
books. He was a lover of the austere who had a flamboyant
manner, a collector who railed against the idea of owning
works of art, a man who fell for nobs and stars and who always voted Labour, a strider in shorts and a lounger in a silk
dressing-gown. He was a shrewd observer and a sweet friend.

I first met Bruce Chatwin in 1976 when he was about to
become an author. This memoir sets out to evoke the occasions of his life, to offer an interpretation of his books, and to
say something about what it was to work with him as an editor, a point of view which isn't often given. My title refers
to the title of Bruce's first book, *In Patagonia*, and to the helping hand that friends of the Victorian explorers used to claim
they had provided.

WITH CHATWIN

I

CHATWINESQUE

If Bruce Chatwin had been portly, myopic and mouse-haired his life and reputation would have been quite different. Descriptions of his looks creep into discussions of his work; his profusely illustrated obituaries are studded with dazzled references to his appearance. Some of these references are neutral and conventional enough—"fairheaded, handsome"—though tinged with the notion that it's a feat for a man to hold a pen and not look hideous. Others are charged with a suggestion of destiny: "patrician good looks" implies more than an accidentally happy arrangement of features, though it can be decoded to mean simply "tall and blond"; "abnormal good looks" hints at the extraterrestrial.

Chatwin was much photographed: sunny and round-cheeked as a small boy; spruce and lanky at Sotheby's. Lord Snowdon—who was taking pictures for the *Sunday Times* Magazine when Chatwin was writing for it—showed the traveller's head half-shadowed, slightly furrowed, with thick-soled walking-boots slung round his neck by their laces; Jane Bown's picture shows a gentler, more serene man in an open-necked shirt. One photographer hung Chatwin's illuminated, drawn face on a background of black: it was this photograph that was used when the *Independent on Sunday* constructed what, for all its disclaimers, managed to look like a rogues' gallery of people in the Arts who had died from

AIDS—and it made Chatwin look like Mephistopheles. In one of the pictures taken by his friend the designer and photographer David King, he is open-faced and widely smiling. As portrayed by Howard Hodgkin, Chatwin described himself as "an acid green smear."

He often looked like someone or something else. He looked like the young Christopher Isherwood, with his wide forehead, squared jaw and rather bulging eyes. And he looked German: as a teenager travelling through France, he had to protest his Englishness in old Resistance restaurants before he could be served; to one Jewish woman friend he was "the beautiful goy." One early friend thought he looked like a curate; Howard Hodgkin, who met him around the same time, when Chatwin was about twenty, thought he "looked like something rather different: very young, very beautiful, not terribly sexy-looking. He looked like the Captain of the First XI rather than a curate—the quintessential blond public schoolboy who had reached puberty but didn't know anything about anything." James Lees-Milne has remarked that he had "seldom met a human being who exudes so much sex appeal with so comparatively little niceness." Friends think that Bruce would have been rather pleased by this remark.

Nearly everyone mentions his eyes. They were very blue and they sparkled. To some, lassoed by a compulsive Chatwin story, they were the glittering eyes of the Ancient Mariner; to others, they were the eyes of someone who had "the eye," who would always know a fake; one acquaintance, Chatwin recorded in a notebook, thought them "the MAD MAD eyes of a nineteenth-century explorer." For many people they are the emblem of a handsomeness which they found difficult to describe. The art dealer John Kasmin considered him as a young man "actually impossibly good-looking. You were almost offended by his looks." The eyes, and the talk, held people, so that they didn't notice the awkward gait. It was difficult to think of him as other than young. Until he fell ill, in his mid-forties, Chatwin never looked older than thirty-five—although, sitting close to him at tea over a little Fortnum and Mason table, one acquaintance suddenly saw lots of small wrinkles crawling over his face under his smile, and thought of Dorian Gray. Chatwin, who rarely passed a shop window without checking his reflection and groomed himself in the middle of his roughest trips, took the sort of pleasure in his appearance which generates a sense of well-being. "I thought," says Gabriele Annan, a fellow guest in Greece, "that he was interested in being beautiful." Because he preened? "No. Because he beamed."

He was particular about his clothes; he liked outfits. For travelling there were khaki shorts, which his friends often referred to as "Bruce's little shorts," not so much because they were skimpy as because they were boyishly over-appropriate. And there was a khaki safari shirt with epaulettes and button-down pockets: a picture taken on a trip to Afghanistan shows a young Chatwin, looking mischievous, kitted out in khaki gear, with ankle-length walking-boots and neatly turned-over fawn socks. This was an ensemble which took him into Africa and over the Welsh hills—and which amused grand friends in India with its whiff of the Raj. What took him through Sotheby's were dark suits, silk ties and red-and-white spotted handkerchiefs. He was hardly an unconventional dresser as an art expert: when he took to jeans in the Sixties it was a surprise to some of his Sotheby's acquaintances. On holiday in Eastern Europe Chatwin and his wife Elizabeth made a special trip across the border into Vienna to buy themselves a pair of loden coats: Bruce's capacious dark green garment swirled with the effect of a cape—he was more than once falsely accused of sporting a poncho. In the West of England the couple distinguished themselves as the only two practical people among the friends who turned up to help Howard Hodgkin and his wife convert an old mill and barn: while London ladies slipped off their high heels and poked at tiny bits of plaster, Bruce and Elizabeth bustled in trim white overalls.

There were special, soft, toffee-coloured boots: "You *could* get some decent boots, Redders," Chatwin advised his friend, the explorer Redmond O'Hanlon: "The Russell Moccasin Company. Just say you're a friend of mine." And there was a frameless haversack in dark brown calfskin, custom-made by a saddler in Cirencester, with each pocket carefully devised to house a particular item: "Jean-Louis Barrault had this pack designed just for me," he is alleged to have told a friend. For travelling in the Black Mountains it contained a moleskin notebook, a Mont Blanc pen, Aylmer Maude's translation of *War and Peace,* Strindberg's *By the Open Sea* and a fine pair of binoculars ("Werner Herzog gave them to me," he told O'Hanlon); for travelling abroad Bruce claimed he tucked in a tin of sardines and a half bottle of Krug, which he would consume sitting in a stream if something went wrong.

Blue was his colour. He liked faded denim blue and the dark blue of Breton sweaters: for the cosmopolitan novelist Sybille Bedford, a Chatwin admirer, these are the blues of abroad—she thinks, in a way that would have appealed to Bruce, of his Brooks Brothers shirts as being like the colour of the shirts of Calais railway porters or American workmen. But they were also the blue of his eyes and the ubiquitous blues of the Sixties. In Paris in 1961 his pale grey suit sported a powder-blue lining. At the *Sunday Times* a few years later, David King recalls a different kingfisher item: when Bruce with his yellow hair and blue eyes appeared in an emerald jacket, "it was as if the blue and yellow made the green."

Bruce in person, like a figure observed by Bruce Chatwin, was emphatic and sharply defined. He didn't often stay still—

in the same room, in the same city, in the same country—
and it is natural to think of him in motion: gesticulating,
shouting with laughter, pacing about. His swiftness and
dervish-like animation gave him the effect of gracefulness,
though this was won against the odds: when he came to a
halt, he was physically tense, planting himself on a chair, with
his hands pressed on his splayed knees, as if sitting an examination of his own devising; advised on one occasion to do
relaxation exercises, he was too physically unco-ordinated to
bring them off.

It is also natural to think of Bruce talking: he nearly always
was. He was known to one circle of acquaintances as "Chat-
terbox" and to another as "Chatty Corner." He is remembered, bidden for lunch in Southern Spain, heading up the
path at half-past eleven, already speaking, with no one else in
sight. He is remembered striding up a Welsh hill, telling stories in different voices, as his companions wheezed behind
him. Anyone who put him up or who stayed with him was
likely to be greeted first thing in the morning with Bruce
wanting to perch on the bed and unburden himself of an
anecdote or piece of news. Even the least taciturn friend was
liable to be left trailing verbally: "I have," concedes George
Melly, "to acknowledge a master."

In his life and in his books Bruce was a mimic. His conversation was full of imitations: of a publisher in mid-hype,
of an art dealer in mid-salivation, of the extremely old
French art dealer who insisted on taking Chatwin to an ex-
orbitantly expensive restaurant, brushing aside his guest's
demurrals by explaining: "Ah well, you know, at my age, art I
can't see any more, I've gone blind, and sex is beyond the
question. There's nothing left but the pleasures of the table."
He had fiery dramatic monologues: one featured his horror
of pop-up books, then a speciality of his publisher. He had
musing explanations which unwound through an evening,

such as the one he spent in his room in Albany, the celebrated Piccadilly apartment house, with the novelist Shirley Hazzard: "in the beautiful late light he talked about the structure of Sanskrit, and how it produces its effects by a sort of suggestion, like an aura." And he had plausible fictions, tales which were taken as gospel by some listeners, as jokes by others, and which left many with the sense that they had when reading his books, of being dangled between fact and fiction. He convinced one friend that he had been the model for the rubicund baby on a tin of Glaxo infant food. He spent a large part of a dinner party persuading his companions that one of his wife's relatives had provided the model for Pinkerton, the inconstant lieutenant in Puccini's *Madam Butterfly*.

He also had favourite riffs, subjects to which he returned over long periods, expanding, elaborating and amending his account. One of these concerned the colour red. Why was red the colour of revolution? Did it gain its significance from blood, or from fire? What was the meaning of the colour in the Church? Why did one culture in the South Seas abstain from using it? He came back from Russia declaring that all Russians hated the colour; years later he was still tucking new bits of information into his conjectures. When he met Hannah Rothschild in Paris, at dinner with Rudolf Nureyev, he almost immediately treated her to an exposition of his theories about the colour, asked her what she was up to in the city, and announced that he had a plan for the following morning: "I'll pick you up at your hotel at six o'clock." He turned up at seven—"Right, we're going to the métro"—and throughout the half-hour journey to their stop, which turned out to be the Flea Market, he didn't draw breath. On the way to the Underground, a beggar wrapped in a red blanket set him talking. He spoke about the political use and the symbolic importance of red; he brought in Fascists and Marxists and bullfighters, Uruguayan butchers, Garibaldi and

the Red Shirts, and the *bonnet rouge* of the French Revolution;
when they reached the Flea Market, he was sparked off again
by the flashes of red from disparate objects on the stalls—the
crimson in a Buddhist scarf, the scarlet of a Communist
badge.

Like many of his turns, Bruce's rap on red, delivered with
minor variations to a variety of listeners, was graphic, excit-
ing to hear and not fully graspable. Although Bruce presented it as a thesis, it didn't develop logically or reach a
conclusion: it was a series of observations, a commentary
which made the unexpected connections of the kind he
liked. It was also a performance. Bruce was a talker as well as
a writer: for some people, being a talker was his main point.
Salman Rushdie admires his work but thinks that Bruce was
not in his books "the whole person he was when you met
him," that there was a holding back of emotion, a holding
back which had to do with his secrets. And he thinks it odd,
since being with Bruce meant laughing a lot, that he never
wrote a really funny book. Martin Amis had developed a
craggy resistance to Chatwin before he met him. He had read
his account of being caught in the Dahomean coup and responded disbelievingly to its blasé tone—in which atrocities
are spoken of in the accents of Noël Coward—and he had
heard too many tales of Chatwin's loquacious eccentricities.
When he saw a sleeping-bag the traveller had left behind
him, "a very dinky little sleeping-bag with a Club Class
sticker," he decided: "That just about sums him up." But
when he met him he melted. It was an evening spent with
Bruce at his most delightful, talking about Romantic poetry
(which may also have been Bruce at his most imaginative,
since his gaps in English literature were legion), which caused
Amis's scepticism to crack. "He did," Amis said, more than
six years after Chatwin's death, "remind you how intense the
pleasures of conversation can be."

Much of this conversation can't be recaptured. "He talked for ages," says one publishing acquaintance. "It was all of it brilliant, and I can't remember a word of it." Which is often the fate of brilliant talkers. But much of it was put into print. Bruce—whose speech scrolled out of his mouth with all its verbs in the right place—rehearsed, trimmed and elaborated in conversation the stories that went into his books. In doing so he was at his most bewitching and most vulnerable. Fastidious about selecting his words, he was profligate in dispensing them: his stories came spilling out to everyone—and to some people more than once. When he was in full flood, it was like being in the room with CinemaScope.

As to when or how he'd arrive in a room, there was very often an element of uncertainty. He liked to turn up, and was a skilful manager of remarkable entrances and surprise appearances. Some of his arrivals had the effect of parachute drops or miraculous jettings-in. He showed up, often without warning and with no apparent flurry of arrangements—like a child running away from home. The literary agent Hilary Rubinstein bumped into him at a cocktail party in Katmandu: they made a plan to have supper, but by the time the appointed hour arrived Chatwin had left.

In Gloucestershire David King and the painter Judy Groves went for a walk with Chatwin near his house. Chatwin led the way, striding in shorts "like a scoutmaster," leaving the other two panting behind. After a while, he gave up on them, and vanished ahead. King and Groves ambled on until a little while later they heard a noise from on high. Looking up, they saw Chatwin staring down at them from the top of a hill; he was dressed in jodhpurs, hacking-jacket, riding-boots and helmet. In the early Eighties George Melly—jazz singer and collector of Surrealist art—was in Australia, Good-Time Georging it in check suit and fedora at the Perth Jazz Festival. During his visit to Perth, Melly and

John Chilton's Feetwarmers went out deep into the Bush, to a spot, forty miles away from the city, where an amphitheatre had been constructed around a stretch of swampy land. A stage had been built on stilts; on the far side of the lake the audience sat in seats that had been cut from the ground. Melly was waiting to go on when one of the men on the door came up to him: "There's a man arrived who says he knows you and his name's Bruce Chatwin."

Shirley Hazzard and her husband Francis Steegmuller, the biographer of Cocteau and Apollinaire and the translator and editor of Flaubert, had several New York encounters with Chatwin in the Sixties and Seventies. He was first brought to their apartment, by a dealer in Old Master paintings, when he was still working at Sotheby's in his early twenties—"as young as he later looked"; they later met at a cocktail party at Dwight and Gloria Macdonald's, at a dinner when Chatwin was eager to discuss Steegmuller's recently published *Flaubert in Egypt,* and at a party for one of Bruce's books. In the Seventies Chatwin surprised them by a transplantation of the friendship. Hazzard and her husband used to spend large portions of each year in Naples—where in 1983 a mugging motorcyclist turned Steegmuller's face into "a sphere of contusions"—and on Capri. Here their gatebell rang unexpectedly early one evening and was opened to disclose: guess who?

Sometimes Bruce seemed to surprise himself—to have turned up on his own doorstep: "Hello darling, I'm in *Islington*" was rendered with exaggerated precision and amazement. I bumped into him one morning in Camden Town, as he shot round the corner of Parkway into the High Street. Parkway, a treeless slope running from the stucco and verdure of Regent's Park to the grimy town centre, was ten years later to sprout a Filofax shop, a Japanese restaurant and, in what had been a Barclays Bank, a Jazz Café. But in the late Seventies the street had an air of the Forties, with an Art-Deco café and a non-Art-Deco café, a knock-down-prices linen store and a bookshop which offered ear-piercing. It was the setting for various sartorial splashes by authors: in particular, Angus Wilson's pink tie, splendid on its owner's pouter-pigeon chest. Wilson would pause with his companion at the Park end of the street, beaming down the grey vista as if about to descend a gilt staircase; he had the air of making a present of himself to the place. Chatwin, swishing through the road in his bright green jacket, looked as if he were using the space as a piece of gymnastic equipment.

The world is full of Bruce sightings: few people can have spent so much time turning up at a distance from where they lived. When I was compiling an entry on his life for the *Dictionary of National Biography* I was asked to supply details of his domestic habits. I consulted his wife Elizabeth, who laughed: "Well, you could say he was hardly ever at home." Bruce rented small urban rooms to work in away from the Chatwins' rural houses—and then ran off from those rooms to write in the houses of friends. He was consumed by the restlessness which he made into a theme of his books, and in thrall to the not uncommon fantasy of writers that there is a perfect spot in which to work. But he was also obsessed by the things that he had about him: however little time he spent in a place, he made it his own. His books and company were distinguished as much by his visual keenness as by his verbal fluency. This keenness was evident in the places where he lived, in which a definite taste was projected by a firm will.

The first flat of Chatwin's that I visited was in Albany, the white hive of apartments opposite Fortnum and Mason, whose allure in the nineteenth century is characterised with aplomb in Nikolaus Pevsner's guide to Piccadilly: "The chambers were built for bachelors and had in popular opin-

ion a flavour which was slightly disreputable and wholly en-
viable." Byron lived in Albany, as did George Canning; Sirs
Compton Mackenzie and Arthur Pinero wrote about it; in
one of its bachelor chambers Macaulay produced his *History
of England*—and Bruce Chatwin wrestled with the early draft
of *The Viceroy of Ouidah*. He did so in an attic room which
he had borrowed from the art dealer Christopher Gibbs, and
which had originally been intended for a maid.

Outside was the long covered way known as the ropewalk.
Greetings and conversation are not encouraged here: some
inhabitants claim that the established procedure if you see
someone on the ropewalk is to ignore him (it is usually him
not her in Albany) and then send a note asking him to dinner. This was a convention breached—knowingly or not—by
Chatwin when he approached one of his neighbours, the
actor Terence Stamp, to tell him about a book he'd had published on Patagonia. Stamp, who at that stage thought
Chatwin meant he'd "found someone to knock out fifty
copies," later became a fan of Chatwin's books, though he
had reservations about *What Am I Doing Here*—on the
grounds that the book didn't tell you what he was doing
there. During that ropewalk meeting they "spoke to each
other like famous people do when they haven't been introduced." Chatwin, who had yet to become famous, would
sometimes talk like that.

Inside was a thin white room with a blue-and-white Indian rug on the floor, whose cooking arrangements were like
those of a ship's galley, whose telephone was often not working, and where the huge manuscript of Chatwin's abandoned
nomad book threatened to slither off a shelf; Gibbs remembers there being "veils over things: images covered, books
covered, clothes covered." There is an insulated, self-enclosed
air about Albany: it reminded Chatwin's schoolfriend David
Nash of a boy's dormitory—"but that appealed to Bruce. He

liked that side of it. He liked the fact that there were bicycles chained to the railings." Chatwin's own description of his quarters—given to Steegmuller and Hazzard—was that of a cataloguer, and schoolboyishly proud:

> *L6 Albany (top)*
> *W1*
> *March 21st 1980*

Dear Francis,

You can certainly *borrow*, not rent the above, but I feel I must warn you of the drawbacks. It is *not* a flat, in the English sense of the term, but a one-room *garçon-nière* such as one might find in the Cinquième. My tastes are also rather Spartan. It has a kind of kitchen, a minuscule shower and basin, but the lavatory is out on the landing. It has a painted Directoire bed, 3ft 6in wide—and definitely for Francis: sharing with *anyone* not recommended. It has a smaller, also Directoire, steel lit-de-camp, which can be made into a bed, though it serves as a sofa. In this Shirley would have to sleep. I *have*, on occasions, and found it small but possible.

Otherwise, there are a Jacob chair, a Régence chair, a table, a telephone, the King of Hawaii's bedsheet with a design of fishes (framed), a Sienese cross, and a Mogul miniature.

You will feel very cramped.

The King of Hawaii's bedsheet, which might sound like a Chatwin fantasy, was real—one of the most talked-about of Bruce's objects and purchases. It looked like a Matisse and appeared in a sale at Christie's, in the Sixties; Chatwin appeared on his bike to buy it, along with three others, which made up the set, and a small piece of stone—called "the aspirin" by the Chatwins—which was an item from a Hawaiian game. This particular piece of cloth is lovely to look at: apricot-coloured and patterned only with its jumping shoal of fish. Chatwin would have liked it also for the stories associated with it. It was a tapa cloth, an unwoven length of material made of pliant bark, hammered and oiled to make it more supple. Early accounts of Captain Cook's voyages have it that on the deck of the ship one of the first sounds to be heard coming from the islands was a percussive music: the sound of whale ivory hammers beating the tapas. Tapas have been made into room-dividers for the Oceanic houses on stilts sheltering huge families; in the eighteenth century, the bark cloth was used to make high-waisted crinolines for Pacific Island ladies.

King Kamehameha's bedsheet adorned a number of Chatwin's white rooms. He usually managed to have a perch in London, often in a rather grand area, and always distinctively arranged. When he first worked in town, when he was at Sotheby's, he had a flat in Belgravia, in the long-since squashed Grosvenor Crescent Mews, an area of stable doors and theatre people at the back of what was then St. George's Hospital and is now a hotel; to get to it, his visitors had to pass the back entrance to the hospital, where, stacked up on a window of the second floor, was an assortment of pickled specimens in jars. The flat was a determined display of Chatwin's developing style. A small octagonal room had a round table for the host's minute portions of delicious food. There were two painted Swedish chairs with blue-and-white eighteenth-century saddlecloth on the seats; there was another table made of a slab of marble balanced on two trestles; and there was the Japanese screen which had once belonged to Sir Ian Horobin, a politician who became involved in a homosexual scandal, and which went on to feature in the picture Howard Hodgkin painted of Chatwin. At one point a cut-out frieze of leaping Matisse figures was attached

to a white wall, as was a Max Beerbohm watercolour remembered by Christopher Gibbs as showing "an etiolated
and unwholesome-looking aesthete goggling at somebody."
Fragments of marble were scattered around, and a trunk contained various prized items, such as ancient pieces of lacquer,
bundled up in scraps of silk tied with leather. A drawing was
pronounced by Chatwin to be not by Watteau but by Watteau's aunt.

According to Howard Hodgkin, the most startling part of
the flat was the bedroom: "It was clearly meant to be a se-
duction chamber of a certain kind." On the floor was a futon
and a white duvet—an arrangement which Bruce was to
favour in other apartments. On the wall was an oval bas-relief
of a curly-wigged Louis XV nobleman in a wooden frame
painted to look like grey marble (Chatwin had bought it
without a frame). Shining on it was a tiny light. Hodgkin
remembers these illuminations: "a very rude Australian student of mine used to call them bugger's lights; if they were
floor lights they were called faggot's lights, and Bruce's apartment was full of them. They were everywhere you looked."
Some of the touches in this flat had an adolescent ostenta-
tion: the sheets of blue notepaper fanned out on a table to
show the deeply engraved "Bruce Chatwin, Bruce Chatwin" wouldn't appear in the flats of an older, surer Bruce.
Other features—the futon and the trestle table—were, in the
early Sixties, startling. Hodgkin was surprised by them on his
first visit to Grosvenor Crescent Mews; his fellow guest on
that occasion—an elderly multi-millionaire whose eyes the
painter saw "pulsating with desire"—was almost overcome:
"A remarkable young man," he'd murmur each time his host
left the room. Gloria Birkett, Chatwin's girlfriend for some
of this period, was exhilarated by what produced the plainness: the sessions of chucking things out.

Light and unadorned was the Chatwin model: these were

rooms of great clarity. They were also places of detailed con-
sideration. Bruce, debating with me about whether I could
make use of some cushion covers that he had—he liked giving presents—said that it was important that they should fit
into my other arrangements: the covers were, he explained,
plain and white. Occasionally a friend became impatient with
these precisions. "There was nothing to jar, there was nothing that might grab your heart or your attention too much,"
says Howard Hodgkin, who tried to tease his friend out of
his carefulness. (His friend teased him back when, in writing
about Hodgkin's house, he pointed to "signs of that wilful
vulgarity with which people of faultless taste protect themselves from faultless taste.")

In one of the rooms in the Chatwins' Gloucestershire
house was a beautiful fragment from an Athenian relief of
about A.D. 100; it was set into a piece of wood painted grey,
and the rest of the room had been planned by Bruce to go
with it. There was a carpet the colour of old jeans, striped in
pale cream, and his chairs with their French checks in
washed-out bluey-greys. "It was all chic as could be but it
was the kind of setting you would expect of a New York lady
of a certain age with a little black dress and a lot of diamonds
sitting very carefully on the edge of her chair," Hodgkin told
me. Bruce kept wondering why the room looked so much
better in winter. Perhaps, suggested the artist, scanning the
neutral tones of the furniture, "it's because with a grey sky all
the colour is indoors." In Bruce's tiny flat in Mount Street
opposite the Connaught Hotel—then in the middle of art
dealer's London—Hodgkin exacted a more practical tit-for-
tat on his friend's taste—and on his tendency to interrupt: it
was, he says, "the only time I ever felt I got my own back."
Chatwin had burst into his studio one day and announced
that he was looking for a colour for his bathroom: "looks to
me as if you've got several colours here," he said, picking up

a tube. Hodgkin doesn't welcome visitors to his studio, so ushered his friend out, then squeezed a bit of pure cadmium yellow paint onto a postcard, and took it down to Chatwin. "That's the colour for a bathroom," he told him. "It's wonderful for human skin." And added that the walls must be shiny—"enamel paint, then gloss." Chatwin took him at his word—to the tune of a then bitter £125. Cadmium yellow isn't flattering to the human complexion: it was, said Chatwin, "a bit like living inside an egg."

In Mount Street there was a white lacquer Ming altar table—grubbily Parthenon-coloured rather than gleaming—and on the wall above it a Persian textile, a piece of silk with a geometric design in very pale blues and creams; there was a small bamboo stool, and a glass-topped table. There were few obviously decorative pieces: ornament and muddle made Chatwin anxious; he liked things which had a purpose and a history and which weren't obviously artistic. He made pictures by cutting coloured drawings—executed by an anonymous draughtsman—from the catalogue of a brush and broom manufacturer. There were rows of pinky-red and of white toothbrushes, double-headed or with a single tuft of bristle, with diagonal ends and with club ends, with straight handles and with curved handles. They were precisely, lightly drawn—elegant and comic.

I first saw those ranks of toothbrushes in the last of Chatwin's London flats. This apartment, at the top of a tall stuccoed house in Eaton Place, showed Chatwin's taste at its most developed—that's to say, at its most restrained. Eaton Place was bright and compact and immaculately planned. It had been designed by the minimalist architect John Pawson to Chatwin's specifications—"I told him I wanted a cross between a cell and a ship's cabin. I wanted my books in a corridor, and plenty of cupboards"—and it worked like a piece of origami: a small area folded in on itself to make separate pockets of space. There was a main room, with off-white Venetian blinds, a table and a pale grey sofa; a square kitchen; and a cube of a bedroom, with a mattress on a low platform and a white duvet. The main room also contained another celebrated Chatwin find. Hanging on one wall was a big pattern of brilliant turquoise and yellow rectangles, which looked as if it were the work of a twentieth-century abstract painter with a gift for giving his work a distinctive fur-like finish; in fact, it was a design made of feathers from Ancient Peru.

Bruce liked the flat not only for what it displayed but for what it concealed. The place always appeared tidy and untroubled, because, although its compartments were barely divided, their functions were kept distinct: they didn't spill into one another. There weren't any reference volumes scattered around the grey sofa, but to the left of the entrance to the flat was a narrow white cubicle, a space smuggled from the main area and lined with books to make a secret library. The writer liked this arrangement because of what it did for the rest of his flat. Looking around his living-room, he was gleeful: "Not a book anywhere."

Like many of Bruce's concealments, this was a partial one: he was happy to display his books elsewhere and to talk about them. "There are books you read for pleasure and books you read for plunder," he once explained, his face gleaming in a parody of Sotheby's acquisitiveness: "Every writer is a cutpurse." Some of these plunderings are declared in his books: in the bibliography to *In Patagonia*, in an epigraph from Jeremy Taylor, and in the quotations from his moleskin notebooks used in *The Songlines*. As soon as he'd finished writing a book, he got rid of many of the volumes he'd used for research, so that his sources would be hard to track from the library that his wife has kept. Alan Moorehead's account of *Darwin and the "Beagle"* would have been consulted when he was working on *In Patagonia*, and Gilbert Freyre's *The Master and the Slaves: A Study in the Development of Brazilian Civilisation* when he was writing *The Viceroy of Ouidah*. Other books on these shelves are favourites: Nabokov, Borges, Poe, Tsvetayeva, Kilvert's *Diary*, Doughty's *Arabia Deserta* and *Wanderings in Arabia*, Tolstoy's *Diaries*, Dante, lots of Hemingway, Gorki, Robert Frost, Turgenev, lots of Edmund Wilson, Donne, Nadezhda Mandelstam's accounts of her husband and of the Stalinist purges. Alongside a range of European dictionaries, there is a Persian vocabulary, *Teach Yourself Arabic* and a book about Sanskrit.

While I was working with him he gave me a Penguin Classics edition of Heinrich von Kleist's *The Marquise of O*. He looked rather glazed when the English classics were mentioned—as if he considered them the literary equivalent of the English brown furniture he disliked—and forgot or discounted his public-school studies, which included an essay on *Pride and Prejudice*, when talking of his early reading: "The great English novelists were left unread, but were heard, very much heard—*Oliver Twist*, *Wuthering Heights*, *Pride and Prejudice*—on gramophone records, in plummy English accents." He described himself as a youthful porer over atlases, and once told me extravagantly that he had read nothing but encyclopedias and art books until he was in his twenties.

Elsewhere he wrote of his youthful reading habits: "The first grown-up book I read from cover to cover was Captain Joshua Slocum's *Sailing Alone Around the World*. This was followed by John C. Voss's *The Venturesome Voyages of Captain Voss*, by Melville's *Omoo* and *Typee*, then Richard Henry Dana and Jack London. Perhaps from these writers I got a taste for Yankee plain style? I never liked Jules Verne, believing that the real was always more fantastic than the fantastical." In the same piece he offered descriptions of other influences and altogether less plain styles. From Edith

Sitwell's anthology *Planet and Glow-Worm* he derived "a number of literary fixtures—Baudelaire, Nerval and Rimbaud, Li Po and other Chinese 'wanderers,' Blake and Mad Kit Smart, the encapsulated biographies of John Aubrey and the seventeenth-century prose music of Jeremy Taylor and Sir Thomas Browne." It was from Smart's *Jubilate Agno*—the passage beginning "For I will consider my Cat Jeoffry"—that he chose to read aloud to friends on a country weekend. From a great-aunt who had lived on Capri and painted naked boys, Chatwin as a child heard Gerard Manley Hopkins's swooning "The Windhover"—

> *My heart in hiding*
> *Stirred for a bird—*

and Walt Whitman's "Song of Myself":

> *The beards of the young men glisten'd with wet, it ran from*
>   *their long hair,*
> *Little streams pass'd all over their bodies.*
>
> *An unseen hand also pass'd over their bodies,*
> *It descended tremblingly from their temples and ribs.*

This aunt also read him a book about Marie Curie by a distant relation, Eleanor Doorly: "the story of Curie's self-inflicted radium burns affected me greatly." The aunt proved "a tireless reader of modern fiction. One day she looked up from her book and said, 'What a wonderful word "arse" is!'—and for the first time I heard the name Ernest Hemingway."

Chatwin's taste was dominant in the houses he shared with his wife—in the Gloucestershire valley of Ozleworth and, later, in the Chilterns (whose proximity to Henley-on-

Thames he found hard to bear). Elizabeth Chatwin claims that at Homer End in the Chilterns her decorating schemes (though not her shifting troupe of cats and Jack Russells) were exiled to the upstairs rooms. Below, her husband installed his favoured items. There were the curtains made from a bolt of unbleached calico that the traveller had brought back from Italy, and the long Italian-style table the colour of malachite that the student, having borrowed the necessary £270 (and beaten the seller down from £350), had snapped up in an Edinburgh antique shop. There was a small red lacquer tray— from Japan and the fifteenth century—which Chatwin once saved from being used for tea by his mother-in-law. There was a Spanish votive picture featuring an unjustly imprisoned man who prayed to the Virgin Mary, who secured his pardon: Chatwin had bought the picture in Barcelona and was later to fly back to pick it up. There was a long pink fibreglass bow made by John Duff, a contemporary artist liked by Bruce, who was not in general much interested in contemporary painting. And there was a squat pottery beaker with a sad face on the front—a South American Indian cinerary urn. There was an astronomer's chair, bought in Pimlico; a six-panelled gold screen; the dainty ivory hammer which Chatwin had used to auction Antiquities at Sotheby's. And there was the big map of Patagonia—black on a tawny background—that had been painted in gouache by the Irish designer and architect Eileen Gray.

Eileen Gray was a natural focus of fascination for Chatwin. When he visited her in Paris in the early Seventies she was ninety-three and, he reported, still capable of putting in fourteen hours' work a day. She was one in a line of forceful old women—Nadezhda Mandelstam, Penelope Betjeman, Maria Reiche, Madeleine Vionnet—whom he admired and befriended and praised. She was also one in a line of talents which had been obscured from British eyes and which

Chatwin was eager to describe. In the Soviet Union he acclaimed the collection of paintings made by George Costakis, the country's most important private art collector, who was known as the "mad Greek who buys hideous pictures," and, in doing so, wrote about the history of the Russian avant-garde. He praised the Constructivist Rodchenko years before the first British exhibition of his work; he also extolled the architecture of Konstantin Melnikov. In Peru he examined the geometric forms, and the beasts, birds and plants, drawn onto the surface of the desert some two thousand years ago, and looking like "the work of a very sensitive and very expensive abstract artist."

Gray's life-story had the apparently clear outline and the exaggerated sense of self of the exiled lives about which Chatwin liked to write. She had moved to Paris, after studying at the Slade, when she was in her twenties, abandoning her Edwardian frills and ruffles and frizzes of hair for a tailored jacket, a shirt and a bob. She had fallen in with a group of women artists—including the flamboyantly sapphic Romaine Brooks and Natalie Barney—and had formed an intimacy of her own with a dark-browed singer called Damia. And she had always skilfully and singlemindedly pursued her obsession with making things. She had begun as an enthusiast for work in lacquer, producing a series of exotic pieces of furniture: a small red lacquer table decorated with the black silhouettes of charioteers and their horses; a canoe-shaped daybed in textured brown lacquer and silver leaf; panels and screens in purplish blues and greys showing lotus blossoms, abstract swirls and dramatic allegorical figures. In her forties, she changed direction: from decoration to function, luxury to practicality, design to architecture. She planned and built an entire Modern Movement house near Monte Carlo stocked with her own creations: tubular steel chairs with fat padded seats, tables which could extend vertically or horizontally on the principle of a trombone, an aluminium dressing-cabinet with swivel drawers and glass shelves which also served as a room-divider. Stencilled in the entrance was the instruction *Défense de rire*.

Chatwin's work, which is nothing if not pictorial, has an equivalent in Gray's designs, both in the dark lustres of her lacquers and in the bare functionalism of her later pieces. And behind the output of both was a similar personality and philosophy. Both were determined to live in a compact and economical way. Both were interested in the notion of transparency. Both disliked the idea of ornateness and decoration—in Gray's case, she grew into this dislike. Both of them, while extremely interested in objects, disliked the idea of possessions. And both of them wanted to go to Patagonia. The map which hangs in Chatwin's Homer End house is one of a pair painted by Gray, who often used maps as pictures. Chatwin first saw it when he went to her flat in the rue Bonaparte, thinking to write a piece about her. He told her that he had always wanted to go to Patagonia; Gray said that she, too, had wanted to go there, but was now too old: "Go there for me."

✤ 2

EDITING *IN PATAGONIA*

By the time I met Bruce Chatwin he had been to Patagonia and had written about what he found there. In doing so, he helped to change the idea of what travel-writing could be. The book that he produced—titled in manuscript *At the End: A Journey to Patagonia*—was distinguished by qualities which were to distinguish all his books. It was pungently expressed and it delighted in paradox. It hovered teasingly between fact and fiction. It abstained from personal revelation but was full of autobiographical material. Even its central subject was a contradiction: the Patagonians were, it turned out, not one nation but a multinational collection of expatriates and exiles, many of whom felt most at home with themselves when they were abroad. This was a feeling with which Chatwin was in sympathy: in this and in other ways, his first book was a declaration of faith.

The typescript of what was to become *In Patagonia* was sent to Tom Maschler, Managing Director of the publishers Jonathan Cape, in the drought summer of 1976. Chatwin was thirty-six, older than usual to be embarking on a writing career—but this wasn't the only book he had talked of submitting to Cape. Seven years earlier the literary agent Deborah Rogers had written to Maschler enclosing a copy of a Chatwin essay about nomads: "Can he come and see you? I am sure he is worth your spending half an hour with. I have a good feeling about him." Kasmin—who travelled with Chatwin and shared his enthusiasm for antiquities—had introduced him to both agent and publisher, hoping to help his friend release some of the bees in his bonnet before they drove him mad: he thought of Chatwin at this time as in danger of becoming like a clerical eccentric of the nineteenth century, dedicating himself to one all-embracing idea. The idea with which the 28-year-old Chatwin was buzzing was human restlessness: he wanted to answer the question "Why do men wander rather than sit still?"—an answer which would have supplied an explanation of himself. An agreement to publish a book called "The Nomadic Alternative" was drawn up; competitively enthusiastic letters were exchanged (Maschler to Rogers: "As I said before, I have a hunch; as you said before, you have a hunch"); a drift of manuscript pages accumulated. In 1970 a reader's report gave an equivocal welcome to a chapter from the book, finding it "lively-minded" and "contentious" but marred by its "wilder digressions" and "outrageous statements." When Chatwin came to hand in his manuscript he had lost his zeal for what he had written: Cape turned the book down.

Those pages have never been published as a unit, though their influence can be seen ducking and diving throughout Chatwin's books, with fragments breaking surface in *The Songlines*. They remained as Chatwin's alternative work: a project which was never quite relinquished but never quite addressed anew, and may well have been too over-arching and all-encompassing ever to have been realised. The failure was a liberation: with his attempt at large-scale speculation put on hold, Chatwin turned to doing what he did best—describing what he saw and heard about him, without feeling the need to summon a higher seriousness. He never did this with more snap and sparkle than in *In Patagonia*. Nevertheless, the report—by a different reader—on that manuscript was anxious:

11.8.76
AT THE END: A JOURNEY TO PATAGONIA Bruce Chatwin
typescript from Deborah Rogers

This *is* very extraordinary—and a possible problem. Basically, it's a collage-like collection of impressions, memories, histories and stories about Patagonia, loosely bound together by an intermittent first-person narrative, but mostly functioning more or less autonomously. Accounts of Elizabethan sea-voyages lie side by side with memories of Butch Cassidy; the farms of Welsh Patagonians are meticulously described—as are revolutionary uprisings and the hunting of Indians. A possible source of "The Ancient Mariner" is identified; the Giant Sloth investigated.

The most striking feature of this mixture of fact, fantasy and folklore is the very high quality of the writing. There are pages of outstanding prose—with some lovely pictures. The trouble is that it is very much a page-by-page read: I was impressed by each bit as I read, but didn't feel impelled forward throughout the whole 350-odd pages. Though I think the author would probably feel the massiveness was central to his conception, obviously cutting would help. Even then, it would hardly be an easy proposition—and if I weren't so impressed by the matching of informativeness with intelligent description, I would say a sad no. As it is, I don't feel able to dismiss it—particularly since this may mean saying goodbye to someone who may well have other good books to come. But I don't think it's on as it stands: I'm afraid it has to be more reads, and possibly some discussion with Deborah Rogers and investigation of the author's position.

I was the author of that report. And, after the weekly editorial meeting at which it was decided that the book should be pursued and that work should be done on it, I became its editor. Bruce first shot into my room at Jonathan Cape in the late summer of 1976. He was carrying his haversack—in it were a French paperback by Blaise Cendrars, *L'or: La merveilleuse histoire du général Johann August Suter,* a World's Classics edition of Sydney Smith's letters and a manuscript of *In Patagonia;* he was already talking. The room was very small, and next to the Ladies lavatory on the ground floor of 30 Bedford Square. The contrast with the Olympian splendour of Tom Maschler's room on the first floor was dramatic—as if designed to make a point to any authors who picked their way up or down the stairs. On the first floor were moulded ceilings, walls packed with file copies of Cape books, a big desk and large dividing doors into the next office—at party time these were peeled back to show the tall windows which looked onto the plane trees of Bedford Square. One floor below, my office had three metal shelves bracketed to the wall, on which were stacked the books waiting to be looked at by the firm's readers: in the Seventies the readers were invariably part-time; they were almost invariably women— they needed, after all, to combine literary judgment with modest expectations of income. I had a desk, a small table with a manual typewriter on which to type reports, a wooden bookshelf with olive-green or pink proof copies, covered with the brimming white urn of the Cape colophon; there was an oblong mirror (provided by me), a window overlooking a central dankish well, and a jolly windowbox tended by a prospective Liberal MP. With Bruce and me in it, the space was packed.

In time Bruce extended his area of operation at Cape. He used the waiting-room, where file copies of books were kept, as his lending library; he cajoled the operator into putting through calls from—and perhaps to—Australia; he was later to spill his Australian stories to Maggie Traugott, the young woman who was compiling the Cape catalogue and who thought, as Bruce twinkled in her doorway, stroking his cheek catlike against the jamb, that he was flirting and winding her up "by describing what *The Songlines* was going to be about."

Since Cape was cramped, we decided to divide our working time between my office and a flat belonging to Kasmin, with whom Bruce was staying. This flat, carved from the ground floor and first floor of a house, was on the north side of Regent's Park, near the zoo and the Danish Church. Downstairs a big light room with white linoleum tiles looked onto the park: this was where Bruce most often read, though in all the houses in which he stayed he was a peripatetic browser. Upstairs, what had once been a ballroom had been made into two rooms. In the large sitting-room, with a white marble fireplace and two huge sash windows, Bruce and I worked.

Bruce was among the most responsive and appreciative people I've ever worked with—and one of the few authors who seemed actually to enjoy the process of being edited. He liked turning his composing into a conversation, and got ideas as he talked. He made up his mind quickly and, without being alarmingly acquiescent, would cut a whole section without a minute's brooding. He would also write a new section overnight: his haversack was heavy with fresh pages.

The task posed by the manuscript was considerable. It was huge and it didn't have a clear sense of direction; it sprawled, and on occasion it got stuck. The book, of course, was always intended to be made up of byways: it was meant to slope off, to jump backwards and forwards in time, to slip from description to speculation, from history to evocation. This was what Bruce was like in conversation—it was how his mind worked—and it also reflected some of the intricacies and peculiarities of the country he was examining. It was obviously important not to streamline the loops and extravagances out of existence. It was also important to provide readers with a way of dealing with them. The book was not to be an adventure story, but nor should it be a series of cameos.

The first change to the typescript was strategic but straightforward. The published version of *In Patagonia* is made up of 97 numbered sections—too small to be thought of as chapters—arranged in a roughly chronological sequence, but with ample excursions. The early versions of these sections were not numbered but named: "A Piece of Brontosaurus and Other Early Interests," "Introduction to a Country of Exiles," "Mammals in Exile," "Heading South," "The Scot," "On the Río Negro," "The Man who was a King and the Later History of a Throne in Exile." These headings had the quaintness of a Victorian manual; they made the book look like an encyclopedia; they didn't help the flow of narrative. As soon as we decided to remove them, the question of what counted as a section was exposed. Why did a piece begin or end where it did? How many episodes or portraits could each carry? Sometimes extra information was needed, to explain what the title of a section had previously made apparent; most often this was slid into the opening or close of an episode. The least colourful lines of the book were written at this stage: "I left the Río Negro and went on south to Port Madryn"; "Anselmo told me to go and see the poet"; "A mile outside the settlement there was another exile"; "I left the soprano and went to call on the Germans." These sentences served the purpose not only of explaining what was happening but also of pushing the story on: in a small but significant way, they helped to pace the book differently. But there was never any attempt to supply what had from the beginning been strikingly absent: a continuous commentary.

Bruce once spoke of *In Patagonia* as being an attempt to give a "cubist" picture of that country, a description which catches the book's structure and character: its angularity, its many small scenes and surfaces—one tilting away from another. The earliest manuscript was organised in this way, and in the process of editing—during which some sections went through as many as four versions—the book became still more angular. Before the first meeting, I had gone over the manuscript marking the points where I thought it sagged or meandered or was baffling. By the time of our last meeting, material had been cut at some of these points; at others, new sections were started. What had begun as a big book with a short style ended by being short in every respect: short sentences, short paragraphs, short chapters. Various manuscripts have sums scrawled in the margin by Bruce when he was trying to work out how much had been cut: 548 times $200 = 109,600$; 300 times $200 = 60,000$. My calculation at the time was that we reduced the length by between a quarter and a third of the original. Before long I was hearing that an old friend of Bruce's was complaining that his editor at Cape was taking all the good bits out of his book.

Bruce was quite capable of taking out the good bits by himself. He got as much pleasure from ejecting an adjective from his manuscript as he did from expelling an ornament from his flat. He was eager that the narrative shouldn't be strewn with reaction shots of the author as sensitive traveller—this was to be a book about what he saw, not about what he felt—but his vehemence in this matter didn't much affect the manuscript: although Bruce made much of casting out anything that smacked of his mooning or moping or thrilling, there was very little of any of this to begin with. He was also eager to get rid of any redundant links from paragraph to paragraph, scene to scene, which disposed of odd sentences along the lines of "They asked me to join them." But there never were many of those links that Paul Theroux missed when, in welcoming the book in a review for *The Times*, he commented that the author rarely explained how difficult or otherwise it was to do his travelling. His first draft was written freely and was sometimes flaccid: "Imagine my excitement on seeing a green tree . . ." Bruce's adjustments on the manuscript that he took away from our editorial sessions—which he returned to me at the next meeting sometimes scribbled over and sometimes retyped—were designed to correct this. He threw out sentences in the main because he thought them silly or flat or superfluous.

There were hardly any extended passages in the first draft that were totally limp. The large cuts that we made were administered not to get rid of duff stuff but to tighten the book's shape, give it more pace and focus its subject-matter. Occasionally this made for an easy exclusion. Bruce, keen to be hospitable to as many stories as possible in his first publication, came up with a few implausible candidates. On the back of one version of the first page, he drafted an account of a meeting on a train with a rabbi's son, "so shy he found it hard to undress with anyone else in the compartment": this man and his father, having fled from Romania and the Nazis in 1941, had years later been traced to Vienna by the Gentile servant who had helped them escape, and now wanted to return to Romania. This story was eventually published in a slightly different first-person form in *The Songlines*: its setting—a European train—meant that it was always an unlikely episode for *In Patagonia*. Most of the cuts were more difficult than this.

Even when it was clear that a section went on too long,

with one meander too many, it wasn't always easy to know what to lose. Bruce and I would sit over one manuscript, sometimes over two duplicates; Bruce would get up and pace around and sometimes—damagingly, for he made everything seem equally entertaining—read bits aloud. He would take pages home marked up with queries from me, and return them annotated with questions and notes by him: "Delete?" "Consider replacing." Some decisions took several goes. In a book which was all anecdote and illustration, the line between illuminating example and excrescence was often hard to draw.

One line was drawn at Bruce's memories of childhood monsters. In one draft, the beast with which the book starts is given a more extensive biography: a spirited piece of writing but one which delayed the point at which the book got to Patagonia:

> Already I had a Museum, a cabinet with Roman glass, a miniature penknife, a Tsarist rouble, a real piece of eight and the skull of a field mouse, waiting only to receive its prize exhibit. But my mother, and other relatives, had swooped on the house of the dead, had captured the valuables, and thrown away the piece of brontosaurus. I have forgiven them, but not forgotten. For I am a man who still walks up and down the earth looking for a lost piece of brontosaurus.
>
> Every boy constructs legendary geographies in far-off lands. By the time I was ten, I had composed my version of the brontosaurus story, based on misinformation, fantasy, and scraps of knowledge from encyclopedias, atlases and charts of evolution. The brontosaurus was the biggest animal in the world. It had a very small brain and an enormous humped body. It was a placid beast and each day ate tons of weed in

lakes, while pterodactyls sparred above. It died out many years before Christ, when Noah could not ship it, let alone a breeding pair, aboard the Ark. My own special brontosaurus lived on an island at the end of the world called Tierra del Fuego, the Land of Fire. Here it got stuck in a glacier, perhaps when the Flood froze. Prisoned in a womb of blue ice, the deep-frozen brontosaurus travelled inside the glacier for thousands of years. Finally, it emerged, miraculously preserved, at the bottom, where my grandmother's cousin Charlie Milward the Sailor found it.

More than one of Bruce's stories about beasts was left out of the final manuscript: in 1976 details about the young Chatwin had yet to be coveted. Twenty years after the publication of his first book the considerable biographical interest of some of these excluded tales is more evident.

"I once made the experiment of counting up the lies in the book I wrote about Patagonia," its author claimed. "It wasn't, in fact, too bad." Here, from an early version, is an account of how his brontosaurus stood up to scrutiny:

When I told this heroic tale at school, they accused me of lying. A schoolmaster said I had got it mixed up with the story of the Siberian mammoth. Years later, in the Museum by the Neva, I saw the Beresovska Mammoth sitting upright like a dog begging, where it had fallen hind first into a pit. I read Pallass's discovery of the woolly rhinoceros; I handled a few crumpled remnants of dry tattooed skin; and in a basement of the Hermitage a curator of archaeology told me a story, equally apocryphal perhaps, but resonant with familiarity, to illustrate the intransigence of Soviet bureaucracy, about the frozen man from Pazyryk. In 1933 the archaeologist

V. I. Rudenko found, under a domed cap of stones
(which acted as a refracting lens), the frozen tomb of an
Altaic nomad chieftain. His wife accompanied him to
the grave, with a marvellous paraphernalia of silks and
felts, a tent for inhaling the fumes of Indian hemp, and
twelve hot-blooded horses of the finest near-eastern
strain. A bestiary of tattoos covered the man's body; a
catfish up the calf of his leg. His insides were stuffed
with Indian hemp lingeringly green. Rudenko packed
the man, his wife and the horses in railway trucks for
Leningrad and hoped for cool weather. The Hermitage
did not have a refrigerator and referred the consign-
ment to the city's meat storage plant. The official in
charge said Niet to the human couple and referred
them to the morgue. The official in the morgue said
where was their birth certificate, and on being told the
man had died two thousand four hundred years ago also
said Niet. No corpse in the Leningrad morgue without
a certificate of death. This is why you have to handle a
few crumpled fragments of skin in a drawer in a basement of the Hermitage.

In Patagonia was Bruce's début and his showcase, touching
on subjects and notions which he returned to and expanded
throughout the next twelve years. It is a book about being
abroad and walking abroad which is structured, as all his
books were structured, in clear-cut episodes. It takes an interest in the culture of an expatriate Welsh community, just
as, five years later, *On the Black Hill* was to take an interest in
an indigenous Welsh community, and talks of a fascination
with prehistoric creatures which was to recur in a darker
form in *The Songlines*. It has things to say, as *Utz* has things
to say, about collectors and archaeologists and Eastern
Europe.

These prefigurings are more evident in drafts than in the published version. In one early manuscript a section describing rival women archaeologists is headed "The Collectors." In the same manuscript, passages about the Welsh community at Chubut are surrounded by jottings about early Celtic nature poetry: "the light flickering through the poplars, the light flickering on the page of a manuscript . . . the unspiteful elder, the melodious birch . . . rather like Japanese haiku but more moving in that they are less clever and artificial." These were the verses to which he turned when writing *On the Black Hill*. And one long passage, cut from the manuscript because it held up the drive of the opening chapter, was later transformed into fiction in that novel:

> There were two principal walks of my childhood. Two walks detach themselves from the chaotic sequence of movements, two paths, two ways, as two sites on which I still may build. One led up onto the Derbyshire moors behind the cottage, little more than a shack, that had once been a tobacconist's shop, in which we stayed when my brother was born. "My path" led up between stone walls through a wood of wind-stunted oaks, past a line of white hawthorn trees, an abandoned orchard overgrown with pink rugosa roses and golden privet, folds of red sorrel, white marguerites. Skylarks in the wind. On the far valley a great house in a park. Past the last wall, where the sheep nipped the grass fine. Crawl along colonnade of bracken stems, up over a linear granite escarpment, until we came on the moor. A Celtic cross to the Duke of Wellington. There was a stone called the Eagle Stone, eroded at the base, sitting in the brown moor where threads of white cotton grass blew in the wind, and you felt the endlessness of the softly undulating horizon. This is a landscape I have found again in Africa. When I found other walkers on

my path, I was very cross and told them to get off. I do not think I felt that way about strangers in the house. I never felt that way about a house.

The second path led along the south bank of the River Avon, below Stratford, where I stayed with my great-aunts, two spinsters, Janie and Gracie. Gracie was a warm motherly figure, who had been matron in a school. She was very deaf and you spoke to her through a little black box she carried like a handbag. The other aunt was an artist, longing only for Italy and the sun. As a girl she had known the painter Van Dongen in Paris. She had lived in Capri in the days of Lenin and Maxim Gorky and painted watercolours of Capriot boys in the nude. Now she copied the great masters. She painted Pollaiuolo's St. Sebastian against a bright cobalt sky. I wanted to know why that beautiful young man was pierced through and through with arrows and could still stand up. In their garden was a statue, made by my aunt, of a beautiful Greek god gazing at his reflection in a bird bath.

To walk along my other path, you crossed the river over a footbridge by a granary that we all thought spoilt the view of the church. You passed under the railway bridge out over two or three fields, with an island of pollarded willows in midstream. You followed the path as it plunged into a wood, hazel scrub, brambles, the muddy path leading forward, anemones in the spring and violets, in summer big yellow evening primroses that I thought very exotic. You used to think of it as a jungle path, looking to the right you could see the brown water of the river, eddying round branches and mats of reed, sometimes there were moorhens and ducks and sometimes a heron and water rat. I loved this path very much. My aunts said it was definitely the path on this bank that Shakespeare was thinking of when he wrote "I know a bank whereon the wild thyme blows . . ." but though I found oxlips and violets, I never found any thyme there and sadly decided Shakespeare was thinking of somewhere else. On our way back we would look in on the church, and if there were any GIs or other important visitors, I would show them Mr. Shakespeare's tomb. Sometimes they would give me sixpence, and my aunts took it and put it into the collection box. I liked this path very much, but I did not love it like I loved the moorland path. Sometimes my aunts would read poems, from a green book called *The Open Road*, and the poem I liked best was about a gipsy woman who lived upon the moor, caring for nobody. Her name was Meg Merrilies, and I thought how fine it would be to live alone, outside, all the time, on the moor.

This passage was heavily influenced by Proust, whom Bruce had wanted to quote in *In Patagonia*. I had argued against this idea on the grounds of pretentiousness, but it is certainly possible to find, in the deleted passage, the Proust of *Swann's Way*, with its two walks, its aunts and its memories:

> We used always to return from our walks in good time to pay aunt Léonie a visit before dinner . . . there were, in the environs of Combray, two "ways" which we used to take for our walks, and they were so diametrically opposed that we would actually leave the house by a different door according to the way we had chosen.

Bruce was ardent and obsessive about his memories and ideas: he adapted them, recycled them and transplanted them. He reproduced some of this autobiographical data in pieces of journalism, but the idea of the two contrasting walks found a different route into print. *On the Black Hill* explains that "the twins loved to go on walks with their grandfather, and had two particular favourites—a 'Welsh walk' up the mountain, and an 'English walk' to Lurkenhope Park." The childhood memory that was dropped from *In Patagonia* went into the novel, where it fitted snugly alongside the book's other twinnings and splittings. Much of the detail remained unchanged. In both the autobiographical and fictional versions there is a high, rough, bracken-strewn walk and a gentler walk with lush flowers; in both versions a grandfather whose name is Sam is associated with the idea of walking, a grand house in parkland is glimpsed, and small boys object to anyone else walking on their paths; in both, there is an ancient stone—called a menhir in the novel— known as the Eagle Stone. The Patagonian pages had a further effect on Chatwin's Welsh fiction. When he came to draw the picture of the wild nature-child who lives at The Rock, the farm on the moor, he was drawing from life, from the figure of a friend. But he was also drawing on John Keats, on the gypsy poem that his aunts had read to him as a boy— and through him on Walter Scott. He created a character who, like Keats's Meg Merrilies, is mostly out of doors, wears a battered hat and old clothes, produces garlands, and has an affinity with trees. And when he came to name her he called her Meg.

Despite Bruce's admiration for Flaubert and his attempts to espouse a Flaubertian impersonality, his books are full of stories about himself. In the flesh he could seem reticent, and people found him awkward to hug, but he would talk compulsively about things that had happened to him. On the page he abstained from personal comment but wrote—with varying degrees of openness—about what he had done. I heard one acquaintance claim that during his imprisonment in Dahomey in the Seventies Bruce had been raped, and too traumatised ever to mention it. Francis Wyndham has pointed out: "If that was the case, he would have talked about it." But there were things that Bruce didn't like to talk about, and he did confide in his wife that such a thing had happened at about that time in the Côte d'Ivoire.

There were also things in his travels that he didn't write about, and few authors can have been so upbraided for what they didn't say. Paul Theroux, whose *Old Patagonian Express* was published two years after *In Patagonia*, has been a worrier at his friend's omissions: in his *Times* review of Bruce's first book and, some fifteen years later, in a piece that was published in America as a preface to *Patagonia Revisited*, the short volume based on a talk that Chatwin and Theroux gave jointly to the Royal Geographical Society. Here, Theroux treats the obliqueness of *In Patagonia* as symptomatic of its author's evasiveness. It was, he says, "original, courageous and vividly written" but

> full of gaps. How had he travelled from here to there? How had he met this or that person? Life was never so neat as Bruce made out. What of the other, small, telling details, which to me give a book reality?
>
> I used to look for links between the chapters, and between two conversations or pieces of geography. Why hadn't he put them in?
>
> "Why do you think it matters?" he said to me.
>
> "Because it's interesting," I said. "And because I think when you're writing a travel book you have to come clean."
>
> This made him laugh, and then he said something that I have always taken to be a pronouncement that was very near to being his motto. He said—he screeched—"I don't believe in coming clean."

Bruce's pronouncement, screeched or not, was itself a sort of coming clean: at any rate, he was telling the truth. He wasn't much given to confiding or to blurting in life or in his books—though his discretion was obscured by the stream of stories which came from him; the accusation that he was mingy with detail must be unique. The gaps that Theroux disliked in *In Patagonia* seem to relate to the sorts of thing— explanations and links—which he most often chose to leave out, considering them "boring," and to omissions of material which was not boring but which would have entirely changed his narrative. There was no reference to his wife, to his profession, to where he had come from: it was as if nothing had happened to him between his childhood and the moment he put a pack on his back and set off for South America.

There were whole Patagonian encounters that weren't mentioned at all, amid the many things that were left in. *In Patagonia* describes with approval a surprising painting by the French artist Raymond Monvoisin which shows a gaucho lying "cat-like and passively erotic." It sketches a close and stormy friendship between a farmer and his peon. It observes the relationship between two men at the Bahai Institute of Trevelin:

> "How you like my friend?" asked Ali.
> "I like him. He's a nice friend."
> "He is *my friend*."
> "I'm sure."
> "He is my very good friend." He pushed his face up to mine. "And this is *our room*." He opened a door. There was a double-bed with a stuffed doll perched on the pillow. On the wall, strung up on a leather thong, was a big steel machete, which Ali waved in my face.

It is a book which is alive to homosexual feeling, and to female beauty, but which never shows the author as a sexual presence. It nearly did. In one early manuscript a section which begins with a chap spinning a yarn about a priest who was "hot for boys" goes on to show Chatwin getting a lift with a lorry-driver who, at first suspicious, had later become "a bit too friendly." This phrase was scored out by Bruce, probably because of its coyness. Another incident was never intended for publication. When an old friend wrote to Chatwin to praise his first book he commented particularly on the passage featuring a young pianist—half-German, half-Italian, and adopted by the Patagonian Welsh—who asks his guest about Wagner and Liszt and plays him Beethoven and Chopin. Chatwin wrote back:

> The pianist! Ah! the pianist! E. Hemingway, who knew a thing or two though it's fashionable to put him down, said if you take something OUT of a piece of writing it always shows. What I took OUT of that story was the head falling backwards at the end of the mazurka, automatically with no hint of it before, and lifting him off the piano stool into the bedroom.

Chatwin, who was married at twenty-five and had male as well as female lovers, was not generally forthcoming about his partners in conversation, and never in print: in a book designed to be about a country, he could hardly be required to be so, though he has sometimes been talked about since his death as if not spilling all his beans were tantamount to suppression. No reader can ever have supposed that *In Patagonia* told the whole truth: it is clearly partial and idiosyncratic. It is also clear that it is composed. Francis Wyndham has written about his friend: "Reading Chatwin, one is acutely conscious of authorial *control*—and therefore, simultaneously and intoxicatingly, of the alluring danger of *loss* of control, of things getting out of hand." This suggests something of Bruce in person: the exactness of his speech was at odds with the gusto of his delivery, his laughter and grimaces.

In Patagonia crams into a short space a large number of diverse lives. It does so by treating each encounter as if it were a short story: shaping it, giving it a turn or twist. The glide from fact into fiction has not always been appreciated by the Patagonians he describes. Several of these men and women have complained that they or their friends and relatives, often appearing in the book under the penetrable disguise of changed names, are nicer or less eccentric than Chatwin has made them seem. Another English traveller in Patagonia, John Pilkington, has taken up his pen on their behalf and written a book in which he berates Chatwin for a culpable vivacity, a vivacity purchased at the expense of truth. "I believe," Pilkington reveals, "Bruce Chatwin knew very well, as he wandered through Patagonia in early 1975, that he was not going to give its residents a fair hearing. Indeed, having met them superficially, he may have been afraid to delve too deeply, suspecting that underneath they might be rather dull. To liven up the narrative of *In Patagonia*, he focused his attention on an array of larger-than-life characters—Patagonians, to be sure, but extraordinary ones—and where details were missing he made them up."

Bruce didn't, in fact, go about suspecting people of being dull. His inclination was in the opposite direction: to be fascinated, beguiled, amused. He certainly overdid his enthusiasms on occasion, and saw the point of some dodgy people, but it should be some comfort to any disgruntled Patagonians that the people in his pages are interesting: his excitements can make a reader want to see through his eyes. The fabrication of details, cited by Pilkington, is not deeply damaging: Pilkington found a number of inhabitants less concerned with their country of origin than Chatwin thought; one woman wanted to sue for libel for an uncomplimentary picture of her father-in-law; when Pilkington visited one resident he didn't, as Chatwin did, find a sprig of mint on the bar of his restaurant.

It is, of course, true that Bruce exaggerated, that he was,

as any writer is, selective about details and that sometimes he got things wrong. Nobody reading *In Patagonia* could mistake it for an attempt to give a comprehensive or balanced view of its characters: it is a series of quickfire, impressionistic pen-portraits written by someone who is clearly drawn to the unexpected, the self-contradictory, the sharp-edged— and who likes to turn a tale in a small space. Chatwin had become skilled at such portraits while he was writing for the *Sunday Times* Magazine, where he produced articles of a similar length and structure to the individual scenes in his first book.

One model for the conciseness to which he was drawn was provided by a writer whose *Brief Lives* Chatwin described as being a staple item of his library. The seventeenth-century biographer and antiquary John Aubrey—a spinner of many schemes and a student of archaeology—was as pervasive an influence on Chatwin as those authors of the volumes of travel, history and adventure listed more predictably in the bibliography to *In Patagonia*. Aubrey was a diner and a drinker and a gossip: his short *Lives* of poets, philosophers, divines, travellers, scholars and speculators were written pell-mell, often with a hangover; he was unbuttoned and breezy and outspoken. "A better instance of a squeamish and disobligeing, slighting, insolent, proud fellow, perhaps cannot be found," he wrote of the Earl of Oxford's Secretary: "No reason satisfies him, but he overweenes and cutts some sower faces that would turne the milke in a faire ladie's breast." Chatwin is less familiar in his treatment of his subjects, and his work is shaped with far more care: Aubrey explained that he "set things down tumultarily, as if tumbled out of a Sack." Nevertheless, *In Patagonia* bears the imprint of Aubrey's biographical brevity: vivacity and piquancy are prized more than comprehensiveness; there is no moralising and a lot of humour; large events and tiny incidents, facial tics and political schemes are discussed in one breath; anecdote and first-hand observation are given more prominence than documentation.

More evident influences were exercised by practitioners of the short sentence and clipped utterance. Bruce—who often used full-stops as a way of reining in elaborations and qualifications—spoke more than once of Hemingway in connection with his style. He also talked admiringly, sometimes extravagantly, about Noël Coward: "For writers who want to write dialogue, I can recommend nothing better than the breakfast scene in *Private Lives*." Coward's measured languor and tense, comic understatement can be discerned in Chatwin's prose, as, occasionally, can Hemingway's gruffness. But his vocabulary was rarely constrained. When Bruce described his style as "bleak" and "chiselled," he was telling only half the story. Although his syntax was pared down, his words were not—or at least not only—plain. He liked the varieties of specialist terms for flora and fauna: his first book features the toxodon, the astrapotherium, the Su, the water-tiger, and the Yemische, "a kind of ghoul"; in trying to identify the kind of albatross shot by the Ancient Mariner, he points out that one candidate, the Sooty Albatross, is also called the Prophet and the Stinkpot, and that the other, the Black-Browed Albatross, is sometimes known as the Mollymauk. And he had a huge palette of colours at his disposal: *In Patagonia* has cobalt and turquoise, steel blue and sapphire blue, porcelain-white and papery-white, silvery grey and grey-green, wine-red and blood-red and scarlet; one seven-line paragraph lists purple, orange, lime-green, lilac and rose-pink. His prose is both spare and flamboyant: its mixtures and contradictions brought him readers who identified with his style and with what they saw of his life; the lives of some of these readers overlapped with Chatwin's, providing coincidences which he might have used in a book.

There is the story, for instance, of a young man called Nicholas Rankin. A few days after the Falklands invasion, on 7 April 1982, Rankin was researching the background to the war in the extensive library of Canning House in Belgravia—a centre for British-Latin American societies. In the Patagonia-Argentina section Rankin, who was later to write a book about Robert Louis Stevenson, found a number of books on Patagonia described as having been "donated to Canning House by Bruce Chatwin"—Bruce always gave a lot of his books away. As he read, he heard Chatwin announcing himself downstairs, explaining that he had to research a talk for the BBC World Service (for which Rankin himself now works) and asking if he could use the library. Rankin, an old Argentine hand and a fan of *In Patagonia*, went to introduce himself. Bruce was in his loden coat, jeans and running-shoes. As he sat at his desk he muttered and continually sharpened his pencils. Later, in a pub called The Star around the corner from Canning House, he delivered one of his torrents of tales, on this occasion largely sepulchral; Rankin noticed that when he got particularly animated he had a habit of rubbing his thigh. Bruce talked about the interred body of Queen Victoria's gillie, John Brown, having been exhumed—he said one of his ancestors had been a minister at Ballater Kirk, though he didn't explain as he usually did that the exhumation had been at the command of Edward VII, who on his accession had the gillie's bones thrown over the fence. He told stories about Wilfred Thesiger and the Samburu warriors with whom he stayed, and a tale about a man from Lloyds Bank who was kidnapped in Argentina: the person negotiating for his release was sent by the kidnappers on a tour of gay bars in Buenos Aires. In particular, Bruce talked about one of his chief Patagonian interests, the Western outlaw Butch Cassidy whose exploits at the turn of the century were made into a film, and who supplied several of these corpses of Bruce's. He gave an account of René Barrientos, the President of Bolivia, who had an obsessional interest in Cowboys and Indians and arranged for the body in Butch Cassidy's grave to be dug up—it proved to be that of a Swede. Rankin, who was thinking of writing a novel involving Butch Cassidy, contacted him later for more stories, not all of which turned out to be true. There was, for example, the tall tale of a Pinkerton detective who arrived at the Sundance Kid's hideout at Cholila and was killed by him and buried. Shortly afterwards a second scout showed up, and was greeted by a dog carrying in his mouth the dead agent's hand—the image comes from Kurosawa's film *Yojimbo*. Bruce also showed Rankin a photograph of himself—a photograph which he was to make into a deckle-edged postcard and send out to his friends—in which his hair was dyed black and he wore a black moustache; he explained that he had used this rig as a disguise while researching *The Viceroy of Ouidah* in Brazil.

A little while later, Rankin rang up the Eaton Place flat. The telephone was answered by a "rather camp" voice which reported that Chatwin wasn't there. "It's about Butch Cassidy," Rankin explained. "Butch Cassidy?" responded the voice. "Is *he* in town?"

For all Bruce's mysteries, his writing is full of details about his own life. These are sometimes elided with the life of another. When he came to write about Robert Louis Stevenson, he used him as a surrogate self; towards the end of his life he spoke with a dark and intimate excitement about Rimbaud, whom he planned to make the subject of a play. An early manuscript of *In Patagonia* contains another portrait of a Bruce-like figure in the shape of an anthropologist in flight from picture collections and fascinated by nomads, foreign places and the Australian Aborigines. By the side of these paragraphs, Bruce has written "Delete?" and I have an-

swered, it now seems to me mistakenly: "Yes." These are the
paragraphs, which followed Chatwin's account of the young
Fuegian boy taken to England on the HMS *Beagle* in 1830
and called "Jemmy Button" by the ship's crew:

BY THESE STRAITS TO DIE

Rooting about in the bookcase of an English estancia
among unread sets of Scott and Bulwer Lytton and
Edwardian manuals of physical fitness, I came across
a copy of *Spencer's Last Journey*.

A proper young man from photos, and an athlete,
Baldwin Spencer was an Oxford biology student in the
1880s. He took part in Darwinian debates and read a
paper on the Pineal Eye of Lizards to the Royal Society.
He was appointed Professor of Biology at Melbourne
and found himself drawn into the Australian deserts.
With the help of his friend, F. J. Gillen, he enjoyed the
confidence of the Australian Blackfellows. For forty
years he trekked the spiny wastes, from the Australian
Bight to the Gulf of Carpentaria, recording the lives of
Stone Age men. His findings gave Sir James Frazer the
raw materials for his theory of totemism. He acted as
advisor to the Australian Government on how to settle
these primitive nomads, but could not settle himself.

At sixty-nine, Baldwin Spencer looked as an English
anthropologist should look—sun-beaten, silver-haired,
with sensible hands and tweeds. But something in him
rebelled against his academic distinctions, his knight-
hood, his family's concern for his health, his own picture collection and the dust of museums. He had felt
the call of the Far South.

He and his lady secretary sailed to Punta Arenas. It
was his ambition to follow Darwin's tracks; his excuse

to compare the last of Jemmy Button's people with the Australian Aborigines; his evident intention to die among them.

It was winter when they reached the Murray Narrows. Snowbound in a hut on Hoste Island, where he had gone to interview a shamaness, he spent his last days dissecting the wing muscles of a steamer-duck and reading his beloved Charles Lamb. His diary records, in scrupulous prose, Yaghan kinship relations, the Latin names of local wildlife, a watercolourist's description of scenery, and the onset of his disease: "Passed nothing but colourless, odourless, slimy fluid all day and night at short intervals."

Sir Baldwin Spencer died in the hut at 12:30 a.m. on June 14th 1929 of *angina pectoris*. His body survived a tremendous storm at sea and was buried in the British cemetery close to that of Charlie Milward.

Directly autobiographical snippets were also cut out of early manuscripts of *In Patagonia*. The draft version of the opening section was so busy with anecdote and description that it was difficult to see what the book was telling the reader: it was a succession of vivid moments. As Bruce and I combed through the pages, we made purposefully plodding lists of what had to be in. What mainly remained of the opening section was a story about a boy and a brontosaurus and a remote land. What was largely excised was Bruce's absorbing account of his own childhood.

❧ 3

SCHOOL

My grandmother's house, in a suburb of Birmingham, stood back from the road behind a hedge of yellow-spattered laurels. It was of dark red brick and had tall chimneys and pointed gables painted a dull green. In the garden, among blood-coloured roses, I learned that my father, that occasional visitor in dark blue and gold, had failed again to bring my banana from the country where the black men lived. He had tried to bring a banana before. This time he had towed a bunch of green bananas in a watertight container behind his ship. They had again gone bad. I had seen plaster models of bananas in shops that sold a few, tired, wartime apples. At nights I tried to imagine how real bananas tasted. I envied the black men who ate bananas all day long. When, after the war, the first bananas arrived, I tried cautiously to eat one, and was sick.

I remember the smell of Anglicanism in that dingy house. I remember ship models, indestructibly ever-green plants, photographs of the family's ketch, the *Aireymouse*, dipping her clipper bow into a tranquil sea, and a painting of blue rollers smashing on a beach. My grandmother sat, immobile, in a wide armchair. The furniture, surrounding her, seemed to have been constructed for giants.

That was how *In Patagonia* opened in one of Bruce's drafts. Parts of this description did appear in the published version, dispersed throughout the first section and expressed slightly differently. Other parts were relinquished from draft to draft, along with further anecdotes about his family and childhood. Bruce was fascinated by his own infancy and by his ancestors; his eagerness to get away from England at intervals and to be apart from familiar surroundings was matched and perhaps prompted by a preoccupation with his origins which he once called "morbid." He found a metaphor for his contradictory fascinations in his own surname, tracing it to the Anglo-Saxon word meaning "a winding ascent" ("a winding path," according to Chatwin), a derivation which gave him a travelling destiny and also yielded a prediction of his writing style. These coincidences or resonances seemed always to be falling into Bruce's lap: how could anyone so loquacious, and so interested in identical brothers, be so well-named? How could the last house in which the odyssean author lived just happen to be called Homer End?

Bruce's imaginative world was marked by correspondences and overlappings, by talismanic correlations. It was a world in which the things he noticed and chose to write about had significance, in which, as his wife put it, "all his geese were swans." When he came to talk about his ancestors he was conscious of picking on those with the most adventurous or lurid lives: on uncles and cousins who had travelled in the desert, been shipwrecked or committed bigamy. On occasion their histories were burnished by Bruce. His father's family, button-makers in the mid-nineteenth century, produced a line of solicitors and architects, "Birmingham worthies," Bruce liked to boast. A plain account of the life of his great-grandfather J. A. Chatwin, written by his son and privately published, records an architectural career devoted to the design of Birmingham churches, Birmingham banks, Birmingham tunnels and Birmingham bridges, and a glass palace for a maharajah. As a young man J. A. Chatwin had been articled to Sir Charles Barry, whose design for the Palace of Westminster was in the process of construction, and Philip Chatwin's short book also describes how his father delivered a lost London policeman and a gathering crowd from bewilderment in a thick fog by groping his way along the surfaces of the buildings in Regent Street until his fingertips identified the familiar mouldings on the front of a club designed by Barry.

This story would certainly have appealed to Bruce, though he didn't include it in the more dashing outline of his great-grandfather's life that he offered me in the Eighties. According to Bruce, J. A. Chatwin had been a button-maker and a friend of William Morris: he did collaborate and correspond with Morris on the enlargement of what was to become Birmingham Cathedral, but it was this Chatwin's father and brother who were the button manufacturers. According to Bruce, his great-grandfather walked from Birmingham to the London office of Sir Charles Barry seeking a job with the simple explanation, "I can draw"; Philip Chatwin's book prints a letter from Barry accepting Chatwin on trial, but doesn't mention the walk. According to Bruce, those years of tracing the intricate patterns on pearl buttons enabled him to sketch with perfect accuracy the elaborate pinnacles of the House of Lords: his designs provoked wistful murmurs of appreciation from John Betjeman: "Ah, Chatwin . . ."

Bruce's accounts, adorned with what his brother Hugh calls the "few extra whistles and bells" which he hung on his stories, often had something of the flourish of the auctioneer who wants to establish an interesting provenance for one of his objects. Hugh himself was given some of these whistles and bells in his brother's accounts: "He wants to be a big-game hunter," Bruce confided on one occasion; on another, Hugh was fancifully described as living reclusively with an

Irish labourer in an overgrown cottage in the East End of London. The Hugh Chatwin of real life is a sober professional man—darker, rounder and more blazered than his brother, but with a disconcertingly similar voice, and with a bold spirit. When at an evening organised by PEN in memory of Bruce, Michael Ignatieff talked about his wish to claim his friend for liberal scepticism, Hugh stood up to confute him.

Bruce credited his great-grandfather with his own quick eye and massive walking capacity; when he spoke of his maternal grandmother he fastened on her affinity with gypsies, expressed in her love of fortune-tellers and horses, her dark looks, long nose and big earrings. An affectionate portrait of this grandmother and her husband was one of the passages that was taken out of a draft of *In Patagonia*:

> My maternal grandmother was very Scottish, but she belonged to the conspiracy of gigglers. Sometimes she and my mother would giggle so loud and hard they couldn't stand up. She had a remarkable range of metaphors. Farting was "bluebottle scent." When she disliked someone she'd say: "That woman has the face of a bull's behind with no tail to hide it." I used to repeat her wisecracks at infant school and thought they were very funny. She usually wore a cairngorm that her father had worn when he won the tossing of the caber at the Braemar Games, at the age of 72, and died of a stroke . . . My grandfather, Sam Turnell, was a thin man, with infinitely sad eyes. His mother had brought him up to be useless, which was just possible until the slump wiped him clean.

These vignettes of Bruce's childhood were innocent of the sort of data required by biographical dictionaries: his date and place of birth (13 May 1940 in Sheffield) were missing, as were his father's profession (solicitor), his non-working mother's maiden name (Margharita Turnell), his place in the family (the elder, by four years, of two brothers), and his academic progress: various nursery classes, followed by a prep school at seven—Old Hall in Wellington, Salop—and Marlborough College. In re-creating his early years—in *The Songlines*, in *In Patagonia*, in pieces of journalism, in his talk —Bruce lingered over his memories of wartime, when his father was away in the Navy. He described the women who cared for him and entertained him: his mother and grandmother, the great-aunt who painted St. Sebastian so enthusiastically, and the remotely related Irish teacher called Eleanor Doorly ("my passion," according to Bruce) who wrote instructional books—*The Microbe Man*, *The Ragamuffin King*, *The Insect Man*—and practised a liberal teaching regime, inviting her hatted and gloved boarding-school pupils to "Go and worship God under a tree." Another great-aunt provoked in her young nephew a powerful dream which would have set a Freudian aflame: "One evening, when I'd misbehaved in the bath, she cried, 'Stop that, or Boney will get you!' and then drew on a piece of paper a dreadful black bicorn hat on legs. Some time later, in a nightmare, I met the hat outside Hall's Croft, the home of Shakespeare's daughter, and it opened like a furry clamshell and swallowed me."

He also described what he remembered as the perpetual motion of his early years with his mother. This passage, from an *In Patagonia* draft, is not much different from Bruce's other rehearsals of the experience, but unusual for him in echoing so strongly in its first sentence another writer's words: Wilfred Owen's "My subject is war and the pity of war":

> My early childhood was war and the feeling of war. We were homeless and adrift. My father was at sea, my mother and I wandering from place to place, travelling up and down wartime England to stay with relations

and friends. Our temporary stopping-places are less clear than the journeys between them. The houses are unreal. I still have a horror of home. The real things are the slamming of train doors, the comfortable rumble of railway carriages, moquette-covered seats smelling of stale tobacco, canvas kitbags thrust through windows, or the white smile of a black GI across a half-lit station. My world was one of tank crews, searchlights in a night sky, canteens with steaming urns of tea, corned beef and sugar sandwiches. I remember an operations room with maps, model aircraft and women in uniform with telephones coming out of their necks. I think I also remember the words "We have won a great victory" coming out of a brown plastic radio set in the left corner of a blacked-out room, and clinging onto my grandmother's legs as she and my mother danced. But this is well before my third birthday. I certainly remember the fleet, a line of silvery grey ships and barrage balloons, strung out over the horizon, and I remember sitting on the beach when a German fighter dived out of the sun.

A few years after his death, the *Evening Standard* gloatingly misread one of Bruce's evocations of his time as a toddler— "I lived in NAAFI canteens and was passed around like a tea urn"—as a confession of sexual promiscuity.

Of course not all of Bruce's early life was movement, but it was the moving which he remembered, and moulded into his sense of what he was bound to become. These years were imbued with a wartime vocabulary. When he first went to nursery school, before the birth of his brother, he was accompanied by a small imaginary friend called Tommy, about whom he often spoke, telling his mother "extravagant things." When he went to a private infant school—whose blazers could be bought for thirteen shillings and sixpence and caps for half a crown—the name of the school, in Crescent Hill, Filey, was the Blue Bird School. Here in the "delightfully situated" house and garden, Chatwin and his peers were taught Scripture and Arithmetic, Geography and Nature Study, Dramatic Activity and Handicrafts, receiving "special attention and careful training with the help of attractive modern methods." The school also boasted "an excellent air-raid shelter." When the infant Bruce admired the banners strung across doors to greet returning soldiers, his mother strung a bath-towel between two trees and pasted letters on it to spell out for Odysseus: "Welcome Home Bruce."

During his first leave from the Navy Charles Chatwin found a house for his family in Birmingham, where they lived for three years. In 1947 they moved to the country some twelve miles south of the city, to a place with the confusing name of Brown's Green. Here, on a large estate, in the shadow of a big house which claimed to have one window for every day of the year, the Chatwins had a small-holding with pigs and poultry, kept cats and briefly a Staffordshire bull-terrier, and liked to say of themselves that they lived "in a clearing in the Forest of Arden." Here Bruce lived out an aqueous country childhood of the Forties: fishing, damming up streams, taking part in competitions in sailing dinghies on a local reservoir. He and his brother bicycled around, delivered parish magazines, marched the sow up the road to be serviced, designed and put together model catamarans. Bruce, who had long had "The Walrus and the Carpenter" off by heart, developed a taste for the "Flower Fairies" series, those pretty pocket collections of illustrated poems in which a water-coloured sprite, its face poking from a circle of petals and leaves, talks about floral qualities:

> *Scilla, scilla, tell me true,*
> *Why are you so very blue?*

There were flower fairies of the woodland, the garden, the mountains, the valleys.

For Bruce, the Arden idyll was interrupted when he was sent to prep school. There are two rather different accounts of his attitude to first leaving home. His mother remembered him as untroubled, and one of her son's earliest letters from his new school, Old Hall, is chirpy:

> Dear Mummy and Daddy,
>
> I am thoroughly enjoying myself here and I am set-tling down well . . . I have made several friends already. I get on very well with Edwards. I have made friends also with a boy called Ghalib whose father is a Turk. The food in Priory is excellent and I have had no need to delve into my tuck box yet. Don't bother to send on the cycle clips as we have to cycle in shorts . . . Please will you send me some books because for an hour in the evening we have to read . . . Most boys here play the trombone. But I don't think I will have enough time . . .

But forty years later Bruce was to offer, in the guise of fic-tion, a more clouded version of what it meant to leave what he would sometimes claim he always wanted to discard—his home. In the spring of 1988 I went to visit him at his house in the Chilterns. He was ill and bedridden but was produc-ing a flurry of short stories and articles. One of these was about a boy going away to school. He had written it out in long-hand on one of the American legal pads—foolscap, bright yellow, with green lines—which he always used for drafts, and he read it out one morning to me and to Kevin Volans, the South African composer who was staying with Bruce and Elizabeth, and to whom the story is dedicated. Volans had some points on the piece: he thought there was

altogether too much about haemorrhoids, and Bruce immediately took out a sentence or two; he also thought that one
phrase should be turned round, and Bruce turned it with
alacrity, pleased to have a musical ear attending to his prose.
Then he said he would give me the story to publish in the
magazine on which I was then working, the *London Review
of Books*. This was in the nature of a present: I had been nagging at him to write another piece for the paper, but the
book that he most wanted to review—the letters of Anna
Akhmatova—was not due out for another year. I prepared to
type up the story on Bruce's manual typewriter, sitting at the
small table near to his bed, where a massive manuscript from
an exigent young novelist waited for Chatwin's opinion ("I
haven't read it: he thinks I'm abroad. Don't say anything if
you see him"). As I pulled the typewriter towards me, a small
painting of an Indian musician in a tawny shift and orange
trousers fell on its gold-framed face; it had been propped up
against the machine like a postcard. "You'd better move that,"
said Chatwin. "It's worth thirty thousand pounds."

"The Seventh Day" was published in the issue of 2 June
1988. Unlike some of the other stories he wrote at that time,
it did not find its way into *What Am I Doing Here*, the collection of pieces compiled under Chatwin's eye and published in May 1989, four months after his death, and has
never appeared in a book. It is a dark, troubled tale, in which
a boy's experience is rendered apocalyptically, and in which
scatology becomes eschatology. The title is based on the last
few lines, which provide a Biblical recital of a crisis: the small
boy, who is constipated, is persuaded by his classmates that he
is going to die in seven days, as another boy had done before
him; a toll is kept of the passing days as in the First Book of
Genesis. However, most of the brief piece—which runs to
about 1100 words—is concerned with the routine life of the
boy, who is not given a name. He is eight, has fair hair, is thin

and comes from Birmingham; his father was on a mine-sweeper during the war and, after it, supplements his income by keeping a few pigs. The boy is in a state of anxiety: he dreads going back to his boarding-school and makes himself sick in order to stay away:

> He hated school because no one would leave him alone. Because he was so skinny he hated being tickled by the headmaster at bedtime. He hated the boy who stole his marbles, and he hated the boy who rubbed his chest with his hairbrush. After lights-out, the others whispered plans for the future. They wanted wives and children. He hid under the sheets and saw himself as the last man alive after the bomb. He saw himself in white cloth walking across a charred landscape.

The tale has two brooding landscapes: the cooling-towers and chimneys and smoke of the Black Country, which the boy finds comforting, and the desolate, blackened, bomb-flattened place of his nightmares, in which he searches for a woman but finds only a wizened person stirring "thick brown liquid in a pot."

"The Seventh Day" is autobiography barely disguised as fiction. In it, Bruce included not only the evident facts of his boyhood, but also incidents to which he attached signifi-cance and to which he often referred. The boy is given a book by the postman at his home, "an account of Sir Wilfred Grenfell's Mission to the Labrador Indians." The small Bruce received a book on this subject from his local postman when he was living at Filey: it was called *The Fisherman's Saint*. The boy is terrified by Guy Fawkes Night at his school, when guys with faces made out of pumpkins are burnt on the bon-fire: "One guy was Mrs. Attlee in a scarecrow hat. Mr. Attlee had Hitler's moustache. He hated the masters for working up the boys. He went into the dark and cried for Mrs. Attlee." Bruce always said that it was this inflaming of the boys against Labour which determined his politics: that ever since crying for Mrs. Attlee he had felt "honour-bound—I *have* to—to vote Labour . . . Never, even in my capitalist phase, was I able to vote Conservative."

The gloom of this raw story was generated only in part by Bruce's early memories of school. The piece was written in the last twelve months of his life and is marked by the pre-occupations of those months. Bruce was taken up with religious questions, as he had been for a while at school. He had the sick person's concern with his bowels. He talked about walking into the desert to die, and he discussed ideas about pairing and marriage and being alone. He was attacked for not acknowledging his illness, or for not reporting on it. He hated the attention he attracted. The end of "The Seventh Day" offers a graphic glimpse of this state of mind: both fearful and hopeful. The boy doesn't know what is the matter with him, detests his schoolfellows watching him as he struggles, and is eventually saved—by an all-powerful matron and, it seems, by his own concealment: "He did not tell about the purple bulge, and soon it went away."

But, however shadowed by his circumstances when writing the story, "The Seventh Day" does offer an insight into Bruce's attitude towards his schooling. The sunniness of his letters may not have been assumed, but it wasn't unbroken; the docility of his pastimes—while he was at prep school Bruce embroidered with flowers a set of round white place-mats still used by his parents forty years later—could be perturbed. Some of his introspections may have been provoked by the importance placed on religious instruction at the High Church Old Hall: his brother—who did well in his Scripture examinations—remembers sung creeds, a lot of church-going and learning of the Bible, and an emphasis on original sin. Some of his disturbance must have come from not being a natural team-player—while having no taste for playing the outcast. He was to withdraw intermittently throughout his school career.

Chatwin had been put down for Marlborough College when he was seven. His contemporaries remember the school with more or less enthusiasm as a place of spartan arrangements and orderly habits: towels frozen with ice in the mornings, substantial breakfasts of porridge and kippers, quite a lot of beatings administered by prefects, Chapel once a day—there were very few Catholics or Jews. David Nash, a future expert at Sotheby's, recalls the "macho masochistic pride" taken by those who, like Chatwin, lived round the claustrophobic central well of the college, where arrangements were "a little bit more rugged, the dining accommodations even more rough and uncomfortable and troughlike." He also recalls the detailed regulation of the uniform: grey flannel trousers, a white shirt with a detachable collar, a lovat-green jacket (and a very scratchy green outfit on Sundays), duffel coats: "If you got to be a prefect you were allowed to wear a waistcoat. There was a whole hierarchy of what you were allowed to wear. There was a point at which you were allowed to wear coloured socks, a point at which you were allowed to carry an umbrella—that was a great status symbol."

"You could be a rugger bugger if you wanted to but you didn't have to," says Hugh Chatwin. His brother abstained. Michael Cannon, a keen hockey-player and future South American expert, had, in a school of mostly Southern boys, the bond of a Midlands background with Chatwin. They went on bicycle rides together: to the beautiful grey stones of Avebury, said by John Aubrey to "as much exceed in bigness the so renowned Stonehenge as a Cathedral doth a parish church"; to the mysterious prehistoric lump called Silbury Hill; to Stonehenge on one Midsummer's Night. They took part in cross-country runs to a neolithic standing-stone known as the Devil's Den, through downland and Savernake Forest. Archaeology was an interest in the school, particularly in the house of the chaplain, Perceval Hayman, which offered the less hearty boys a retreat from the austerities of communal life: the chaplain's daughter remembers Chatwin sloping into the elegant dining-room, trying out an Elvis Presley scowl.

In the sixth form, when they were studying for their A Levels, Cannon and Chatwin were allotted a study together which was to feature in Chatwin's reports as a decorative item. It had lime-and-white striped wallpaper, purple curtains and Italian oil paintings; it contained a chaise-longue and a huge chair lugged by Chatwin from a local antique shop. This was certainly the study of the boy whom his parents remember as an Edith Sitwell reader among a lot of Nevil Shute fans. Chatwin himself recalled that the proprietor of the local Marlborough bookshop gave him Sitwell's anthology *Planet and Glow-Worm* for his seventeenth birthday. "What," he asked his teacher in a free reading period, "is an ornamental hermit?"

Some of his recollections of school—"I tried to learn Latin and Greek and was bottom of every class"—have a dramatic clarity which isn't borne out to the letter by his reports, which pronounced him dreamy, not straining himself and, when coming eleventh in a class of thirteen, "a cheerful worker." But he was no scholar. Escapes rather than escapades mark his reminiscences of his schooldays: "There was, however, an excellent school library, and I seem in retrospect to have come away quite well read. I loved everything French— painting, furniture, poetry, history, food—and, of course, I was haunted by the career of Paul Gauguin." Encouraged by one of his teachers, he had begun to collect furniture, visiting a shop in nearby Ramsbury which stocked half junk and half antiques, and hauling back items on his bike. A confident and misspelt letter to his parents bears out the French influence:

> Thank you very much indeed for the wonderful surprise. It really is a wonderful book, and on really looking at it closely it seems even better. Like many French books it is eminently sensible in that it does not deal exclusively with those fabulous rarities that are locked behind glass cases in museums, and on that account are apt to be dull . . . I have been rescued on several points. Firstly, that it is justifiable to refinnish French furniture completely, and secondly that the two chairs are definitly genuine (though I'm not entirely happy about the table, but anyway good reproductions of a century ago are now nearly as valuable). The second chair really is a rarity, it appears; square-backed Louis XVI bergère chairs with that standard of carving and those spiral legs are very highly sought after, and even in that book there are few that have its elegance.

It is a letter which also suggests a possible future career. Few of his other pastimes yielded such a hint. At home the teenager took to flower arrangement and when he was sixteen won second prize at the Royal Leamington Spa Horticultural Society for a "bowl of flowers and foliage arranged for effect." At school he took to crooning Noël Coward melodies, swathing himself in a silk dressing-gown. The music that he loved at Marlborough was less the rock'n'roll of his contemporaries than the songs that his mother had grown up with——Fats Waller and Jack Buchanan as well as Coward. These songs had a perceptible effect on his delivery——his clipped diction held an echo of his Master's voice——and his demeanour.

"Is that Lord Chatwin's brother?" Hugh Chatwin, four

years younger than Bruce, remembered hearing of himself as he arrived at Marlborough. The story wouldn't have displeased Chatwin—nor most young aspirers—but his patrician bearing, developed early on, had not always served him well. A cluster of school reports show one headmaster worrying over his pupil's lack of clubbability. At eleven he was "frank and responsive, full of good will. I am sure he is straight and dependable. But he is not popular at the moment with his fellows and appears to be regarded as conceited." The headmaster was sanguine: "It should not be difficult to put this right and I hope he will do so. I much admired his fighting spirit in the boxing. He very nearly won the Junior Cup, being just outpointed by a cleverer opponent, but his 'do or die' spirit was good to see." So it seemed that if Chatwin did or died his popularity might soar. In fact, he seems not to have found it easy to fight his way out of this corner. The next term's report notes that "he seems to be a little unpopular with the other boys, who regard him as rather boastful and self-important"; over a year later, "a sense of his own importance" is being held against him by his peers, if not by the masters who praised "his cheerful disposition and frank and open personality."

Chatwin the marvellous boy appears to have beamed his way through this problem: his attentive parents thought him always happy at school; his photographs show a blond serenity. But there were always those who found Lord Chatwin, as an adult as well as a child, too much, too goldenly himself. He was never an overtly rebellious schoolboy, nor an obviously sensitive abstainer: he did "splendid work" with the Combined Cadet Force. But he held himself apart—and this irritated some people, while alluring others. When, in the course of an interview in the Eighties, I asked him what he made of school, he said that he "rather ignored" it. As far as his headmaster was concerned, any difficulty was resolved in a typical public-school practical manner, by giving him boots large enough to be big in: "I am going to make him a dormitory prefect next term."

He sometimes liked to be apart; he didn't like to be out of sight. He was a notable schoolboy actor. He was cast—against type—as Bottom, in scenes from *A Midsummer Night's Dream*; in *Twelfth Night* he reverted to type as the Duke Orsino. He appeared in *The White Sheep of the Family* as "James Winter, JP," and produced the farce *Tons of Money*: nearly forty years later an oil painting that he manufactured for the play ("it wasn't my paint so I used a lot") hung, thick with luxuriant purple and yellow foliage, in the kitchen of his parents' house. But his biggest moment on the boards was in *The School for Scandal*, when he was fourteen. The critic in the *Wiltshire Herald and Advertiser* thought that all the cast played well, "with the possible exception of Rowley, who was inclined to fumble his words, and Crabtree who was not convincing and had what could only be described as a dirty face." Chatwin, performing in Sheridan's play as one of the female cronies of Lady Sneerwell and Sir Benjamin Backbite, got a rave: "In spite of a rather deep voice, her expressions and remarks went well and she swayed and sailed magnificently across the stage. Indeed, on occasions, it was difficult to realise that a boy was taking the part." The *Herald* headline proclaimed: "Chatwin's Mrs. Candour a personal triumph."

His housemaster managed to turn some of these successes against his pupil, while himself turning a phrase: "the undoubted success he had on the stage . . . shows that he is extremely capable of organising other people, while the undoubtedly unsatisfactory reports in this folder show that he is not very capable at organising himself." But one schoolboy contemporary of Chatwin's had no reservations about his abilities: Anthony Ellis explained in the *Independent* after Chatwin's death that "the memory of his performance at the age of 16 as the Mayor in Gogol's *Government Inspector* even now produces a glow of pleasure." Ellis also remembered Chatwin—bewilderingly widely read, he felt, and "having more than a hint of Rupert Brooke"—as Secretary of the school's Shakespeare Society, "fearfully select and membership by invitation only (to ask was taboo)." At the end of 1957 the Secretary, displaying some of the levity of which his masters disapproved, reported on the Society's activities:

> We read *A Midsummer Night's Dream* beside the Kennet. It was intended that members should recite their parts perched up trees, or floating on the river in a boat. This could only partially be realised, and it was unfortunate that the ground was quite sodden. However, it was a most delightful meeting: the fairies sang so charmingly in a deep bass, even the moorhens on the river felt that they had to join in.

Chatwin's English assignments in the Classical Lower Sixth at Marlborough—average age sixteen years eleven months—included a Shakespearian sonnet about spring, a piece entitled "Cars and Character," and an attenuated page and a half on the "comedian" Jane Austen. "She was unusually preoccupied with her own sex," Chatwin wrote with confidence about the peculiarity of the phenomenon he was describing, "for in *Pride and Prejudice* there is never a scene without women present." Marlborough in the Fifties was full of the sons of the Southern English professional classes: "whereas the owner of a black Rolls-Royce—or, just permissible, a midnight blue or olive green one—gives clear indication of his or her social respectability, the owner of a red or white one most certainly does not; indeed he is probably a property speculator in Birmingham," suggested the schoolboy from Brum. And Marlborough was traditional,

Classically-inclined: a place in which Tin Pan Alley turned into Gin Lane. "Effective work, amply imbued with a sense of horror," was the master's comment on Chatwin's commendably patrician poem about working-class youth, which was awarded an alpha double minus:

THE TEDDY BOY

When gin was cheap, and sin was rife,
In bed-clothes grimed and torn,
His mother, aged fourteen, expired
The moment he was born.

With sunken eyes and boot-lace ties,
With leer and lecherous grin,
In coffee bars and cinemas
He bathed himself in sin.

The crooked prodigal of the earth,
Depraved and loose in will,
He cannot help but swear and drink
And some day come to ill.

Poor fool! He met his reckoning hour,
The hour that such must meet.
He felt a knife cut through his back
And crumpled on his feet.

Most of Chatwin's surviving schoolwork is fluent and conventional. But every now and then a fin of originality shows itself. An essay called "Swimming Underwater in the Mediterranean" is corny in its descriptions and vague exclamations—"The blue was a blue beyond the range of an artist's palette . . . The landscape was like some conception of

life on another planet"—though alive with besotted pleasure
at spikes and corals and petals and sponges, greens and oranges and pinky-greys. There are some lofty adolescent
touches in his pages on "The Age of Wren"—Chatwin for a
time considered following the Chatwin architectural tradition, but would never have had sufficient mastery of mathe-
matics. None of it smacks of parroting, however. More
striking is an essay on the Dutch painter Kees van Dongen.
This was a likely topic for him, in part because there was a
biographical link of the kind he relished: years later when he
came to chronicle the exploits of his dashing great-aunt, he
included among varied bohemian adventures her partying at
Kees van Dongen's Paris studio. The artist's history also provided what were to become recurrent themes of Chatwin's:
foreignness, exile, a clash of high and low life, a delight in
strong colour, ridicule, an attention to women's dress, escape.
Despite its sententiousness and local muddles, in the Van
Dongen pen-portrait there is the beginning of *In Patagonia*.

> His paintings of political figures leave a pitiless report
> which condemns a period and a class. By his paintings
> he created the type of woman that makes that period
> remembered, the queen of the boudoir, with an ex-
> aggeratedly thin body, swathed in transparent tulle,
> adorned with glittering jewels, her pallor only broken
> by a gash of brilliant lipstick.
>
> It was his audacity that endeared him to those
> people, his audacity in wit, the subjects of his paintings
> and his use of colour. He once had to paint a woman
> to whom he objected very strongly. She insisted that he
> included in the portrait her favourite lap-dog, a yap-
> ping little hound which Van Dongen loathed. He
> painted it green. The woman was furious and de-
> manded why he had painted it in such an outrageous
> colour. "Dogs aren't green in nature," she declared. He

replied: "Why should I paint it differently? Your hair isn't violet in nature." He became richer and richer, and moved from studio to studio; everyone flocked to his parties. Suddenly he completely forsook high society, bought a farm in Provence, and has been painting what he wants to paint ever since. None of these paintings have ever been exhibited, and he insists that they will not be until his death, which probably will not be for many years, so vigorous is his old age.

By the time these essays were written he had fallen under another influence. The enchantments of abroad were delivered to Chatwin in a heady burst when he was in his early teens. Neighbours at home had arranged an exchange of visits between their son and a Swedish boy, but when it came to his turn their son didn't want to be swapped. Chatwin stepped into the gap, and onto a boat called the *Patricia*. He went carrying a present of liqueur chocolates which his mother had been given by a friend; according to his parents, "after a month, he came back a year older."

Sweden offered various kinds of excitement. Chatwin was staying with the family of Ivan Bratt, the politician responsible for bringing in Sweden's stringent legal restrictions on drink; Hugh Chatwin describes him as "a socialist baron of the most wealthy variety"; his mother used to savour the memory of a picture of her elder son accompanying his hosts which appeared in the Swedish equivalent of the *Tatler* captioned "Count and Countess Bratt, with a fellow passenger." There was a summer house in Nichoping and visits to Stockholm and Denmark. A friendship was formed, not with his teenage counterpart, who was teenagely and Fiftyishly absorbed in playing jazz and reading detective novels, but with his uncle, a connoisseur of furniture and fine art; back in England, Chatwin was to post him copies of *Country Life*. It was, his brother explains, his first taste of the "good life" and "he came back full of ideas." Chatwin's own account of the adventure was suffused with the light and leisure of a latter-day *Cherry Orchard*:

> One summer when I was thirteen I went alone to Sweden to talk English to a boy of my age whose family lived in a lovely eighteenth-century house by a lake. The boy and I had nothing in common. But his Uncle Percival was a delightful old gentleman, always dressed in a white smock and sun hat, with whom I would walk through the birch forest, gather mushrooms or row to an island to see the nesting ospreys. He lived in a log cabin lit by crystal chandeliers. He had travelled in Tsarist Russia. He made me read Chekhov in Constance Garnett's translation, also Duff Cooper's biography of Talleyrand.

These recollections suggest an infatuation with a person as well as a country—but not, perhaps, with Uncle Percival:

> On the first day of the crayfish season we rowed to the fisherman's hut and rowed back towing twelve dozen crayfish in a live-net. That evening, they came in from the kitchen, a scarlet mountain smothered in dill. The northern sunlight bounced off the lake into the bright white room. We drank akvavit from thimble-sized glasses and we ended the meal with a tart made of cloudberries.

There was certainly a change. The old Chatwin had gone. He grew up a bit, and the episode seized his imagination with consequences more practical than the touch of Slavic mist in his memories might suggest: Chatwin had a way of turning his fantasies and fairy-tales into projects. This visit helped to alter the way he looked at things and the way he thought things should look. He enthused about eighteenth-century Scandinavian houses with their clean lines and scrubbed floors. He loved the Swedish use of colour: when looking at a piece of furniture, his wife began to anticipate the announcement that it "would look terribly nice if it was painted pale grey." Thirty years after his trip Uncle Percival's chandelier was translated from a Scandinavian memory into a London flat: when Chatwin went to Sweden in the early Eighties he came back with one made of eighteenth-century glass, which still hangs in his Eaton Place flat. He invited Howard Hodgkin to come and see it: "He said: 'You must wait outside while I light it. It is so beautiful, you can see that it was made in a northern country where there was ice and snow.' It was very remarkable, but the aura with which Bruce had surrounded it was somehow lessened by the fact that the wax was dropping onto the floor below." This was one of several visits. On another occasion he brought back a mineral used on Swedish barns which, mixed into a Chatwinesque pudding with boiled linseed oil and reindeer soft soap, was applied to the front of Homer End. The house—built in the Thirties and previously used as a school—is modelled on an American barn (one with confusing Thirties porthole windows in the front door) and has an Edward Hopper appeal; it also has the uncluttered look of a wooden house in the depths of the Scandinavian countryside. Chatwin liked its long windows and its lightness and enthused about its un-English appearance. Thanks to the Chatwin mineral pudding, it changed from its earlier creosote brown to the—startling for Henley—maroon of an American barn.

The summer term of 1958 was Chatwin's last term at Marlborough. "I hope he finds a field where his verve and constructive imagination are not so restricted by the kind of exacting demand that is made by the Classics," wrote one master on his final report. How much did he hope it? These reports of Chatwin's are like school reports in a novel, in their urbanity and their ability to carry more than one meaning.

They could be represented as the manifestation of school-masterly sticklerishness, with the future novelist butterflying around the pin-sticking pedants: "he finds difficulty in remembering facts and only the bizarre or trifling really appeals to him. His historical approach is far too free as yet and he must try to control it more carefully"; "too often in school and, it seems, in preparation, he is led astray and his mind goes off at a tangent, usually interesting but usually irrelevant." They could also be read as a vindication of a schoolmasterly percipience. They are remarkably acute and consistent in their identification of the traits which were to characterise their pupil's published work: "Very much alive. I think he likes the trees more than he likes the wood—and, after all, that's natural among non-professional historians"; "he has a smooth and elegant style but is still too fond of the byways of historical accident. He would much sooner write an intimate memoir of Julius Caesar than a factual account of his Gallic War. But then who would not? Unfortunately the examiners require fact." "Vague" is a word that occurs more than once in these comments, and is a quality which obviously bemuses these definite men; "insouciance" and "levity" are disdained. Their remarks can also be read with some pleasure as the exercise of a particular prose style. These magisterial sentences, with their balanced clauses and careful qualifications, seem not to have affected—unless by way of producing a reaction—Chatwin's snappier style. But he must have responded to the friendliness which informs even the least encouraging of these remarks. "He has developed his gift for literary expression," wrote a teacher of the Classical Lower Sixth: "his gift may be slender, perhaps, but it is genuine."

4

ART WORLD

Chatwin's literary gift took a subterranean, twisting path. In the winter of 1958 he joined Sotheby's auction house as a porter. His A Levels had not been good enough to win him the scholarship to Oxford which had been dangled in front of him by his Marlborough masters; his interest in antiques and old furniture was undiminished; a friend of his father's with a link to the auction house arranged an introduction. As so often, Chatwin's timing was perfect. The late Fifties and Sixties were a period of huge expansion for Sotheby's: the lifting of post-war restrictions on the movement of money and goods in and out of Britain, the resulting growth of business abroad and especially in America —clinched in 1964 by the acquisition of the New York salesroom Parke-Bernet—and the sudden boom in the price of Impressionist paintings meant that a small auction house, which had from its foundation in the 1730s until the 1920s specialised in books, changed into a house of international pre-eminence. One chairman effected this.

Peter Wilson, who was to transform the London art world and become an important figure in Chatwin's life, had joined Sotheby's in 1936. Wilson had a terrific eye for works of art, an eye which was very much in tune with Chatwin's. He had a gift for attracting interesting experts to Sotheby's—scholars and charmers. And he had a flair for promotion: he advocated glamorous sales, beautifully produced catalogues and extensive publicity. He was very tall and fleshy, with big cheeks, receding hair, immaculately tailored suits and drawling upper-class vowels. Howard Hodgkin remembers him as a person who, while not handsome or at all sexy, had considerable presence: "He had that pale from-under-a-stone sort of Old English look which I think particularly abroad went down very well." He had an edge to his talk and a penchant for catty stories while also having an extravagantly unctuous way of extolling objects: Chatwin was to develop a good line in mimicking his former boss's "It's *simply* marvellous, wonderful, oh it's simply *wonderful* . . ." Wilson was charming and he was chilly. He was a giggler, thought of by some of his staff as imperturbably amiable, who from the cosy chaos of a tiny office—a room stacked with piles of dust-covered objects and dying tulip bulbs in boxes—contrived Sotheby's rise. But not everyone was susceptible to his charm. The art dealer Julian Agnew has said: "He destroyed everyone who came near him."

There is no dispute about his enormous appetite for dealing in works of art or about the skill he deployed. A good art dealer is supposed to know where everything is, observes Christopher Gibbs, and Wilson "really did know where almost everything was. He would travel round dim princely families in Germany, ferreting about in their cellars and jewel boxes and coin cabinets and libraries." In true dealer fashion, his commercial zeal extended to his own possessions wherever they were; no guest could be certain that the same bed would be there to sleep in two nights running; vans would arrive at his house in the South of France at all hours to scoop up mirrors and chandeliers.

There is also no dispute that his voracity—a voracity which, as Gibbs puts it, caused Wilson to have "a worrying regard for people who had enormous amounts of money"—

led him into several shady areas, generally concealed from his colleagues by his disarming comic touch and his patrician air of honour. In 1988 Chatwin described the effect of Wilson's avidity on a Spaniard known to Bruce:

> "I've left Sotheby's," I said to the Duke of M _____.
>
> "I'm glad to hear it," he smiled. "We had a most disagreeable experience with a man from there. Wilson, I think his name was. He called to ask if he could see my collection. Of course, after *our* agreeable experience, I invited him to lunch. But he started to tell me the price my Guardis would fetch at auction. I had to show him the door."
>
> "In the middle of lunch?"
>
> "Yes."

The art journalist Geraldine Norman has described Wilson as being "up to every possible trick in the art world." He was adroit at circumventing legal and fiscal restrictions, at manipulating offshore trusts and numbered accounts; he was associated with faked export licences and a clandestine syndicate. Norman wrote of his smuggling art from Russia, and gave as her authority a Sotheby's employee "who carried the briefcase of gold sovereigns to Finland." In 1991, seven years after Wilson's death, a Sotheby's administrator, subsequently sent to prison for stealing £50,000 worth of antiquities from the auction house, claimed that his dealings with Italian, Swiss and Indian smugglers had been approved by Wilson.

For years a story circulated about Wilson's being a Russian spy. It was a story that Chatwin—who himself claimed to have been approached by British Intelligence while travelling in Eastern Europe—embraced eagerly, claiming that he expected his ex-boss to be unmasked each time there was the discovery of another Soviet agent: "I *know* he's going to be

the Third/Fourth/Fifth man . . ." To some of Wilson's acquaintances it seemed improbable that he had any interest in
politics at all, and that if he did have any political opinions
they could only have been those of a right-wing ultra. This
was the line he himself took when quizzed about his activities by the tenacious Geraldine Norman. Waving at an office
equipped with bronzes, Impressionist paintings and fine
wines, "he laughed and said: 'Do you think it's likely? I mean,
would you say I show any signs of left-wing leanings?' "
What signs there were have to be looked for elsewhere.

During the war Wilson had worked for British Intelligence, on a joint Anglo-American operation directed at the
Japanese; he had shared an office with Guy Burgess, and was
close to Burgess, to Anthony Blunt, and to Victor Rothschild. The official Sotheby's biographer reports in an arresting footnote: "Peter Wilson was, in fact, asked to remain on
the staff of MI6 at the end of the war and for a time felt
tempted to do so." A story circulated that he had not been
knighted because too much was known about him in government circles.

There was more than one sense in which Peter Wilson, the
spotter of fakes and searcher for the real thing, was not as he
appeared. Though married with children, Wilson was homosexual. The often repeated phrase "Peter Wilson's boys"
carries a reference to this—though it also reflects Wilson's capacity for attracting young talent to the firm, talent which
was mostly male but not exclusively homosexual; his personality lent Sotheby's a hothouse atmosphere which one
Church of Scotland secretary found overwhelmingly orchi-
daceous: "Catholics and gays," she believed, "really ran the
place." It was an ambience which fascinated Bruce Chatwin,
and which, along with other aspects of the business, finally
repelled him. When, at the end of his life, he came to write
about the art world, the influence of these Sotheby's years
was apparent, though not explicit: he produced in *Utz* a

book which associated works of art with smuggling, with Eastern Europe and with a suggestion of sexual ambiguity.

Chatwin's employment as a porter at Sotheby's was lowly, though not as beefy as the title suggests. There wasn't much of the boiler suit about the young men in grey overalls flitting with their costly objects through the labyrinthine corridors which linked the Sotheby's offices in St. George Street with those in Bond Street. Although a porter's work was not itself particularly taxing—it mainly involved numbering items with labels and moving them around before sales—it constituted an informal practical education in looking at paintings and objects. Before the introduction of systematic instruction—a Works of Art course in the Seventies, to train people to become experts, and, later, an intensive Bursary Scheme for graduates—it was quite usual for school-leavers, more males than females, to join Sotheby's at sixteen or eighteen in a fairly modest capacity and to go on to promotion within the firm. Chatwin's Marlborough friend David Nash, who started as a porter in the Impressionist Department in 1961 and went to New York to start the Impressionist Department there three years later, was to become International Head of the Impressionist and Modern Art Department. Chatwin's ascent through the firm—from porter to cataloguer to expert to director—was unusually quick, but not unique.

Two of his jobs there didn't develop. He had a brief stint as a porter in the Furniture Department. He also worked for some months in the Ceramics Department with Marcus Linell, who is now in charge of several departments. Linell, who had started as a porter at Sotheby's a couple of years before Chatwin, was beginning to catalogue the porcelain and glass and needed an assistant to take over numbering the pieces. The job involved taking a galley proof with all the descriptions of the various objects, matching each description to an object, dusting off each piece, putting a lot number on it and placing it on a shelf ready to go upstairs on view; any-one who came to view the sale ahead of time had to be cher-ished—and might hand over half a crown as a reward. These were tasks for which Chatwin was equipped but ill-suited. He could tell whether something was good or not—even in porcelain, which didn't interest him and about which he knew very little: "Show him four things and ask him which was the best and he could always tell you," says Linell. "On the other hand, he was completely undisciplined. At a certain point, I had to say, 'This simply will not work—he's absolutely bril-liant in regard to works of art, but you've got to find someone else that I can bring on as the numbering person.'"

The two departments in which Chatwin soared had little in common. The objects in the Department of Antiquities—with their unexpected looks and their winding histories—were what finally interested him most; the paintings of the Impressionist Department gave him a chance to show his mettle and to take part in the new dash and cash of Sotheby's. The Fifties were a decade of boom for the auction house: everything did well. In particular, those years marked the rise to dominance—within the firm and throughout the art world—of Impressionist and Early Modern painting. When Chatwin first sought an interview at Sotheby's he was not able to be seen because the place was convulsed by early preparations for a sale which was to be instrumental in the in-ternational growth of the Impressionist market. He started work in the year that the sale took place.

The Goldschmidt Sale of 1958 is the sale described by Michel Strauss, current head of the Impressionist Depart-ment of Sotheby's in London, as "*the* great Impressionist sale of all time." A year earlier a sale of modern French paintings from the Weinberg collection had rehearsed some of its fea-tures: closed-circuit television had allowed potential buyers who couldn't be accommodated in the main gallery to follow the proceedings and make bids from other rooms; an outside advertising agency had handled the public relations; there had been massive press coverage—and a visit from the Queen, escorted by Sir Anthony Blunt, on the day before the sale. "The flower of the intelligentsia, divided fairly evenly between the opulent and the impecunious, crowded Sotheby's rooms yesterday," fluted *The Times*. "The scene was extraordinarily animated, adorned by half a dozen feminine hats—perhaps chosen to vie with the charming confection worn by the Renoir lady of one of the paintings." The Weinberg Sale was an illustration of Peter Wilson's flair and showmanship, and a pointer to the future. But it was the Goldschmidt Sale which established London as the centre of the art market.

There were seven paintings—three Manets, two Cézannes, one Van Gogh and one Renoir—announced for sale at 9:30 p.m. on 15 October; it was the first evening sale to be held in London since the eighteenth century and those attending were asked to wear evening dress. A huge public relations exercise, helped by the Central Office of Information, had meant coverage of the sale in twenty-three countries a month before; when the *Daily Express*'s attention seemed to be flagging, Peter Wilson had rung up Lord Beaverbrook—an old friend of his father's. The paper's subsequent coverage was extensive. "At 9:35," wrote its correspondent,

> tall, dinner-jacketed Mr. Peter Wilson, Chairman of Sotheby's and auctioneer of the night, climbed the steps of the pulpit-like rostrum in the green-walled main sale-room. Chubby-cheeked Wilson blinked in the glare of the massed TV lamps, ran his eye over the mink and diamond-dappled audience, rather like a nervous preacher facing his first congregation, and rapped firmly with his ivory gavel. The sound, amplified by

the microphones, stilled the chatter. Then to a great movement of anticipation and craning of necks, the first picture was carried in by two cerise-coloured attendants. It was Edouard Manet's self-portrait.

The first three paintings were sold within five minutes, all for substantially more than their reserve prices. The *Express* reporter, who seems to have liked colouring people in, observed: "the grey head of Somerset Maugham shook slowly in amazement. Dame Margot Fonteyn, in an off-the-shoulder, eau-de-nil dress, stood on her famous toes craning with excitement. An iron-grey man dropped his monocle under foot." Cézanne's "Garçon au Gilet Rouge" was sold for what was then the highest price ever paid for a modern picture at auction, with laughter greeting Peter Wilson as he exclaimed with plaintive surprise: "£220,000. £220,000. What, will no one offer any more?"

The Goldschmidt Sale lit Chatwin's entry into Sotheby's and affected his whole career there. Before it, all paintings that weren't Old Masters—everything from 1800 to the present—had been handled by a single department. The success of the Goldschmidt Sale led to the formation first of a separate departmental division for Impressionist and modern paintings and eventually to an independent Impressionist Department. Chatwin became the first full-time Impressionist cataloguer. The account he gave to me of his rapid rise was singular, anecdotal—and perfect copy for the *Harper's & Queen* article I was writing. While performing his porterly tasks, he had been loitering near a gouache of a harlequin by Picasso, the subject of a dispute between two visitors, when he was approached by a man "looking like a birdman, in a blue fedora and suede shoes." What exactly is a birdman? At all events, this one asked him what he thought of the picture; the porter said he didn't think it was genuine, and was then obliged to account for his opinion. He was right. And fortunate. His inquisitor turned out to be the noted connoisseur Sir Robert Abdy, who spread the word about the talented youth, and eased his way within the firm.

Like many of Chatwin's descriptions, this report—with its baroque detail and consequential encounter—crystallises and dramatises. It doesn't—and doesn't claim to—tell the whole story. Chatwin's eye for works of art was remarkable: he'd always had it ("I don't know *how* I know. I just *know*," he'd replied in exasperated bewilderment to his father when choosing antiques as a boy), and it was this that caused him to be regarded as a star at Sotheby's. Having "the eye" is sometimes spoken of with quasi-mystical reverence—as in the account of another of Chatwin's fortunate meetings as a porter, in the Department of Greek and Roman Antiquities, with a collector who seems to have rolled an interested eye in the direction of young men.

One morning there appeared an elderly and anachronistic gentleman in a black Astrakhan-collared coat, carrying a black silver-tipped cane. His syrupy eyes and brushed-up moustache announced him as a relic of the Ottoman Empire.

"Can you show me something beautiful?" he asked. "Greek, *not* Roman!"

"I think I can," I said.

I showed him a fragment of an Attic white-ground lekythos by the Achilles Painter which had the most refined drawing, in golden-sepia, of a naked boy. It had come from the collection of Lord Elgin.

"Ha!" said the old gentleman. "I see you have The Eye. I too have The Eye. We shall be friends."

He handed me his card. I watched the black coat recede into the gallery:

Paul A——— F——— Bey
Grand Chamberlain du Cour du Roi des Albanis.

For some art experts, having "the eye" is "like having faith: you can't explain why you have it or how you have it." Others have a more pragmatic attitude. Michel Strauss, who worked with Chatwin in the Impressionist Department, explains: "You know what an artist's work looks like and the way he uses the brush and the colour and the drawing. Really, it's like somebody's handwriting—when you get a letter from somebody in the morning you can recognise who it's from by the writing on the envelope. It's that keen recognition, and some people are very slow and never can learn it. Others have just got a natural talent."

It was a talent which had a practical—and cashable—use: not only in identifying what was good, but in recognising what was not. All young Sotheby's entrants—all those who had the ability to do so—taught themselves as quickly as possible to spot the difference. Strauss, who estimates that about ten per cent of the pictures he sees at Sotheby's are faked, sees the problem as having shifted in recent years from fakes to questions of attribution, with the rise of scholarly research revealing more and more cases where a student or follower, working very closely with a major artist, leaves a work which is subsequently signed with his master's name. Nowadays heaps of evidence needs to be sifted to solve such a question. Thirty years ago, there were only a few experts on each artist, less documentation, and more reliance on gut feeling. Strauss still remembers his and Chatwin's excitement when they realised that two paintings supposedly by Jackson Pollock, sent in for sale within a few years of the artist's death, had been produced by the same forger.

Michel Strauss joined the Impressionist and Modern Art Department as a cataloguer in November 1961, after Chatwin had been working there for about a year. Strauss was at that stage a rarity at Sotheby's in coming from a scholarly art-historical background—he had been doing postgraduate research on the Impressionists at the Courtauld Institute of Art as well as writing art criticism—and wasn't at first entirely welcome to his colleague. This was Chatwin's period of greatest ambition in the art world, and, accustomed to being the only full-time cataloguer in the Department, he wasn't pleased that another young man was to share his duties.

Strauss was made aware of this early on, with the first collection of paintings to come in for sale after his arrival. In the Villa Mauresque at Cap Ferrat on the French Riviera, Somerset Maugham had on display works by Renoir, Matisse, Monet, Rouault and Toulouse-Lautrec; to avoid death duties, he had bought many of his pictures in the name of his daughter, to whom he intended to leave them. In his beleaguered old age—alarmed by news that a gang of art thieves was working the Riviera—he decided to sell his paintings. The Somerset Maugham Collection reached Sotheby's one afternoon in January 1962 and Strauss and Chatwin agreed that they would begin to catalogue them the next morning. But when Strauss turned up at the appointed hour he found that Chatwin had been there since five o'clock and had finishing cataloguing.

The sale took place on 10 April 1962. A Blue Period Picasso, "Death of a Harlequin," which showed a harlequin lying with folded arms on a bed, and had another picture on the back, was sold for £80,000; the entire collection fetched £523,880. "That's rather a lot of money for a single gentleman to get," commented Maugham. Which proved to be the point. Maugham's daughter, learning that her father had decided not to let her family have any of the money, sued Sotheby's for the proceeds of nine of the paintings. "This has nothing to do with us," Peter Wilson told the press. "When asked to sell paintings we do not ask for legal evidence that they belong to the owner. As far as we are concerned, they belong to him." But Maugham's daughter had receipts for the paintings, as well as letters from her father telling her that they were hers, and the case was settled out of court two years later; Maugham paid the legal costs.

Chatwin had seen Maugham's pictures before they arrived at Sotheby's. Casting him in the role of acolyte and of ambassador, Peter Wilson had set the blond boy to entertain and charm clients into buying and selling. In order to secure Maugham's paintings for sale at Sotheby's, Bruce had been down to the Villa Mauresque—with its marble staircase, its statue of the Chinese goddess of mercy, and its four dachshunds named after characters in Wagner operas. He was sent to the house with instructions to delight the wizened author. Peter Wilson told him to be sure to wash his hair.

Chatwin—who was not an admirer of Maugham's books—told his tales of the Villa Mauresque with varying inflections. He had enjoyed the trip to the South, the paintings, and the excitement of the business. He was glad of the chance of observing Maugham, who, over dinner at the Dorchester, "told a story about a temple boy, himself, and a baby elephant." He enjoyed mimicking Maugham's secretary Alan Searle issuing instructions: "Bruce, do let Willy play with your hair." But he found the atmosphere surrounding the author "seedy," "grotesque," "murky." He recoiled from the prospect of Maugham's last, dark, luxurious years—quarrelling with his nearest relatives, encircled by toadies, his mouth drawn ever more firmly downward—and almost as soon as he met Maugham's grandson, Jonathan Hope, told him how he felt about his forebear's arrangements. He did so, Chatwin explained towards the end of his life, in order to stop the young man from being overwhelmed by his relatives, but Hope, an expert in Far Eastern and other esoteric textiles and artifacts, was upset by the zest with which Chatwin chronicled his distaste for the world of Somerset Maugham.

For a time Chatwin took some pleasure in being used as bait as well as expert. "You'd flirt with man, woman or dog," Howard Hodgkin accused him. "It didn't stop there," Chatwin responded, with a lift of the head. But there were those who said that it did. "He's amazing, that boy," commented one art critic: "He keeps so many elderly millionaires on heat and yet he never delivers the goods." He was delivering skill. Having settled into friendly and productive competitiveness with Michel Strauss, he was sharing the work of the Impressionist Department with him: looking at pictures, seeing clients, cataloguing, selling, travelling. "I was an instant expert, flying here and there to pronounce, with unbelievable arrogance, on the value or authenticity of works of art. I particularly enjoyed telling people that their paintings were fake."

He went to New York: "On Park Avenue, a woman slammed the door in my face, shouting, 'I'm not showing my Renoir to a sixteen-year-old kid.'" He also went to Switzerland. And many times to Paris. In Paris he helped to catalogue the diverse collections of Helena Rubinstein—which ranged from twentieth-century European paintings to African art—slipping up when he came to describe Brancusi's huge bent needle of a bronze, *Bird in Space* (he didn't say how many there were of the sculpture), but excelling with the African catalogue. In Paris, while staying at the Louisiane—a hotel made famous by the New Orleans jazz musicians who stayed there—he is reported to have gone dancing with a live python around his neck. And in Paris he visited an elegant dealer and aesthete, the son of the Abdy who had helped him at Sotheby's and an early collector of Art Nouveau pieces. In the middle of their discussions, the dandy pushed his way past a decorated commode which was arranged against the William Morris wallpaper and pulled from a cupboard an Egyptian granite head of one of the

Pharaohs. "Can't you see the similarity?" he asked his guest. "Look at my face! Look at this head!" Chatwin said: "I had to admit there was a remarkable similarity. I also had to admit that the head was a fake."

I had suspected the python of being a fake too, an exotic fabrication. But there was a python in his life and it did go to Paris. Sue Goodhew, a snake-hater who worked as Chatwin's secretary until she left Sotheby's for a while after a hunting accident, remembers it clearly. She used to listen to her boss's accounts of its meals (mice), its living-quarters (a suitcase by the radiator in Chatwin's Grosvenor Crescent Mews flat), and its personality ("terribly friendly"). On one occasion when Chatwin was going away for the weekend he asked her if she would go in and feed the pet—he'd show her where to get the mice. When she rejected the idea of going near the "beastly" thing, Chatwin flared up, threw a reference book across the room—and hit her. Penitence followed immediately, and slamming doors, apologies, running feet, a lump on the head, a steak bought to put on the lump, sandwiches and sweetness—and, on Chatwin's return from France, the presentation of an orange box done up with brown ribbons, and inside it a white Hermès scarf patterned with *Les oiseaux des champs et des bois*. When asked how he'd coped with the snake, Chatwin explained that he'd taken it with him to Paris, carrying it underneath his shirt on the plane; on the way back, a Customs officer had spotted it squirming there; the creature ended up in a Paris zoo. The autobiographical hero of George Moore's Fin-de-Siècle novel *Confessions of a Young Man* kept such a snake in his Paris apartment. No doubt George Moore was imitating someone else, and here was Bruce imitating him. Snakes within snakes.

During Chatwin's Sotheby's years Bill Haley and his Comets were ceding pride of place to the Beatles, and drainpipes and full skirts were giving way to collarless jackets and mini-dresses. But not in Sotheby's, where suit and headscarf prevailed—along with the protective garments required by the conditions of the workplace. In the front of the auction house a man in a hat handed people out of Daimlers and helped Elizabeth Taylor in all-over ocelot across the threshold; behind the green baize doors were small rooms with grimy windows, dusty shelves and bare floors stacked with paintings. The cold drove some secretaries to swaddle themselves in ski-jackets and extra pairs of inelegantly thick protective tights (which had to be whipped off if they entered the most public areas of the auction house); they typed in gloves. The dirt meant that the entire kit had to be changed daily.

Chatwin occasionally sported a beret with his sharp suits, and was given to entertaining his colleagues with imitations of Bea Lillie and with his rendering of "A Bar on the Piccola Marina"—the Noël Coward song which describes how love came to Mrs. Wentworth Brewster and sent her round the bend; he sometimes dictated letters in the Master's voice. He dashed from one end of Sotheby's offices to the other, helping to run both the Impressionist Paintings and the Antiquities Department, then lodged in a vaulted basement, well away from fresh air and light. When, at the beginning of the Sixties, he first visited Kasmin, to inspect a tiny Indian bronze about which the dealer was suspicious, he was well on the way to becoming "a wizard." The barely adult expert in Antiquities was full of self-confidence and bluff: he took a pin from the lapel of his jacket, scratched the patina, and declared that the object wasn't good. According to the author in one of his most ornate moods, the high spots of his time at Sotheby's were: "1. A conversation with André Breton about the fruit machines in Reno. 2. The discovery of a wonderful Tahiti Gauguin in a crumbling Scottish castle. 3. An afternoon with Georges Braque, who, in a white leather jacket, a white tweed cap and a lilac chiffon scarf, allowed me to sit in his studio while he painted a flying bird."

Each of these high spots could have been the occasion for a short story. In fact, it was more than twenty years after he'd left Sotheby's before Bruce wrote about the art world—in *Utz*, and in some brief sketches collected in *What Am I Doing Here*. But his time there had an indelible effect on what he wrote. Most of the Impressionists' subjects—their scenes of domestic life, their European landscapes and cityscapes, their frilled and parasoled ladies—were not especially congenial to him, but he responded to the boldness of their colour, their light-flooded surfaces and the attempt they said they were making to record objectively. His time with Antiquities confirmed his appetite for the rare, the overlooked, the unadorned object. And from the procedure of cataloguing he developed a way of looking and a way of describing what he saw. The cataloguers' habits—of close attention, the chronicling of a mass of physical detail, the search for a provenance and the unravelling of a history—can be seen in the structure of his paragraphs and plots, and in his project of objectivity. In an admired 1964 catalogue, compiled with his wife Elizabeth—for the Ernest Brummer Collection of Egyptian and Near Eastern Antiquities and Works of Art—can be seen the beginnings of the dense, exotic, precise vocabulary of his descriptions.

❧ 5

OBJECTS

Chatwin liked clear outlines, plain surfaces and un-expected bursts of colour. He liked things that were finely wrought and things that were functional. He liked histories and narratives. A clutch of the postcards he sent—gathered from the Museum of Modern Art, Hereford Cathedral Library, the New Moree Motel in New South Wales, the Musée de l'Annonciade in Saint-Tropez, the British Museum and elsewhere—shows a taste for surprises, for stories, and for a graceful line. He sent a boggle-eyed Mexican mask, a mural of the Last Supper and John White's sixteenth-century watercolour drawing of a soothsayer, with winged head and dancing fingers. He also sent the grey, lime-green and pink Matisse called "Piano Lesson," which shows the artist's son at the keyboard—wide-browed, light-haired, with something of Bruce's look. Snaps of satellite dishes and bright green spa baths were designed to tease and ruffle the sensibilities of Francis Steegmuller and Shirley Hazzard, accustomed to receiving self-evidently aesthetic offerings from their friend: he also posted them a picture of the Hereford Breviary, a Bonnard nude and an Altdorfer battle-scene the colour of embers.

One of the cards he despatched featured paintings by the subject of one of his best essays, a subject who had some things in common with Chatwin. The American artist

Donald Evans created thousands of tiny watercolours in the form of postage stamps—for which he invented the countries of origin. He arranged his miniatures on the pages of stamp albums in trim rows, displaying them as a stamp collector displays his specimens—or as the anonymous designer laid out his sketches of toothbrushes in the catalogue whose pages Chatwin hung on the wall of his Mount Street flat. Chatwin's crisp and attentive account of the painter's short life— he died in a fire when he was thirty-one—tells of a child, born in the Forties, who bent over maps and encyclopedias and who dreamt of desert countries and the South Seas. It characterises Evans as a man who felt liberated by being away from his homeland and who, in recognition of his outbursts of wandering, named one of his imaginary capitals "Vanu-pieds" ("Barefoot Vagabond"). According to Chatwin's essay, Evans was secretive and given to "slotting friendships into compartments"; his work was cool and self-contained. But despite his reserve, he produced in his philatelic pictures what Chatwin calls "a painted autobiographical novel of forty-two chapters."

Chatwin described Donald Evans with unequivocal warmth and admiration—unlike some of the other figures through whom he traced aspects of his own life and work. He is fascinated by Evans's working methods: when the artist embarked on his stamp pictures at the age of ten, he produced the perforated edges by using his mother's pinking-shears. He honours his draughtsmanship, his sense of colour and pattern. He also enjoys the virtuosity of his self-expression. The "countries" of Evans's stamps reflected moods, stages, events or relationships in the painter's life: one set, issued by an imaginary archipelago of coral, was called "Coups de Foudre"; "Yteke," a frosty land, gained its name from a dancer friend of Evans's who was able to dance only in chilly conditions. Chatwin's essay discusses an imagination which is drawn to the far-flung and the wildly romantic, but also illustrates "zeppelins, barnyard fowls, penguins, pasta, a passion for mushroom-hunting, Sung ceramics, shells, dominoes." In celebrating this art, Chatwin was registering his own appreciation of the austere and tranquil as well as the sumptuous; he was also drawn to the idea of creating a world in small discontinuous scenes. The Evans card that he sent to Shirley Hazzard is coloured in muted blue-greys, brownish reds and sharp greens: it shows hens, and is called "Poultry."

Chatwin often went a long way for his simple things. One of his obsessions for some time was wood: he loved things made out of it. From the top of some cupboards in his Eaton Place flat a large round tray poked out, painted red, with a stripe of bright blue around the rim, and made of wood. This lovely thing—unembellished, shaped like a very large garden sieve but shaded in crimsons and pinks as subtly as a colour chart—was a tabla, a fish tray which Chatwin had brought from Istanbul. He liked to explain that the design hadn't altered for five hundred years—prints in the Topkapi museum show fishermen using these trays to fan out their catch so that they can sell fish from their boats. They are still in common use: David King was greeted with bafflement and mirth when, going east in his friend's footsteps, he approached some fishermen to buy one.

King shares Chatwin's passion for wood and, like him, thinks that objects like the fish tray (one now hangs on his Islington wall) are "just as good as paintings." He makes wooden things—slatted beds and angular Constructivist armchairs. Some of his productions were the subject of disputes with Chatwin, who thought that wood should always have a matt finish, and that a shiny surface, even in a kitchen, was a mistake because it looked like a plastic coating. One of King's items in particular became an object of desire for Chatwin: the Black Lamp. King had made a black wood col-

umn, about six feet high and one foot square; sunk into its
top is a 25-watt bulb; the glow this sheds is faint, and it's not
easy to know where the light is coming from; King had
wanted to make the thing as unlight as possible. The idea of
a dark light is quintessentially Chatwinian: he was intrigued
by paradox and inconsistency. He was interested in rich
Communists, in sensitive artists who were brutal human beings: artists like Albrecht Altdorfer, whose intricate, lumi-
nous *Battle of Issus* Chatwin pressed David King to see at the
Alte Pinakothek while he was in Munich—and who was
active in a pogrom against the Jews. Chatwin fell for the paradoxical black lamp, longed to have it for his house in the
Chilterns, then decided black wouldn't fit in with his colour
scheme, and asked if he could have it in dull grey. King, who
didn't mind parting with the lamp, wasn't going to budge on
the colour, so Chatwin never owned it. In the end, its maker
found it frightening in a small room; to prevent the black
lamp giving him the creeps, he stowed it under a table-tennis
table.

King and Chatwin also shared an enthusiasm for utilitar-
ian structures, basic buildings, "sub-architecture," in which a
good design couldn't be ascribed to a named designer;
Chatwin was particularly keen on a book called *Architecture
without Architects*, which concerned itself with the refined and
complex culture of societies such as the Dogons of West
Africa; he also favoured a volume about the concrete fortifi-
cations constructed during the Second World War, *Bunker
Archaeology*. The two men spent a weekend in Diana Melly's
tower in the Welsh Borders looking at constructions of
corrugated iron in the countryside, particularly at Nissen huts
(Chatwin also prevailed on his wife not to demolish a concrete air-raid shelter which gapes outside their kitchen window at Homer End). And not far from the tower—or from
the Black Hill—they found a building that pleased them

both. In the village of Pembridge, near Leominster, is the fourteenth-century Church of St. Mary the Virgin: it contains a Jacobean pulpit, a thirteenth-century reading-desk carved with a fighting dog and dragon, and some Medieval stained glass; it does not have a spire or a tower. Next to St. Mary's is an odd, dumpy structure with a broad octagonal stone base and two smaller storeys made of weatherboard and topped with a little shingled spire. The building looks as if it were on its knees, or as if it had just landed. This detached bell-tower is one of seven in Herefordshire, but it is unlike the others—or any other belfry in England. The bells have seventeenth-century inscriptions; inside are eight huge oak beams and narrow loopholes in the very thick walls—it was used in early times as a place of refuge; it may originally have been simply a framework of timbers built to support the bells while the church was being built. Chatwin would have liked the use of timber in this building, as well as its clumpiness, its plainness, and its Scandinavian structure. A remark by Penelope Betjeman, to the effect that the only time she had seen a construction which looked like the Pembridge tower was when she was in the Western Himalayas, may also have added lustre for him. Later on, David King found a belfry on Romney Marsh which reminded him of Pembridge and of Bruce, but by that time his tower-collecting companion was dead.

These zealous tastes determined David King's arrangements when he came to design what was for some people Chatwin's most unexpected book: the collection of his photographs that was published, together with extracts from his notebooks, four years after his death. Few of his acquaintances associated the author with photography, and not many of his travelling companions remember his taking a large number of pictures: he didn't make a production of it. Nevertheless, he was snapping away all the time: in compiling the book—which runs to some ninety prints—King used only a tiny fraction of the whole. Chatwin took pictures freely and treated the results cavalierly: scrolls of film were tipped out of his haversack; heaps of photographs lay unlabelled around his rooms. But he thought about them seriously and talked about wanting to display them, in a book or an exhibition. One of his pictures appeared on the cover of *What Am I Doing Here*: in the first edition it was unattributed, since when he handed the photograph to Tom Maschler, Bruce neglected to say he had taken it. It shows a shopfront of corrugated iron in Nouakchott, Mauritania, painted all over— the top half a tomato-soup red, the bottom partly sage green and partly golden yellow; the doors are coloured over without distinction, and are detectable only as lines cutting through the great slabs of rippled colour. In his notebook Chatwin describes the painted structures in the old town of Nouakchott, and decides that "Rauschenberg could not do better." *In Patagonia* also contained a few black and white photographs: informative interiors and evocative landscapes. Rebecca West amused Chatwin by telling him that these were so good they rendered superfluous the entire text of the book. King reproduced some of the best of them, including a shot of a deserted railway station, plonked in the middle of an enormous vacant plain, and—enhanced by enlargement— the ghostly white hands painted prehistorically on the wall of a cave in Río de las Pinturas.

There was no obvious sequence for the photographs: when David King came to decide an order for them in the book, he had scarcely any documentation enabling him to group the pictures reliably according to chronology or setting. Not that he wanted to. The book is illuminating about Chatwin's imagination not only because of the individual pictures but because these are arranged according to a principle he applauded. One of the art books he most liked—

more than one of his favourites featured "without" in its title—was a 1937 volume by Ludwig Goldscheider called *Art without Epoch*: this places side by side objects and paintings which have an affinity though they were made in different ages and countries. A bronze from Benin is put next to a Mazzoni terracotta head; a crayon drawing by Titian appears alongside a mask for the Japanese Noh drama. In King's book of Chatwin's photographs the beams and slats of an East Anglian windmill—its body clinkered and its sails stretched out against a blue sky—are sandwiched between the similarly ridged expanse of a tin roof in Senegal and a disused mine in the Butch Cassidy region of Wyoming; the figure of a woman—Maria Reiche—seen from the back, setting determinedly out across the huge and empty Peruvian desert, is placed immediately before a shot of a solitary tree stump in the middle of a grey and misty Patagonian river; a shop window in Katmandu containing false teeth, fairy lights and the picture of a glamorous Oriental woman is followed by a Lisbon window displaying a television set which has been converted into a cage for budgerigars.

King's arrangement brings out varieties of that difference-in-similarity, and similarity-in-difference, which interested Chatwin. Similar shapes made up of contrasting materials are put together: the arch into a courtyard echoes the mound of a temple's dome on the facing page. There are juxtapositions of similar-looking materials which have been put to widely different purposes: a gleaming pile of corrugated iron lies in a merchant's yard; opposite, shine the decorative ridges of an ornate mausoleum in Afghanistan. King made his own vegetarian point when he put on one spread pictures of gentle long-muzzled goats and a butcher's shop adorned with hunks of red flesh.

In his introduction Francis Wyndham suggests that this book could have been called "Art without Artists." There is hardly anything here that would be shown in a gallery; few of the objects on display were consciously created as works of art. Chatwin took some trouble in composing his shots and his pictures don't look like casual snaps, but they weren't set up, and weren't presented by him as art photographs. He used his camera much in the way that he used his notebooks, as an aide-mémoire of things that beguiled or bemused him, and King has done for his friend's pictures what Chatwin himself would have done—what he did when he used material from his notebooks in his published works. He has cropped—many of these pictures are expansions of only the middle section of the original shot, from which a large amount of repetitive blue sky and desert sand has been cut away. And he has edited, selecting and ordering the photographs to point up particular preoccupations.

Chatwin liked frames and angles and arches: his book is full of windows and includes a series of doors, the last of which is a weather-made hole in a rock looking onto the sea. He also favoured looking aslant at a subject. He was intrigued by the use that Russian avant-garde artists such as Malevich and Suetin had made in the Twenties of dynamic composition, creating pictures constructed around a diagonal so that the eye of the onlooker is drawn from corner to corner of a canvas, and beyond. King's book emphasises Chatwin's diagonals—as a band of rusted iron reaching across a door, or as the beams of a skeletal roof rocketing off the edge of the page.

Other Russian interests of Chatwin's are also represented. One photograph shows an icon leaning (on a diagonal tilt) against a pale blue wall inside a derelict Russian Orthodox church: Chatwin was long interested in icons—one of his favourite movie scenes came in Tarkovsky's film about the icon-maker Andrei Rublev, when a bell is made by a child who doesn't know what he is doing; towards the end of his life he was also drawn to the Orthodox Church. Another picture—fuzzier than most—was included by King not because of its quality but because it demonstrated one of Chatwin's enthusiasms. A detail of a saint's robe from a fifteenth-century icon shows a pattern of white crosses with black counter-crosses—a pattern which jumps as the eye moves from one set to the other. Extracted from the rest of the image, these crosses could be a piece of geometric abstract art from the twentieth century: they might have come from the brush of a Suprematist, and show exactly the sort of epoch-leap which pleased Chatwin.

Photographs were not Chatwin's only unexpected accomplishment. The first time he came back from Africa he decided that what he wanted to do was make boxes with objects inside them. He made three—but destroyed two of them. The surviving box may have been inspired by the enigmatic productions of the American artist Joseph Cornell, who at his death in 1970 left hundreds of glass-fronted boxes in which he created controlled micro-worlds featuring his many obsessions—Greta Garbo, Victorian toys, Mallarmé, prison bars, items from the five and dime stores. Chatwin's box, which is about a foot square, has a green painted frame and a glass front; on the outside are stencilled the words "God Box." It encloses a small mirror, a horned creature, and a pinky-grey spiralled mass, curling round like the caterpillar in *Alice in Wonderland*, with feathers growing from the top; the background is made of patterned wallpaper. It could be a model theatre; it could also be a laboratory showcase. In fact, the objects—which Chatwin bought from a medicine shop in West Africa, and wrapped in a beautiful blue and white cloth now lying on a day bed in Homer End—are gris gris (African amulets): a lion's ear-drum, a pair of bird's talons joined with a strip of indigo cloth, a guinea fowl's feather, a dried iguana and a creature's intestines.

Some of his objects might have escaped from the work of Elizabeth Bishop, who is asked by an acquaintance in one of her poems: "What's that ugly thing?" The answer is "an empty wasps' nest,"

> *small, exquisite, clean matte white,*
> *and hard as stucco.*

In another of her poems an extended description of an ambiguous structure—a tumbled stack of boxes or perhaps a purposeful arrangement of fretwork and worn timber—turns into a eulogy of wood. During a trip to New York in the Sixties Chatwin contracted an enthusiasm for Bishop's writing, which was not widely acclaimed in England at the time; he particularly admired her prose. He shared with her more than a passion for disregarded objects. Bishop, who spent much of her life outside her native North America, settling for fifteen years with a woman friend in Brazil, was a meticulous chronicler of land and seascapes. In the titles of various collections—*Geography III*, *North and South*, *Questions of Travel*—she made apparent a theme of her work, which asks why human beings travel. "Should we have stayed at home and thought of here?" she asks in one poem—vindicating her own restlessness by the vigour of her observations, while raising Chatwin's recurring question:

> *What childishness is it that while there's a breath of life*
> *in our bodies, we are determined to rush*
> *to see the sun the other way around?*

Chatwin has often been recalled to his friends by the things that he liked. He had the paradoxical mysteriousness of the very definite person: he has been censured both for being elusive—for not being "really there" even though physically present—and for being over-present, for being "too much." But his visual taste was always recognisable. From time to time he uttered sweeping edicts on the subject: his worst nightmare, he told David King—who isn't sure that his friend was the first person to say so—would be to spend a night locked up in a room full of Rubenses. More often his enthusiasms were transmitted to his friends quite casually as he went along—a transmission which was a kind of intimacy. Everyone who knew Bruce had a forceful sense of him when looking at the items belonging to the collector George Ortiz which were exhibited at the Royal Academy of Arts at the beginning of 1994. In seeing piece after piece it was impossible not to think of Bruce. He would have delighted in the Cycladic marble egg (of unknown purpose) from the second or third century before Christ, and in the Etruscan votive boots, made of terracotta and varnished black, which may have been used as libation vessels. He would also have loved the tiny zoomorphic weights from Babylon: the frogs and squatting baboon which were used as amulets. He had owned such weights—including one in the shape of a duck.

It's not surprising that there should be a sympathy between Ortiz's eye and Chatwin's, though the intensity of this sympathy is striking. The two men were friends. In the Sixties they went to the Soviet Union together, visiting archaeological museums and getting drunk at an Uzbek banquet; according to Chatwin, Ortiz's excitement at the holdings of the Hermitage swept him away when he talked to the Deputy Director of the Museum: "This is the greatest museum in the world, right? I am the greatest collector of Greek bronzes in the world. If I leave you my collection in my will, will you appoint me director of this museum for a number of years?" Chatwin, who had a flair for improbable though not necessarily inaccurate evocations of friends and acquaintances (he once characterised Susan Sontag as "a brick"), was to describe the supremely cosmopolitan and sophisticated Ortiz as "innocence at large." It is impossible that the figure of this friend didn't come to his mind when he was writing about the collector Utz.

Bruce's taste went on affecting his friends after he had died: he made people look at things differently and made them look at different things. David King knows that Chatwin would have loved the book he has found which examines paintings and drawings on the backs of pictures in the National Gallery. Five years after his death, the same gallery put on an exhibition of thirteen huge paintings by Zurbarán which would certainly also have intrigued him, particularly after the strictures in his notebooks on one display of Spanish painting: "The Prado does not qualify as one of the world's great museums in my world picture. Nature banned. Religion, aristocracy and lunatics—often all three—the only subjects considered worthy of painting and collecting." The Zurbaráns in the National Gallery show were sane, dignified and scriptural, statuesque but full of individuality: the life-size images of Jacob and his twelve sons, gorgeously turbaned or humbly hooded, variously regal, judicial and fierce, hung on the walls like giant playing-cards. And King is sure that Chatwin would have taken pleasure in a new enthusiasm of his for tin plates, decorated with an abstract design, which were made in Asia just after the Second World War specifically for the African market. The Chinese who made them followed their plates to Africa and set up factories there; they were bought by Americans and taken to Europe. King thinks some of the designs are better than those of the Russian avant-garde which they resemble. Chatwin would have liked them because of this resemblance, and because of their history of movement; he would have liked the fact that they were made out of tin—and he would have liked their modesty as objects. These plates are, as King says, "such a Bruce."

Encounters early on in Chatwin's art-world career helped to
determine what it was that made something "a Bruce," and
encouraged him to combine taste with trade. John Hewett,
the doyen of Antiquities dealers at the time Chatwin met
him, was particularly influential. Hewett, who had been a
Scots Guards sergeant in North Africa during the war, and a
gardener at Kew, had a strong personality, an imposing figure
and the accoutrements of an old-fashioned country squire: he
sported a big beard, tweeds, a stick and a flat cap. He had
begun to take an interest in Antiquities when few were collecting them, starting off as a runner—a freelance dealer
without a shop who borrows objects from a seller. It takes a
good eye to be a runner, as well as a thorough knowledge of
where to find things and what prices they might fetch and a
reputation for being trustworthy; but it doesn't take much
money. After a few years Hewett had opened his own shop
in Chelsea, and was advising the Robert Sainsbury family on
what to buy for their collection in Norwich; he had developed a network of contacts who brought him things—pieces
of sculpture, pottery and stone—from the Continent as well
as from England; he had become friendly with Peter Wilson
at Sotheby's and acquired a top-drawer partner, Sandy Martin, who was deeply embedded in the object-owning and
object-shedding upper classes. He and his wife had bought a
property called Bog Farm in Kent. He had also developed a
distinctive and impressive demeanour. Howard Hodgkin,
who remembers Hewett as a Plymouth Brother from Upper
Norwood, thinks of him—perhaps by association with
Conan Doyle's story "The Norwood Builder"—as being
"just like someone out of Sherlock Holmes." The Hon.
Robert Erskine thinks of him as "a very frightening and also
very frightened person. He didn't have the confidence of

someone who'd grown up in this way. He made it himself, behaving in this immensely distinguished way without antecedents for it."

Hewett also dealt in small objects in a scarcely furnished room. In an eighteenth-century house in Park Street, Mayfair, he had a drawing-room which looked onto a street full of dentists, with a smaller room behind it. Howard Hodgkin remembers the main room in detail: "white Indian carpets, white walls, stripped eighteenth-century mantelpiece with emblems of the arts—pallets, lyres, brushes, little busts of the finest quality; a huge Chippendale desk with three or four drawers on both sides, one black angle-poise, three non-matching eighteenth-century chairs, no curtains but, just to stop people being able to see in, white cotton nets over the windows. There was a modern sofa, covered also in white material. It was all white and full of light. It was like going to see a shrink. Once in a fury I said he'd copied his showroom from the abortionist set in *Carnet de Bal*."

The delight in small objects and the spareness of the room were not lost on Chatwin. Nor was Hewett's gift for bestowing an identity and history on the objects in which he dealt. Hewett once said of a contemporary picture-dealer that "like all really good dealers, he makes his own market." Indeed, "he makes his own things." This was what he himself did when he got people interested not only in his huge Benin bronzes, but in tiny objects such as Pre-Dynastic Egyptian heads which could be held in the hand. He would play his desk like a piano, opening and shutting different drawers, peering in and discarding. Two plain but not matching eighteenth-century rummers were brought in with Scotch or champagne, and Hewett would finally pluck out an object. "This," he would announce, in his strange amalgam of a voice, in which the tones of Peter Wilson could be heard, "is really rather interesting. It might have been held by"— long pause and lowered tone—"Cleopatra."

It was at John Hewett's Park Street rooms that, soon after he had left Marlborough, in the late Fifties, Chatwin first met Robert Erskine. Hewett had spirited up a bronze necklace from his hoard and Erskine, seeing that the blond boy was "very wet behind the ears," airily hazarded a provenance: "Crimea—or somewhat west of there"; it was years before an impressed Chatwin realised that he had been taken in by a bluff. "Everything visual delights me," Erskine had once declared as an undergraduate: after his archaeological studies, he had gone on to be both a televisual presence and, at the time of his meeting with Chatwin, an expert on ancient coins and a publisher of modern British painters' prints. Erskine's St. George's Gallery Prints was just round the corner from Sotheby's, and in the same building as a bookshop which John Hewett visited almost daily, and Erskine would go regularly to nearby Park Street to buy objects. An informal cabal was established, made up of people who liked the same things. There was lots of buying and selling among its members, who would sometimes hand over a particularly admired object as a gift, with a proviso adapted to what Erskine considers the "magnificently venal" propensities of the group—that no such present should be sold for at least six months.

Chatwin was drawn to this small world. His liking for stories and researchable histories, as well as his eye, attracted him, as Hewett and Erskine were attracted, to the sort of thing that is more likely to be found in the Museum of Mankind than in the National Gallery or the Victoria and Albert Museum. The friends that he made at this time also impressed themselves on his taste in a practical manner: many of the pieces in his flats had originally belonged to them—in Eaton Place there were a host of small objects from John Hewett, and from Howard Hodgkin a stool, the Régence chair with its original covering and a little Indian painting of a building with flags. Hodgkin thinks that Chatwin's best effects in his rooms and in his books rested on a use of precedent—"Everything has a precedent," and Bruce was good at putting it all together. "Suddenly he, in the middle of all this, is throwing things around—and one is completely dazzled. And rightly."

He didn't mind going to market with his enthusiasms. "There's nothing about the commercialisation of art that I don't know," he was to reassure one of his editors, Elisabeth Sifton, who had been tentative about subjecting her aesthetic author to the onslaughts of himself being marketed. Sotheby's provided him with some of this knowledge; his extra-curricular activities supplied the rest. He had, from his earliest days at the auction house, always bought and sold things on the side. As he explained in a late essay published in *What Am I Doing Here*,

> I had next to no money. The Directors at Sotheby's assumed that people like myself had private incomes to supplement our wretched salaries. What was I to do? Exist on air? I earned myself a little extra by trafficking in antiquities—until the Chairman told me to stop. It was wrong for members of staff to deal in works of art because they actively hindered a possible sale at auction.
>
> I felt this was unfair. Almost everyone in the art business seemed to be at it.

Much of his dealing had been done in conjunction with the swashbuckling Robert Erskine, who had put up the money for several shopping expeditions overseas, while Chatwin found customers for their purchases through his Sotheby's contacts. When the two men went together to Afghanistan, they stopped in Persia, arriving shortly after a buried hoard of twelfth- and thirteenth-century pottery had been discovered, preserved by the dry soil. They bought about two dozen glazed, decorated pots, some turquoise, and some potsherds, and got them back to England to sell: fragments of pots travelled wrapped among the socks in their suitcases.

When Erskine, who had been filming with the BBC in North Africa (and glimpsing his second wife for the first time), found himself in Tunis, he visited a dealer to seek out coins and saw that one room of his big shop had been turned into a gilded forest: it was crowded with hundreds of small gilt chairs—the kind of dainty chairs that might be hired for a wedding reception. Peering through this jungle of upturned spindly gilt legs, he made out in the background "a huge great grimacing piece of wood," a piece of wood which he examined and recognised as one of the great New Caledonian door panels which used to stand outside a hut to keep away bad spirits. It was carved with enormous chevrons and on its back bore a French inscription in black paint naming the ship and the captain who had carried it in the mid-nineteenth century, a definite dating which made it extremely valuable. The dealer had another such panel, and named for the pair the not cheap but affordable price of £2,000—but Erskine had no money with him and was due to move to Algeria in the BBC Land Rover. He got in touch with Chatwin in England, described the panels, the inscription and the dealer, and asked if Chatwin could fly out and pick them up. Erskine was left with the impression that Chatwin had done a Bruce swoop, arriving in Tunis the next day, buying the panels, and returning to England immediately. In fact, the money for the transaction had to be borrowed from Elizabeth's mother, which took a little time, and when Bruce went to Tunis he went with his wife: they had a two-week holiday before returning home. Chatwin sold the panels to John Hewett, who sold them to George Ortiz. Erskine and Chatwin split the profits half and half.

In Egypt, after their first trip abroad together in the early

Sixties, they struggled through Customs with "a huge great, bloody great stone head"—consigned to a plastic bag wrapped up in newspaper—trying to look as if the heavy bundle weighed nothing at all. A Cairo dealer had assured the Englishmen that if they bought from him, he would bribe the Customs so that there was no chance of their being stopped. The officers didn't stir from the benches on which they were lying as the men and the head passed by.

Erskine was well up to a swagger on these occasions. He was exhilarated by the scrapes and derring-do of their excursions abroad, and even relished the effect of their partnership on Chatwin's employers: "Sotheby's finally rumbled the whole thing and when they renewed his contract they wrote into it quite literally that one of the conditions was that he didn't do any further dealing with Robert Erskine! Named! Not with any other party! Which I was rather pleased with." When engaged on his heists his companion was less robust. Chatwin, playing the pirate, tended to quiver and dream of jail and reach for a pill: "He'd go absolutely grey, and I'd think: 'Christ, Bruce is going to pass out on me.' I'd never seen anyone look so guilty."

But Bruce was sometimes prepared to brazen things out by adopting a disguise. On the way back from one Middle Eastern trip with Erskine, he proposed that since the Australians had a reputation for ferocity in Cairo—the Anzac troops having rioted there during the Great War—the two of them should buy bush hats to carry them through the Cairene Customs. The disguise was penetrable, not to say silly, as both men had British passports. Nevertheless, bush hats were worn, and they got through scot-free. One of Bruce's own favourite tales of effrontery in foreign places concerned an episode at Sotheby's when he was sent by Peter Wilson to France to collect a painting by Cézanne—a painting for which an export licence would not have been granted; like most Cézannes, the picture was unsigned. According to Chatwin, he borrowed a collapsible easel and a paint-box with an old palette full of squeezed-out tubes of oil paint. He wrapped the picture up in oil-cloth and tucked it under his arm. When challenged by Customs to explain his parcel, he declared: *"Moi-même, je suis peintre."*

Such were the adventures of an aesthete. Chatwin's life-story could be compared with a certain "talented young aesthete who transformed himself into a great man." This was his description of André Malraux, a man of many modes who roused him to scepticism and to sympathy in a complicated and sparky essay. Chatwin jibes at Malraux's grandiosity of manner—"he deliberately confuses the event with the archetypal situation"—and at his verbosely rhetorical style, quoting Cocteau's question: "Have you ever heard of a human reading *La Condition humaine?*" But he is responsive to him as an "adventurer" who is, as well as an archaeologist, a "compulsive traveller and talker." He was also intrigued by the writer's companion, Louise de Vilmorin, whom he was to think of including in a novel.

He cites observations by André Malraux which have the unexpected visual effects of observations by Bruce Chatwin: "Trotsky's white skin and haunted eyes made him look like a Sumerian alabaster idol." He touches on aspects of Malraux's personality which are aspects of Bruce Chatwin's personality: the restlessness which made him unfit for academic discipline, the dandyishness which caused him to wear to the Spanish Civil War a flying-jacket, jeered at as "artistic" by his critics, which was a match for Chatwin's visually pleasing haversack. He suggests that Malraux could be likened to T. E. Lawrence—with his archaeological interests, his desert-dwelling and his different lives—just as Chatwin was to be compared to T. E. Lawrence by friends and by detractors; Malraux—though interested in Lawrence, about whom he wrote—repudiated the idea of an influence, as did Bruce Chatwin. And Chatwin explains how Malraux, in one of his early incarnations, was to set up an expedition to Cambodia to search for Khmer ruins, an expedition brought to an end when the colonial authorities arrested the amateur archaeologist for taking away temple sculpture he had found in the jungle. This incident took place when Malraux was in his early twenties, the same age that Bruce Chatwin went buccaneering.

Bruce's career as "talented young aesthete" was attended by chatter about the prodigious feats of his eye. The hazy excitement of this could bewilder: "What *does* happen when Bruce Chatwin looks at a picture?" Francis Wyndham asked before meeting him. "It falls off the wall," someone piped up. Gossip about the Wunderkind was fed by episodes such as that of The Bottom. As a 22-year-old, Chatwin became friendly with Bertie Landsberg, the elderly Brazilian proprietor of the Palladian Villa Malcontenta outside Venice, who had been drawn by Picasso and had commissioned Matisse to do a picture of his sister; his family owned a great deal of land, "something the size of Belgium." Chatwin had visited the Villa Malcontenta while staying with his friend Teddy Millington-Drake, and had spotted a chunk of stone—a carved lump—lying on the floor under a console. He identified it as part of a Greek marble statue; he dated it to the sixth century B.C.—and he so impressed his host that he was made a present of the piece. Millington-Drake was later dragooned into driving Chatwin, who had developed a raging temperature, back to the Villa to pick it up; Emma Tennant went with them. The object was popped into a suitcase, and sent back to England, where it was given a starring role in Chatwin's Hyde Park flat, the flat which he described with pert defensiveness in his essay about Howard Hodgkin: "the sitting-room had a monochromatic desert-like atmosphere and contained only two works of art—the arse of an archaic Greek marble kouros, and an early seventeenth-century Japanese screen." The first of these items was known to Bruce's friends as The Bottom.

His discoveries could be startling even when his identifications weren't so secure. When Jonathan Hope visited the house where Chatwin was staying on the Welsh borders, he was told by the author with great excitement that in a small Ludlow antique shop he had come across two Sumatran javelins. Chatwin proposed that he should buy one, and Hope the other, but that night he left Shropshire for London, not indicating whether he was disappearing for a day or a year. Hope went into Ludlow and found the shop: in it were two long poles in orange lacquer, covered with a black tracery pattern and labelled by the proprietor of the shop as Venetian candle-snuffers. The South-East Asian expert saw that they were neither snuffers nor spears but processional umbrella-handles from Sri Lanka. He bought them, took them back to London, and was soon being regaled by friends with the story of his purchase as told by Chatwin: according to this, Chatwin had made his amazing discovery but Hope, displaying considerable business acumen, had whipped in before him and made off with the items. When, half-stung and half-amused, Hope explained that he had stuck to their agreement and intended to share the spoils, Chatwin wouldn't take his umbrella-handle: "No thanks. I'd rather have the story."

More than one person was reminded by Bruce of David Carritt, another keen-eyed and quick-witted blond about whom tales were tattled. Carritt was a prodigy, and the art critic John Richardson, who thinks of Chatwin's progress as a Balzacian story of a boy from the provinces who succeeds in the metropolis, has speculated that the prodigy's career could have appeared to the young Bruce as a guiding beacon.

While a schoolboy at Rugby, Carritt, brooding over the pictures in *Country Life*, had written to a selection of local lords inquiring about coming to view their paintings, and astonished them with his youth when he bicycled up. He has been credited with producing alternative renderings of A. A. Milne ditties when stranded in a Stockholm airport with a copy of *When We Were Very Young*:

> They're changing sex at Buckingham Palace.
> Philip Mountbatten is now called Alice.

He spotted a Tiepolo on a ceiling in the Egyptian Embassy and discovered an untraced Caravaggio in an English collection; he swept to a directorship of Christie's in the Sixties, became the art critic of the *Evening Standard*, and founded the international art-dealing consortium Artemis. He died of cancer when he was in his fifties.

Carritt—despite his success with Artemis—was by nature more connoisseur than dealer. Chatwin—whose categories of human behaviour were greatly influenced by the varieties of human specimen he came up against in the art world— had a flair and a relish for dealing: he liked seeing an object move from hand to hand, his pleasure having more to do with the excitement of supervising this movement than with profit. For a time in the early Sixties, when he was beginning to want to get out of Sotheby's, he discussed with Robert Erskine the idea of setting up in business as art dealers: one of Chatwin's schemes was for selling Indian floor-spreads— he had met someone who had a heap of massive cotton sheets printed with big Mogul flowers.

That idea didn't come off, but Chatwin went on manipulating the movement of objects for his own pleasure—and for that of his friends. One night he turned up at midnight, exceptionally drunk, on Howard Hodgkin's doorstep to propose—almost to demand—that his friend gamble his worldly possessions on a painting that had come up for sale at Sotheby's. He showed Hodgkin a photograph of the picture—an unusual, beautiful Matisse, one of his rare cubistic paintings, a still-life of oranges in a glass. He explained that the Marlborough Gallery wasn't interested in buying it, neither was any big buyer, and that Matisse's daughter—the only other customer in the field—would have to sell a later painting in order to purchase this one. He said he thought the oranges would fetch between fifteen and twenty thousand pounds: "How much is your house worth? How much are your Indian paintings worth?" Hodgkin, who spent a sleepless night worrying about the matter, remembers exactly their concluding exchange the following morning. Chatwin rang: "He said: 'This is an opportunity that will never recur in your life. You'll have other opportunities but this won't. I assure you you'll regret it if you don't do it.' And I said: 'I'm sure I will, and I'm not going to do it.' If I had done it I would now be a millionaire."

Although Hodgkin failed to collect on that occasion, the sense of him as a collector was central to Chatwin's idea and description of his friend: "His collection is an essential part of his life's work. Any retrospective exhibition of Howard's own paintings would, in my opinion, be incomplete without the Indian collection hanging beside them." His essay about Hodgkin is affectionate, intriguing, teasing and perceptive. He is eloquent about the expressiveness of the collection:

> I have sometimes thought that Howard's pictures are a declaration of war against his Indian ones. He is obscure where they are explicit. He is mute where they tell a story. He fudges where they are finicky. His colours are deliberately jarring where theirs seek to soothe. Perhaps it is a case of renouncing the thing you love?

Perhaps his "walloped-down" pictures can be seen as an act of total renunciation.

He writes with brio about the mysterious subjects of Hodgkin's pictures, drawing autobiography from their abstractions, tracing favourite colour combinations to an eccentric grandmother and finding erotic tales in "dots, splotches, flashes and slabs of colour." And he touches on the complicated tango performed by the elusive subjects and their precise titles: "it doesn't require much imagination to see that the one called *Red Bermudas* is of a sunbather in Central Park. But who would guess that *Tea*, a panel over-splattered in scarlet, represents a seedy flat in Paddington where a male hustler is telling the story of his life?" The wit that is at work in Hodgkin's titles was to help Chatwin: it was Hodgkin who protested (threatening, he later said, to get out of a moving car) that the author's first book couldn't possibly be called "Oh Patagonia!" and who suggested, on analogy with the titles of many of his own paintings, "In Patagonia."

In the Sixties Howard Hodgkin was a witness to a strange Chatwin encounter in Kensington. Robert Erskine's house, near the High Street, was a place of parties and pop stars—and of resort for the newly married Chatwin and his wife Elizabeth. It was comfortable and skilfully crammed with objects: the big double drawing-room on the ground floor had a door by Robert Adam, two large Boulle cabinets, and glass shelves on which chunks of Medieval urns and Pre-Dynastic Egyptian vases were watched over by little plastic spacemen from Cornflakes packets; the windows stretched down to street level so that passers-by could be called in by a tap on the pane. Here Hodgkin was talking to the future author and to Erskine one afternoon when Erskine's (huge, bronze, Renaissance) door-knocker announced the arrival of a tall bespectacled American man trailing a sexy, sulky, smelly girl:

"she looked very animal and she was obviously terribly rich and very spoilt." Chatwin glanced at Hodgkin and went into an elaborate pantomime of courtesy, "a mixture of a duke and a duchess, a dowager and her old husband," as he was introduced to the girl—and greeted the man as an acquaintance of long ago. When they left the room, he explained: "That's him. The steamer-chair character. My steaming steamer." On a steamboat before his marriage, he had sat on deck next to a blond and blazered American, who had been reading Chekhov. They'd talked; they'd become friendly; they'd had a shipboard romance. And, until the afternoon at Robert Erskine's, that was the last they'd seen of each other.

Some years later the Hodgkins went to have dinner with the Chatwins in Gloucestershire and found them still shocked from a recent weekend visit from the Steamer, now married to his girlfriend. Elizabeth Chatwin had noticed the wife playing with an interesting-looking ring on her finger, and asked her where it had come from. It was a present from her husband. Elizabeth looked again, saw that the stone was a scarab—in fact, an Eighteenth-Dynasty scarab in yellow jasper—and when Bruce appeared pointed it out to him. Bruce fell to grilling the Steamer about where he had got the ring: "In the market? Which market? Which city? At Sotheby's? Would you like to try again?" The Steamer couldn't remember. "Well, I'm now going to make a phone call," said Bruce, "I'm going to call up a mutual friend." He went to the telephone and rang Robert Erskine in London. He said: "I have found the scarab that was stolen from you. It has been made into a ring and is on the finger of somebody who is sitting in my kitchen." The Steamer steamed off into the night.

❧6

EDINBURGH

Bruce Chatwin left Sotheby's in 1966. He had been made a director of the firm and had run two departments—Antiquities and Impressionists. He had established a reputation doing something he was good at—and stood to earn a lot of money. He was secure in his position, and had prospects of advancement. He was in his mid-twenties and could have been expected to stay at the auction house—as his contemporaries David Nash, Michel Strauss and Marcus Linell stayed—and make it his career. Instead, not for the last time, he bolted. And, not for the last time, his actions have become surrounded by a buzz of different explanations.

In *The Songlines* Chatwin gave a graphic account of the reasons for his flight:

> One morning, I woke up blind.
>
> During the course of the day, the sight returned to the left eye, but the right one stayed sluggish and clouded. The eye specialist who examined me said there was nothing wrong organically, and diagnosed the nature of the trouble.
>
> "You've been looking too closely at pictures," he said. "Why don't you swap them for some long horizons?"

After this consultation, he said in *The Songlines* and told me when I was interviewing him for *Harper's & Queen*, he took off for the Sudan, where he met nomads with shields of elephant hide, found a puff-adder curled up under his sleeping-bag, and learned to read footprints in the sand. He decided to leave Sotheby's.

It wasn't quite like this. As so often, Bruce's description dramatises by leaving out links and explanations and by collapsing the time-scheme. But as so often, his account wasn't as far from the truth as posthumous rumour has suggested. Eyes were at the root of his trouble, and travel was to offer a salve. Bruce the visual expert was susceptible to afflictions of the eye in much the way that Bruce the great walker was troubled by varicose veins. As a teenager at the end of a holiday, he had suddenly looked up from reading *The Times* and announced that he couldn't see—an episode which was followed by weeks away from school and a mysterious spell of repeatedly tumbling, laughing, down stairs, but by no final diagnosis. Years later, scouting for Black Hill background with Diana Melly in Wales, he panicked about the condition of his eyes in a hotel dining-room, saying that the sun and wind had hurt them, and sending out a search-party—in the shape of his friend—for Optrex and droppers from a late-night chemist. After a series of long evenings with American collectors had left him with "physical and visual indigestion," he complained: "New York turned me inside out and has left me in a highly nervous state, also without the power to focus my right eye." Throughout his life, after reading or writing for any length of time, he would say that he couldn't see.

The eye specialist whom he consulted on the occasion of his sudden loss of sight was a friend, Patrick Trevor-Roper, who diagnosed Chatwin's trouble as "convergence insufficiency": he had a latent squint which showed itself under stress. Chatwin's symptoms—not quite blindness, but headaches and his eyes drifting off-true—were essentially stress-induced, and aggravated by looking at close range. Trevor-Roper advised him to give up Sotheby's, asked his patient what he wanted to do, and when Chatwin said "travel," encouraged him.

In an unpublished manuscript Bruce was to give another account of his indisposition—one which treated it less as a symbolic act of fate and more as an act of calculation: "I manufactured a nervous eye complaint, which I then came to believe in and later suffered from. This was interpreted in many ways, but achieved my intention—a leave of absence for several months' travel in Africa. The eye complaint evaporated by the time I reached the airport." He didn't explain there or in *The Songlines* that during his time in the Sudan he was not living in the wild but staying with his ex-girlfriend, Gloria Birkett, who was married and living in the region. Nor did he leave Sotheby's immediately on returning to England.

During his last months at the auction house Bruce was at his most luridly fanciful: "The atmosphere of the Art World reminded me of the morgue. 'All those lovely things passing through your hands,' they'd say—and I'd look at my hands and think of Lady Macbeth." Over the years he had accumulated different strata of grievance and unease: he was tired of hearing people fawn over collectors and their objects; he felt oppressed by the heaps of beautiful stuff that surrounded him; he was wary of being caught up in scams; he was weary of being able to tell that an object was good but not knowing the story behind it. And he was piqued. His wife remembers the immediate occasion for his leaving the auction house as the surprise appointment of a considerable number of people as directors of Sotheby's. Chatwin, who was made a director after his return from the Sudan, had expected to be one of a few.

Having an ally helped him to escape. In the summer of
1965, when he was twenty-five, Chatwin had married Elizabeth Chanler, a young American woman who had been
working at Sotheby's as one of Peter Wilson's secretaries.
Elizabeth, small, dark and independent, had studied history
at Harvard, taken courses in Indian art and Rembrandt etch-
ings, and been given a thorough grounding in art history at
school, but claimed she owed her job at Sotheby's, as most
girls did, to qualities of a different order. She knew people in
the firm. She was persistent, nagging at the management
until they gave her a position—at first in the exiguous New
York office, where one of her tasks was to sift through the
obituary columns sniffing out any collections which might
have been left. And her own grandfather had a collection in
which Sotheby's was interested.

The eldest of eight children, Elizabeth came from an East
Coast Catholic family: Bruce used to chide her about her
"awful Pope"—though before he got married he went for
instruction to the Mayfair Jesuits in Farm Street. Her father
was a naval officer; her mother, the daughter of a diplomat,
had spent part of her girlhood in Europe: a picture by the
equine painter Alfred Munnings in her New York flat freezes
her at seventeen, in front of Spanish hills, on a horse called
Morning Light. They made their home at Sweet Briar Farm
near Rochester in the west of New York State, which had
been bought by Elizabeth's paternal grandfather, who liked
to hunt: there were some three hundred acres of land under
wheat and oats; there was a large lawn with big oak trees;
there was an 1890s clapboard house with a capacious terrace.
It was here that Elizabeth was brought up, and from here that
she got married.

Bruce liked to surprise his friends with his marriage, producing information about the event like a conjurer. Over
elevenses in a coffee bar near Sotheby's, he confided in his

friend Cary Welch, the connoisseur of Indian and Persian art, that he was thinking of becoming engaged—but other friends scarcely knew he was seeing someone. He took Elizabeth for an introductory supper at the Hodgkins', and returned alone later to announce: "I think we're going to get married." He yelled the news to Robert Erskine from the window of a block of flats in Chelsea, expanding his account as his friend progressed across the square.

But there was nothing impromptu about the wedding. Two months' solid work produced a gathering of some two hundred guests, and a ceremony, with a Nuptial Mass, in the Chanlers' private chapel. The evening before the wedding a dinner party for ninety relations was held at the house of one of Elizabeth's uncles: there was a drought and no wind and the meal took place on the lawn, where torches shone at night. Elizabeth's three sisters were bridesmaids in pale yellow, with wreaths in their hair and daisies in their hands; her brothers—"She's got lots of brothers. I'm very afraid of those brothers," Bruce used to claim before he met them—were ushers with Hugh Chatwin; David Nash acted as best man. The bride wore white, with a veil which had belonged to her mother's grandmother; her hair had been cropped savagely short and in order to anchor her veil she had to wear a hairpiece—the curls of this were whipped up and coiled fantastically in the manner of Sixties' brides, like ice cream in a cornet.

On their wedding-trip the Chatwins sailed round the coast of Maine in a rented boat; accompanying them in their own boat were friends of Elizabeth's, Billy and Mia Wood, who also had on board Cary Welch and his wife. They holed up for some time in Cape Split, memorialised in the paintings of John Marin, they walked through woods in which the wrecks of cars, used for target practice by the local people, lay among the trees. Bruce and Elizabeth bought badges inscribed with the names Max and Maxine: "Max" stuck through their married life as Elizabeth's pet name for her husband. The Elizabeth Chatwin of today is more recognisable in the energetic honeymooner than in the fondant bride of her wedding photographs. Bruce's widow has been white-water rafting in Alaska, and travelled in her husband's footsteps through Patagonia; she guides expeditions through the Himalayas, and likes to wear Indian indigos as well as sailors' trousers. Bruce, with whom she voyaged to India, Afghanistan, Persia and China, used to assert that they were happiest as a couple when they were travelling.

At Homer End Elizabeth keeps a flock of Black Welsh Mountain sheep. Bruce, in one of his embellishing boasts, used to say that she gave her occupation on her passport as "shepherdess": American passports don't give occupations, but "shepherd" is what Elizabeth calls herself when challenged. Bruce wasn't eager to be pastoral himself, only reluctantly turning out to help with rounding up the beasts, mooching in the corners of fields with his hands in his pockets. The Chatwins differed in their attitude to animals. Bruce was not a lover of pets, though he sometimes took to a creature if it made him laugh. Elizabeth horrified him with the number of animals she cared for: there are always cats in her kitchen, a saddle hanging over her banister rail and in her car a bustle of small dogs—trim Jack Russells and Chinese lion dogs, whose long fringes and plumed tails make them look like two mop-heads tied together. Squinting at one of these dogs—its eyes hidden under its hair, and only a square grin to show which end was which—Bruce objected to his wife that the animal was "so oblique. I can't understand how you know what he's thinking." The breed he liked best were pugs—because their faces stand out so clearly.

"I don't *know* what feminism *is*," Bruce once insisted to me. But he often behaved as if he did. He didn't emit a glimmer of male superiority when I was working with him, and was quick to express his contempt for the patronising airs of liberal publishing men as they clucked over their subordinates—"these girls." He described a similar casual condescension in *On the Black Hill*: "Never, he said, had he met a more intelligent woman, as if this was a contradiction in terms." And he married a woman who, while paying him a great deal of attention—Bruce always liked to be mothered—had an independent life, and an independent tongue: at Homer End there were often two streams of talk, sometimes blending, sometimes clashing, sometimes flowing volubly along side by side.

Elizabeth raised no objection when her husband announced that he wanted to leave his lucrative Sotheby's post and go, at the age of twenty-six, to the University of Edinburgh to study archaeology. He was hoping that his studies would prove fairly science-free: he had shied away from more graph-intensive archaeological courses—it is difficult to imagine a Bruce graph.

A few weeks into his first term at Edinburgh he sent a letter to Stephen Tennant, one of Bruce's ornamental hermits. Tennant was said to have told his father, Lord Glenconner, that he wanted to grow up to be "a Great Beauty"—and he did. He was sculpted by Jacob Epstein, said by Thomas Hardy to walk like Swinburne, adored by Siegfried Sassoon, with whom he had an affair, and much photographed, willowy and mackintoshed, by Cecil Beaton, whose portraits of himself he pronounced "quite perfect, luscious & dazzling & melting & the bare shoulder ones are like a sculpture, too beautiful for words!" He decorated one of his rooms entirely in silver; he endlessly rewrote a book, to be called *Lascar*, about Marseilles, sailors and brothels; he lived as a recluse in his Wiltshire mansion, where he considered installing a pool for seals.

Bruce had corresponded with Tennant while at Sotheby's, where he had written on behalf of a friend, "one of your fervent admirers," to see if he could buy one of Tennant's paintings—"Do let me know if you can spare one, one with Lascars?"—and where he had arranged for him the sale of a picture by Tchelitchew, "Garçon Allongé." In the letter from Edinburgh Tennant was told, with reference, no doubt, to his correspondent's previous existence courting the rich and their valuables: "I have never been so overworked in my life. Even duchesses take up less time than history essays." Bruce issued some cheerfully conceited complaints: "I have learnt never to offend the second-year students, who are immensely full of their own self-importance. One second-yearer leaned across my shoulder and asked me why I was reading a particularly devious book, and then said that first-year students were not able to understand its mysteries. A rigid stratification divides the years and the twain shall never meet let alone have a conversation." And he wrote with some straightforward enjoyment about a fellow student who might have taken Tennant's fancy: "There's a wonderful young man with carrot-coloured plaits who wears a red plastic coat and no shoes even though there's ice on the pavement."

Chatwin was writing from the Canongate, where he and Elizabeth were spending the second year of their married life in a Corporation flat—part of a Sixties wing in a seventeenth-century block; they were on the opposite side of the Royal Mile from John Knox's house, hard by the heart of Midlothian, in an area teeming with curios and tourists. An attempt to buy a flat in the New Town had failed when their solicitor had dithered, expressing disquiet at the idea of a well-brought-up young woman purchasing a flat near which a murder had taken place. Elizabeth Chatwin, who was commuting between the Canongate flat and Holwell Farm, the house which they had just bought in a Gloucestershire valley, hated their time at Edinburgh. She also hated the flat, which had been badly rebuilt and left unfinished: the windows were put in peculiar places, the wardrobes didn't have rails in them, the floors were splintery, and it took four hours for the boiler to heat enough water for a bath. Chatwin bought furniture from the Salvation Army, and sisal mats, and Christopher Gibbs remembers the apartment as being both "stark and elegant and empty" and "full of charming things": it served as an arena for the perpetual battle in Chatwin between his collecting urge and the ascetic instinct which drove him to purge "his own gross appetite for having two ashtrays instead of one." But to Elizabeth the place was never better than horrid; the house was filled entirely by English people who "clung together and moaned." She hated, too, the line of pubs in which you couldn't sit down, the cinema which showed only *The Sound of Music*, and the difficulty of getting a salad.

Her husband had more to divert him. There were all those essays: Chatwin's are remembered as being of a high standard, on-time and typed. He liked eating at the Café Royal—as did his wife, with whom he devised, in the Canongate, a dish using three different kinds of local fish. And he made occasional excursions out of the city. He roved over the countryside near Dunbar with Christopher Gibbs, in search of the spot from which Thomas the Rhymer, the thirteenth-century Scots seer and poet—credited with foretelling the Battle of Bannockburn and the death of a Scottish king—was supposed to have been whisked off to Elfland, where he made the fairy queen his mistress. Travelling on small branchline trains, Chatwin and Gibbs were equipped with luggage of elfin proportions: Gibbs remembers "a rug and some sort of old kettle, and maybe a toothbrush in the kettle. Bruce always had some precious little bundle somewhere—very, very special soap or something."

In Edinburgh Chatwin made friends with his professor, Stuart Piggott, whose teaching had been one of the attractions of the university for him. Piggott, the author of books on prehistory and a study of the eighteenth-century antiquary William Stukeley, was beaky and precise. He was some thirty years older than his student and temperamentally very different: "I'm on the side of the Enlightenment," he said. Bruce "was on the side of the Romantics"; Bruce also had "a vivid interest in people—which I didn't share." But they had in common a fascination with forgeries. This had long been a concern of Piggott's, who had been friendly with one of the archaeologists who exploded the Piltdown Man fraud; the reputation of Chatwin's eye had been a matter of exposing the sham as well as finding the real. Robert Erskine remembers catching a glimpse of his friend shooting through a room in Christie's, pursued by a retinue of young men who were struggling to keep up with him, taking notes while Chatwin was delivering judgment: "That's fake, that's fake, that's a fake, that's a complete fake, and that's a horrible fake . . ." And both Chatwin and Piggott liked food. Piggott relished two Chatwin dishes in particular. There was a boiled chicken served with lemon sauce. And there was Imam Bayeldi, the aubergine dish from Turkey which translates into English as "the imam swooned"—a priest, on first tasting the delicious concoction, was said to have fainted away.

It seems that the professor may have swooned too. Piggott became very attached to his pupil: a friend of Chatwin alleges that his teacher, lapsing into romantic melancholy, had once proposed a suicide pact. When Chatwin, encouraged by a senior member of staff, put in to complete his course in three rather than four years, Piggott refused: he was later to say that Edinburgh was never the same without Bruce. This refusal was one of Chatwin's reasons for leaving Edinburgh. Another was the departure of a lecturer on the Dark Ages whose course he had particularly wanted to take. Another was his wife's misery. He was also discontented with the subject: "I got into the same trap with archaeology that I had in the art world, because of its reliance on things," he explained in an interview conducted a year before his death. "In the Cairo museum I saw all these masks of the pharaohs, row on row. I asked myself: Where are the masks of Moses? I started liking people who had no garbage to leave. I wanted to find the other side of the coin." This turning-point had an aesthetic dimension, reflecting his own preference for very bare, non-glittery objects: he thought the pharaohs looked as if their funerals had been "done by Heal's." He had become fascinated, he told me, by lives that were "invisible to the archaeologist's spade," by the lives of nomads who travelled through history "leaving no burnt layer."

Intrigued by the idea that archaeologists were driven to bury themselves, he and David Nash had collected examples of deaths brought about by collapsing buildings and caved-in tunnels. Bruce drew on this collection in one draft of an *In Patagonia* passage, where he expanded on his complaints about his old studies. He called archaeology "the dismal science" and elaborated to doleful effect the description of Sarmiento antiquities collectors in the book:

> These archaeological ladies had acquired the indestructible patina of the objects they loved. They confirmed one of my favourite prejudices: archaeological ladies are endowed with monstrous strength from grubbing in the earth; the men who are attracted to archaeology tend to wither, to suicide, so that perhaps the crowning glory of their career would be to dig their own tomb. There are two recent cases, one in Santorini and the other in Chile, of archaeologists who buried themselves in their own excavations. Archaeology attracts the depressed.

Near this are the words "never so painfully aware of my own mortality"—although he had also been made acutely aware of this in the "morgue" of Sotheby's. In a talk called "The Morality of Things," which he delivered in 1973 before a charity art auction held to raise money for the Red Cross, Bruce regretted that his old teachers had rejected as "emotional and unscientific" any attempt to deduce from prehistoric objects the beliefs or character of their makers.

Other scholars were also sceptical of these attempts. In the winter of 1970 the Asia House Gallery in New York put on an exhibition called " 'Animal Style' Art from East to West." The material for this was chosen, and the catalogue compiled, by Emma C. Bunker, from the Denver Art Museum, assisted by Ann R. Farkas, from the History of Art Department at Columbia—and C. Bruce Chatwin. In an introductory essay, Mrs. Bunker discussed some attributes of what is known as the "Animal Style," a type of ornament used by early European and Asian warrior-herdsmen. She explained that the term was slippery, and the origins of the style uncertain. She also said that this art may be "intriguing, and, at times, even beautiful, but it is never monumental or intellectual": these barbarian objects, small in size, are also small in importance when set against "the major achievements in painting, sculpture and architecture of the learned city folk."

The catalogue shows an array of graceful, witty, expressive objects, none of which would have been out of place in the exhibition drawn from George Ortiz's collection. There is a perky bronze bird from China with a long straight tail and a jaunty crest: dating from around 1300 B.C., it was made to go on the top of a pole and had a pellet inside its body which converts it into a rattle. There is a harness ornament from Central Asia of the sixth to fifth century B.C. which features a wonderfully fluid ibex, whose folded legs echo the curve of its long horns, and which is just over two and a half inches high. There is a hollowed antler tube carved with an animal's head, which has short ears and jet eyes and comes from Alaska. There is an eight-inch pin from the Caucasus, made to be placed on a tomb, which is topped by a bronze horse with a ball-headed, big-nosed rider in boots and tight trousers. There are daggers, pendants, axeheads, wands, belt-hooks, sleeve-weights, amulets and knife handles. There are griffins, wolves, walruses, eagles, snakes, horses, tigers and dragons.

These were objects which Bruce admired. He shared his enthusiasm for the Animal Style with Cary Welch, who arranged his involvement with the Asia House exhibition, and, although he doesn't say so in the catalogue material, Chatwin would have considered the work of these "barbarians" to be as important and distinctive as the monumental artefacts of the "civilised." What he did say in his catalogue essay, "The Nomadic Alternative," obviously disturbed his fellow contributors. Here Bruce was at his most speculative and all-encompassing; he was also vivid and stimulating. He proposes that shamanism could have been the inspiration for the Animal Style; he suggests that this inspiration could account for the style's appearance among Eskimos as well as Irish, North American Indians as well as Asians. In making his thesis, he outlines his own aesthetic: "nomadic art tends to be portable, asymmetric, discordant, restless, incorporeal and intuitive." He also lays down some lively comparisons. Modern accounts of hallucinations in trance describe "a dis-ordering of space and form, the disintegration of eidetic images into spirals, whorls, volutes, carpet patterns, nets and lattices; colours are of other-worldly brilliance; there are half-faces, faces split in half about a central axis, X-ray vision." In nomadic art "colour is violent; mass and volume are rejected in favour of bold silhouettes and a pierced technique of open-work spirals, lattices and geometric tracery. Animals are depicted from both sides at once, their heads abutted to form a frontal mask. The so-called X-ray style is common."

This theory drew a note of demurral in one of Emma Bunker's catalogue essays, and a reproof from the Director of the Asia House Gallery, Gordon Bailey Washburn, in his Foreword: "Mr. Chatwin, an anthropologist at heart, is inclined to find shamanism the most likely inspiration for the Animal Style . . . Mrs. Bunker and Dr. Farkas are less interested in an unprovable hypothesis and more concerned with the exacting research that traces the movements of ancient peoples and their styles of ornament across the vast face of Asia and the smaller one of Europe." There is in this voice an echo of Stuart Piggott, who, in addressing the PEN meeting about Bruce, amused some of his audience with his magisterial caution: "He would have got, if not perhaps a first, certainly a very, very high second."

Bruce never wrote about his time at Edinburgh, although his work there fed into *The Songlines*. But he did leave an indirect account of the effect that the city and his experiences there had on him. "You must remember that I shall be a nomad, more or less, until my days are done." Not Bruce Chatwin, but Robert Louis Stevenson, writing to his mother in 1874, when he was twenty-four years old. A hundred years later, Chatwin quoted these words in the course of reviewing James Pope-Hennessy's biography of Stevenson for *The Times Literary Supplement*. It is the most disturbing and the most revealing piece of criticism that he ever wrote.

The arresting feature of Chatwin's article is that he dismisses Stevenson both as a man and as a writer, while understanding him and evoking his presence vividly. Five times within four paragraphs he moves in a disagreeable way to find his subject wanting. Stevenson was "a talented story-teller but he was never first-rate"; he was most effective as an author of straightforward books for children, which "is hardly the mark of a first-rate writer"; his life was not "a first-rate performance"; he was "an obvious second-rater"—in fact, "it is Stevenson's second-rateness that makes him interesting."

Bruce rarely took on a book review if he had nothing favourable to say. There is no question that he found Stevenson extremely interesting: he talked vehemently about him to friends; his unprecedentedly repetitive and violent language is that of someone fighting off fascination and complicity. The article is a complicated piece of self-examination and self-dislike.

Chatwin and Stevenson resembled each other in a number of ways, some of which would have been apparent to Bruce when he wrote his review. Both men were self-styled "nomads" who wrote about their journeys and gained reputations as romantic figures. Both were educated, though in Bruce's case for a short time only, in Edinburgh. Both were Francophiles; both married American women. The sexual proclivities of both have aroused public speculation: Chatwin speaks of Stevenson's "gift of making himself irresistible to both sexes." Both died in their forties, surrounded by half-truths and hero-worship. "Whether his acts were genuine or faked is beside the point," Chatwin suggests. "The events of his life and the circumstance of his death have a mythic wholeness . . ." His description of André Malraux as "a talented young aesthete who transformed himself into a great man" has its interest in relation both to Stevenson and to Chatwin himself.

At each point of similarity Chatwin recoils from his subject. Stevenson's travelling is represented as timid, escapist and compromised. "He yearned for adventure, for a 'pure dispassionate adventure such as befell the great explorers.' But he hadn't the stomach for it; on the whole, he travelled in a world made safe for aesthetes." In fact, Stevenson journeyed courageously—and, as Chatwin does say, often in desperately poor health. He went alone from Edinburgh to Monterey by emigrant train and ship, and arrived suffering from malnutrition, eczema and pleurisy; he visited more than forty Pacific islands, and spent a week at the leper colony on the island of Molokai. But what is really striking about Bruce's unfairness is that he should pit the extremes of his own personality against each other. Chatwin himself was a traveller rather than an explorer: he didn't go alone into uncharted regions, and in that sense his own journeyings were circumscribed and "made safe"—though they were none the less spirited, enterprising and open-eyed for that. And they were certainly journeys made by an aesthete. Adventurer and aesthete co-existed in Chatwin—but here the two are depicted as being both ridiculous and self-evidently incompatible.

According to Chatwin, Stevenson "harped on the need for the simple life, alone or out in the open with the woman one loves, only to cumber himself with the hefty trappings of the middle class." Everyone who knew Bruce for any length of time heard his denunciations of acquisitiveness: the talk "The Morality of Things," which he delivered to an audience who had gathered together to bid for works of art, inveighed against the accumulation of art objects, and he was always prepared to deliver off-the-cuff tirades on the subject. There wasn't much that was "hefty" about his own living arrangements, which were designed to seem breezy rather than bourgeois, but anyone who visited his homes was aware of his ability to procure beautiful things. There was obviously a tension between his delight in objects and his distaste for them: "And do we not all long to throw down our altars and rid ourselves of our possessions?" he demanded in "The Morality of Things." Most of Bruce's friends regarded this tension as a benign contradiction, rather than the failure or near-hypocrisy which he seeks to detect in Stevenson. But it seems that Bruce may have been harsher on himself.

Description shades puzzlingly into reproof in his discussion. Stevenson's "predicament is very familiar—the spoilt child of worthy, narrow-minded parents, unwilling to follow in the family business, longing to slough off civilisation in favour of healthy primitivism, yet tied to home by links of affection and cash." This isn't clearly shameful, but worse is to come: "Stevenson is the forerunner of countless middle-class children who litter the world's beaches, or comfort themselves with anachronistic pursuits and worn-out religions. *Travels with a Donkey* is the prototype of the incompetent undergraduate voyage." Bruce here has been carried away by his anxiety—as the travelling child of supportive middle-class parents—to distance himself from his fellow travellers of the Sixties and Seventies, the hippies. It is an anxiety for which the playwright Alan Bennett has taken him to task—and which is part of Chatwin's suspicion that what is familiar is bound to be mediocre.

Elsewhere he gives what could be thought a self-portrait, only to pour scorn on the figure he has drawn. "One side of Stevenson was the perennial boy with the pack on his back, always happier to be somewhere else." This was exactly how many people experienced Bruce—who goes on to denigrate the backpacker as "unable to face the complications of sex, and ready to work it off on a hike." He then blames the writer for also being the boring opposite of this figure: "The other side of Stevenson was the man with the staid, conventional view that he should marry and settle down." This does very little justice to an outlandish match: Fanny was ten years older than Stevenson and, when he first met her, in an artists' colony in the Fontainebleau woods, was still married with two children; his parents did not approve.

Stevenson "liked to think he was free with information about himself." In fact, Chatwin explains, in what could be thought a caustic account of his own procedures in his books and in this article, "he kept tight rein on the confessional; but, consciously or not, he was always dropping broad hints in his stories." It is Stevenson's divisions, contradictions and

ambiguities which fire Chatwin, who represents them as du-
plicities. Edinburgh, he announces, is "the key to understanding Stevenson," and Edinburgh, where both Chatwin
and Stevenson went to university, and where both abandoned
a course of study, is depicted as "a place of absolute contrast
and paradox." The city is New and Old, squalid and distinguished, foggy and airy, puritanical and orgiastic, urban and
rural, full of slums and full of mansions. Edinburgh produced
in Stevenson "a repetitious see-saw of attraction and loathing
that almost predetermined his death in the South Seas"—
although the South Seas saved him from Edinburgh mists and
puritanical fruitlessness. Edinburgh also enabled him to produce his novel about human duality, *The Strange Case of Dr.
Jekyll and Mr. Hyde.* In the most touching sentence of this
painful piece, Bruce puts in a word for the dark partner of the
duo: "It does not say much for Stevenson's understanding or
tolerance that he should bestow his sympathies on Dr. Jekyll
and damn Mr. Hyde."

Bruce's demeanour was that of a clearly directed, decisive,
unusually singleminded man; his sentences tend to be those
of someone who has made up his mind. In writing about
Stevenson and his divisions, he suggests some of the complications and anxieties that accompanied his own definite
manner and unambiguous prose. Stevenson is reproved for
not measuring up to a number of writers. Walt Whitman,
Rimbaud and Hart Crane—the first mentioned by Chatwin
elsewhere as an influence on his own early life, the second
a late obsession—are cited as other "literary vagabonds." A
comparison with Oscar Wilde is less persuasive: Stevenson
and Wilde were almost exact contemporaries—born within
five years of each other and both dying, in their forties, as the
century was turning—but were hardly indistinguishable in
their personal and writing styles. It isn't at all clear why
Stevenson should be compared to Wilde, whose "open-
hearted audacity" he is said to lack. It is clear that one of the

things that Wilde, Hart Crane, Rimbaud and Whitman had in common was that they were evidently homosexual or bisexual. Chatwin is speaking up for this, and for a sexual frankness in which he himself was accused after his death of having been deficient.

But he is not claiming that Robert Louis Stevenson was homosexual. He sketches the occasions which have led some critics to wonder about that: a supposedly strong attachment to his stepson; an admiration both of the handsome Samoan houseboys whom he employed in the South Seas and of the scarred pirates whom he created in *Treasure Island*; his "girl-ishness," and his tender descriptions of male friendship—"his eyes dwelling on those of his old friend like those of a lover on his mistress's." His own conclusion is different. He quotes Stevenson's lines on having his portrait painted by Gugliemo Nerli:

> *Oh will he paint me the way I like, as bonny as a girlie,*
> *Or will he make me an ugly tyke, and be—to Mr. Nerli!*

He goes on, "Had he been a homosexual, or known what it was to be one, he would surely not have written these arch and embarrassing lines." This comment is unusual for Bruce in its seeming to identify him publicly as someone who does know what it is to have homosexual feelings.

The confident intimacy which characterises Chatwin's speculations about Stevenson is noticeable in his discussion of Stevenson's marriage to Fanny Osbourne. He is sure that "there was not going to be much sex in this marriage," sure that Stevenson was besotted with his future wife, and sure about the way their marriage operated: "Fanny was to be the dominant partner. In good times, she was to be companion, fellow-adventurer, sister and mother, but hardly ever the lover. In bad times she was to be the devoted, iron-willed sick-nurse." He is harsh on Fanny—on what he sees as her tantrums, snobberies and "salvationist impulses." At one point he violently caricatures the couple and their marriage, by reinventing the portrait painted of them by John Singer Sargent: "Sargent's brilliant portrait of the pair, painted at Bournemouth, says it all—he the pale, agitated narcissist, twiddling his moustachios and gazing into the mirror, she, a dumpy sedentary figure in oriental costume." He goes on, gnomically: "The Stevensons were in some ways a very modern couple." At another point he responds with enthusiasm and sympathy to their romance: "There is every reason why the gauche, elfin lad, with his 'odd intent gaze,' should have been drawn to an attractive older woman. Furthermore, any transatlantic love-affair holds an extra fascination for both sides, combining the charm of the exotic with an ease of communication." Chatwin is writing here as someone who married an American woman who was, as Fanny Osbourne was, a capable, practical, tomboyish, self-reliant woman engaged in artistic pursuits in Europe.

He is also writing as someone of whom this could be a description:

> in velveteen jacket and straw hat, knapsack on back, he arrived at Cockfield Rectory. At this period he was closely related to a style of youngster already rife in British universities and later imitated in the States with pious Anglophilia—very young, very witty, very impulsive, very cultivated, very promising, very picturesque, very high-strung, very generous, and oh so very sensitive. Rupert Brooke was the peak of the development. Louis's essential charm in his Scottish version of that role seems to have been marked if sociably egocentric; years later a lady-interviewer came near explaining it: "He assumed that you too were alertly alive;

that you would understand and share his interest in all interesting things."

This evocation of Robert Louis Stevenson, in J. C. Furnas's biography of the author, fits Chatwin very well, although he was never as moony as Rupert Brooke. As does Sidney Colvin's memory of his young Scottish friend: "Pure poetic eloquence . . . grave argument and criticism, riotous freaks of fancy, flashes of nonsense more illuminating than wisdom, streamed from him inexhaustibly." In both cases, there was a penalty for exhibiting such ebullient charm. Stevenson's friend, the Classical scholar and fairy-taler Andrew Lang—author of a story featuring Queen Elizabeth I as the Earl of Darnley in drag—was aware of an element of competition in Stevenson's appreciators. He had at first been suspicious of the author, thinking him a poseur in his cloak, but was won round: he wrote that "Mr. Stevenson possessed, more than any man I ever met, the power of making other men fall in love with him. I mean that he excited a passionate admiration and affection, so much so that I verily believe some men were jealous of other men's place in his heart." Francis Wyndham, writing about his friend Bruce Chatwin, has noted a tendency towards possessiveness among some of Bruce's friends—and a wish to claim their version of him as the real one.

Bruce was fired up on finding the verse that Stevenson wrote about Fanny Osbourne:

MY WIFE

Trusty, dusky, vivid, true,
With eyes of gold and bramble-dew,
Steel-true and blade-straight,
The great artificer
Made my mate.

Honour, anger, valour, fire;
A love that life could never tire,
Death quench or evil stir,
The mighty master
Gave to her.

Teacher, tender, comrade, wife,
A fellow-farer true through life,
Heart-whole and soul-free
The august Father
Gave to me.

He used often to quote these lines, in which he recognised
something of his own wife: at the end of his life he talked
about them again as showing Elizabeth's qualities. The piece
he wrote for the *TLS* makes it clear that he saw himself in
Robert Louis Stevenson. But some similarities would not
have been perceptible to him when he wrote it, and there are
moments when the article appears prescient. In 1974 Bruce
wrote about Stevenson's "hysterical gaiety in the face of fatal
illness," and of Fanny Stevenson's industrious nursing. In
1989 Bruce died after a spell of feverish excitement, during
which he was nursed by his wife.

7

EXOTICA

I once met a lord at a party who told me that he knew something about Bruce Chatwin. "The thing is," he murmured confidentially, "he was really a nomad." Chatwin talked fervently and wrote copiously about his fascination with nomads: it was a fascination which cast a vagabond lustre over the journeys he made. He made many journeys, but he often stayed comfortably in the houses of friends—and to some of these friends his perpetual motion seemed like that of a perpetual guest. "For a nomad," commented one host after an extended Bruce visit, "he spends an awful lot of time in one place."

The host in question was Teddy Millington-Drake—Edgar Louis Vanderstegen Millington-Drake—with whom Bruce stayed for long periods, in various foreign houses, throughout his adult life. They had met when Bruce was in his early twenties, and become lovers. Large chunks of *The Viceroy of Ouidah* were written at Teddy's house in Tuscany. On the Greek island of Patmos, the island on which St. John the Divine is said to have composed the Book of Revelation, Bruce pinned up lists of nomadic tribes and interesting places in Teddy's house, and began to compose *The Songlines*.

Teddy Millington-Drake was often ambivalent about his numerous guests: on Patmos he kept a set of special plates, intricately decorated so that, he said, he had something to look at if he got bored during one of his dinner parties. He was some eight years older than Bruce, and much more contained—physically and verbally. He talked about his friend with the tetchy indulgence of the old lover. He would provide a comprehensive guide to the author's limitations as a house guest: he never switched off a light, made lengthy transatlantic telephone calls for which he never quite paid, and was demanding about the furniture in the room where he worked—a remorseless shifter of desks and table lamps. But Bruce was also "a good friend. Every sort of a friend."

Teddy was always more kind and generous than he was welcoming: when he died at the age of sixty-two in 1994, one of his guests, Nigel Ryan, wrote memorably about "the shy, disconcerting, unenthusiastic greeting of the host on the quayside after the long journey from Athens." He would turn up for drinks on his terrace—always immaculate, with his crisp curls, precise features and pressed cottons—looking as if he were rising above a recent irritation or scenting a distant bad smell. His smiles, when they came, were startling. He seldom disguised his sense of tedium: having asked a visiting magnate to explicate the workings of inflation, he became tired of the topic and broke in: "You don't see many Pekinese about in London these days, do you?" But he never stopped inviting people to stay, and he never stopped making it nice for them to do so. He was good at thinking of treats for his visitors, and was helped by money to provide them: on Patmos there was a gardener and a cook, as well as a boatman who took friends and acquaintances, of which I was one, from bay to bay, and collected sea urchins to add to their beach picnics. He was not a host who himself wanted to be the chief source of entertainment: he liked his guests to do the holding forth, and there was an appeal in his querulousness which made them want to raise his spirits and trick him into one of his sudden laughs. Bruce—who was all guest,

who liked to go into a throng and twinkle, and who sometimes went out like a light when left alone with a resident
companion—rose to the challenge of Teddy's manner.

These two Aegean virtuosi had in common their enjoyment of travelling: for an irritable and a pampered man,
Teddy was astonishingly robust on his journeys through the
Far and Middle East—often travelling alone, sometimes
sleeping rough. Each also had an unbudgeable sense of how
he liked things to look. On Patmos, in the monastery village
of Chora, Teddy had two seventeenth-century houses restored under the direction of the interior designer John
Stefanides, making big rooms with timber beams and white-
washed walls; the blue of the painted chairs and the white of
the cottons on the sofas and the muslins round the bed were
the colours of the world outside. There were some murals
painted by Teddy; his studio and sitting-room, the room in
which he died, had windows framing a favourite view of a
hill on the peak of which is a chapel dedicated to the prophet
Elias. On his fiftieth birthday he climbed this hill with Bruce
and Diana Melly, taking food and several bottles of wine,
which they arranged with some care at the top, careful to
catch the best view of the moon. Two minutes after they'd
settled down, Bruce announced that the moon was better
from the other side of the summit: the feast was dismantled
and moved, with much enjoyable grumbling from Teddy,
over scree and boulder into the best lunar light.

In front of his Patmos house he created a gorgeous garden
which spread down the hill, lusciously colourful, dotted with
secluded nooks and concealed seats. He said he thought that
Chatwin probably considered his paintings—graceful watercolours of Indian palaces and courtyards, sketches of Patmos
hills and flowers, some abstracts, a sequence of soft-toned
irises—to be not "particularly as good as they should have
been," though Bruce once came up with some effusive copy

about them. They certainly both responded strongly to quiet brown Patmos, a place of rocks and scrub and low white houses, whose status as a holy island shields it from many modern noises, where goat-bells are a common sound and Orthodox priests, long-gowned and big-bearded, a common sight. Bruce was always drawn to bare, arid landscapes.

At the end of his life, he was also drawn to the Greek Orthodox Church, and to Mount Athos. But the language of St. John on Patmos had entered his writing years before: the verses from Revelation listing the stones of new Jerusalem, verses composed on an island of baking heat and rock, are read out in *On the Black Hill* as the rain comes down on a small Welsh church.

Teddy Millington-Drake turned out to be stoical when the worst came to the worst. When he contracted AIDS and stopped going out—"it's so depressing for people"—he conducted himself calmly: the great complainer ceased to complain, but pointed out to his friends, "I will leave a big hole in your lives, won't I?" He had been valued during his life for qualities remote from stoicism: for kindness, for cheek (booed off the stage of a theatre during his brief attendance at Oxford, he had poked his head through the curtain to declare: "And a big boo to you, too!"), for his tart insights—he had a good line on the Great Tradition of Malice in English literature, presided over by Virginia Woolf. When Bruce was dying he told Diana Melly that he had loved only two men, and that Teddy was one of them.

He must also have enjoyed the stories of Teddy's family: the mother who whisked her son back and forth across the Atlantic with outfits from Worth of Paris packed into thirty trunks, and who, as a widow and Catholic convert in Rome, kept parrots who mimicked her voice perfectly; the handsome father who, when he was Minister in the British Embassy at Montevideo, translated Kipling's "If" into Spanish for the benefit of the Uruguayans. Bruce liked anomalies and extremes. He also liked—at least some of the time—the upper classes. He was susceptible to celebrities and to socialites—while arranging his life to escape from them much of the time, and railing against the baroque sycophancies of his years at Sotheby's. Not all his acquaintances discouraged his tuft-hunting tendencies. "How," one of them asked me, peeping out from under her hat, "can an ordinary person edit Bruce Chatwin?" Bruce, who had taken the ordinary person to dinner, together with the hat, made no audible protest.

Some were more exposed than others to Bruce's social excitements. Emma Tennant remembers him in London at the beginning of the Sixties, in a world in which "being civilised meant being nasty, rude and well-dressed." She had met him first at Millington-Drake's house near Venice, when Bruce was in his early twenties. They had had a brief affair, borrowing a house in Wiltshire for a weekend, and being driven to Paris by a friend in an old Rolls-Royce: "I'll never forget," Bruce told her towards the end of his life, "the scene you made about my knickers on the radiator in our room." In the metropolis, they glided for a time around a circle of the smart, which included philosophers and writers as well as *salonnières*: "If Richard Wollheim was going with Colin MacInnes to a black club in Notting Hill Gate it's perfectly likely that they would all have been to a dinner party given by Anne Fleming." Chatwin and Tennant both became connoisseurs of the glancing insult, of the hostesses whose point was being rude to their guests, of the guests whose point was complaining about their hostess, her food and their fellow guests: "Such a terrible evening: I had to make my own fun." Tennant remembers: "The fashionable thing was to be unpleasant, catty and vile about everybody else and of course to have as many love-affairs as possible without caring at all who might get hurt. It was probably as nasty as the world of *Les Liaisons dangereuses*."

In Millington-Drake's Patmos house some twenty years later, Hugo Vickers, the biographer of Cecil Beaton and Greta Garbo, wrote up his diary, which catches echoes of this society:

> Bruce was sitting at the breakfast table and we had a long talk. He is at work on a book about Nomads which will be a dialogue . . . He used to know Juliet Duff and Stephen Tennant and had good stories about the latter. He'd seen a photo of Cecil and Stephen in bed with a French sailor . . . He said that Cecil once got some Tchelitchews and Indian Mogul pictures off Stephen and put them straight into Sotheby's. It was bad to make so much out of close friends. He got thousands for them. I must check this story. Bruce said that was the reason for the row between them.

In this diary Bruce is reported talking about various remote relatives: "one died a Muslim beggar singing the Koran beside the Cairo mosque. Another got lost in Paris—a friend of Wilde and Lord Alfred Douglas." These are two stories that might also have been checked. He is described telling a tale about Alice B. Toklas and Gertrude Stein, which turns on the suggestion that Stein had bequeathed to her companion paintings that Toklas had herself bought. He is chronicled imitating Noël Coward on the beach, and citing Coward's advice, which he quotes in *What Am I Doing Here*: "Never let anything artistic stand in your way." At another breakfast he is heard discussing Anthony Blunt, the murder of Earl Mountbatten—who he proposes may have known one of his murderers—and "the question of Mountbatten's homosexuality," the Falklands War and "the days of gentleman pirates." Among the period touches that feature in the journal is the information that, the night before Chatwin left for Rhodes, the diarist was woken by the sound of him being violently sick in the next-door bathroom: "I thought Teddy was far from sorry to see him go. He had talked too much and repeated himself a lot."

Bruce's flights and repartees were in fact widely appreciated. "Doesn't she look every inch a duchess?" he exclaimed of a real duchess who was leaning against his Ozleworth mantelpiece. "She did it all herself." "What are you saying about me, Bruce?" asked the lady in question—and extended an admired leg, clad (the other one being in plaster) in an eighteenth-century black silk stocking. His amusement sometimes became harsh ridicule; sometimes it was tinged with self-aware self-parody. In the Sixties he undertook an expedition with Stuart Piggott. After years of teaching the archaeology of the North European Plain, Piggott had decided he should go there: "I don't like talking about areas that I've never seen. I know the rest of Europe. I knew it then pretty well. I knew the Baltic. I knew Germany, Holland, the Low Countries. But I'd never seen the North European Plain and I discovered that you can take a train from Ostend which will take you to Moscow. In fact, we didn't go further than Warsaw on that train, but that was enough. We saw the North European Plain. I never want to see it again. Nor did Bruce."

As they passed through East Germany, their passports and tickets—second-class, since, although Piggott had a travel grant, Bruce did not—were constantly checked. Early one morning—with Chatwin still sleepy—Piggott had got up, tracked down the samovar and had a glass of tea, when the inspector arrived to look at their tickets. There was a kerfuffle: "The inspector was surprised, I think, to find that we were travelling second-class and he said: *'Fahren Sie nicht in der ersten Klasse?'* I said: *'Nein, wir sind zweite Klasse.'* *'Ja, ja,'* said Bruce, just as I was saying *'Klasse.'* I got the chap out and he was satisfied, and I said: 'Bruce, what on earth were you saying? You know we aren't travelling first-class.' 'Oh,' said Bruce, 'that was what he was asking, was it? I thought he said, *"Sind Sie Aristokrat?"*—and of course I said yes.'"

Chatwin's books aren't full of toffs—though some put in an appearance. But he did have stories to tell about them, as this notebook entry featuring Jacqueline Onassis shows:

> Evening at the John Flemings. Called at 85 and 5th to pick up J.O. Apartment splendid. Entirely French. Franco-Anglo-American atmosphere.

> *J.O.'s apartment*
> Workroom pale green marbleised. Exquisite painted 18th-century chairs—easel—work table. Divans with rounded cushions. Company paintings. The library dark brown—Cogolin—straw mat on floor—dove's-nest desk. English house-painting Fernley Wootton? A lacquer table on which piled magazines. An album which said Jack 1962 on spine. Stacking red children's books. She came in: in black and gold pyjama pants. The whisper is conspiratorial not affected. The whisper of a naughty child egging you on to do something mildly wicked. To behave badly without being rude.

> A cupboard full of fur coats.

> The marbleising in the porch. "Oh, it was an Italian. Spent the whole summer while I was away—and now he's gone back to Italy. And he even did the cracks. And they *were* cracks." A Khmer torso and an Old Kingdom standing official. Was it John who came down in the lift in vaguely bike-boy's jacket—thin washed-out face—enigmatic—beautiful distant smile, tight hips in blue jeans, on the way to forbidden pleasures?

Set off in a hired Cadillac. The driver had shaken hands with her and Jack—"but you wouldn't remember?" "Nice of you to remind me."

Dinner. Next to Mrs. O'Moore who was wide-eyed and very enthusiastic about Hemingway. Mr. O'Moore said after dinner that Hemingway had taken decadence to a point never realised by Baudelaire. Mr. Fleming asked me if I went riding with Jackie. Peter Glenville made a slight fool of himself about Ireland. He had come with Mrs. Vincent Astor who has just had important facial surgery. I didn't know this but everyone else in NY did including Jackie. Mrs. Astor wore eight strings of pearls, a slit dress, white gloves, a pillbox hat like Loulou wears, a hugely spotted veil to hide the surgery. As we came in the lift Jackie said: "Brooke, do go first. They're bound to forgive us when they see the veil."

It is surprising that there is no mention here of the food. Bruce was a cook and, though a delicate feeder, very interested in what he ate: *"Qué precioso,"* he would joke before settling to anything particularly delicious. He was once excitedly reported to be walking across Eaton Square carrying a white truffle. The meals that he prepared himself were usually labour-intensive but simple-looking; he favoured the small and exquisite. Preparing to be interviewed for a magazine piece, he went into an elaborate debate about what he should provide as sustenance for himself and his inquisitor, and eventually settled on one *chèvre*: a single, cream-coloured cheese the size of a large pill-box. When I went to supper with him in his Eaton Place flat just after the publication of *On the Black Hill*, he appeared from his tiny kitchen with a savoury succession of courses. The meal began with mozzarella; the main course was lemon sole, with vegetables served from a bamboo steamer; the pudding was a bowl of lychees. Just after we had finished eating, Bruce exclaimed with a sudden recoil: "How dreadful. I've just realised. That was a totally *white* meal."

As a young man, he served his old school-friend David Nash maté tea in little silver cups. Years later he introduced the anthropological writer John Ryle to wild rice, cooked with lemon grass. In Wales, where for breakfast he would dip a piece of bread into olive oil and fry it, he taught Diana Melly how to make the Mexican fish dish ceviche and, further north in the principality, produced for Martin and Stella Wilkinson another Mexican speciality—turkey with a chocolate and peanut sauce—impressing on his hosts that all the ingredients had been bought in New York. In 1980 his Christmas present to the Wilkinsons—with whom he had stayed, as he pointed out in their visitors' book, "endlessly"—was a beautiful illustrated dictionary: *Food* by Waverly Root, a mixture of practical tips and historical information in which "A" is illustrated by a Chardin picture of a jar of apricots, "B" by an eighteenth-century Delft pottery cow, and in which even the goose is from the tomb of Ra.

The food in Chatwin's own books dramatises the differences between the books themselves, with their different Chatwins: from the cottage loaves, dumplings and boiled bacon of *On the Black Hill* to the gumbos, malaguetta peppers, coco flesh and fried cockscombs of *The Viceroy of Ouidah*. When Bruce described Benjamin Jones in *On the Black Hill* surprisingly baking a cake as a boy, he was describing something that he himself had done. When he was leaving Marlborough he broke with the usual practice of taking his housemaster out for a meal, and undertook the catering himself. His mother, arriving to lend a hand with the preparations, found her son making Elizabeth David's orange and almond cake. When in *Utz* he describes his protagonist's disgust at the gourmet profusions he samples, he was describing a fastidiousness he himself felt.

Not that he resisted all sumptuous meals. After she had reviewed *In Patagonia* in the *New York Review of Books*, Sybille Bedford became friendly with him, and gave him a taste of her world. This world, as Angela Carter has pointed out, is continuous with the old Europe suggested in the writings of Elizabeth David, who advocated in Britain the fine and unadorned style of cookery that Chatwin admired—the authentic *bouquet garni*, the splash of rose water, the omelette with a glass of wine; in one of her books Mrs. David recalled one of her sisters arriving from old Vienna "with a hare which she claimed had been caught by hand outside the State Opera House." Ms. Bedford has written about the white and gold ballrooms, the dark mahogany, the coachmen and the butlers of her childhood in pre-war Germany. She has also written about her father cooking goose livers and egg dishes over a spirit lamp in his dressing-room, and about his instructing her as a child how to twirl and sniff the Bordeaux in her glass.

These discriminations were not lost on the small Sybille. When, as a seventeen-year-old, she lived in a maid's room in Albany, as Chatwin was to do, she found that the "spartan" room had some compensations: "a partridge could be roasted on a spit." Her Chelsea flat still features the Grand Cru bottles which impressed Chatwin when he first visited her. And for years she organised splendid dinners, keeping typed lists of the food, wine and guests, together with the occasional comment. In 1982 Bruce was present at what Ms. Bedford considers was probably "the grandest Bordeaux Dinner—$\frac{3}{4}$ Premier Gd Cru—I ever gave." In the same year, he attended another such feast, given in honour of Shirley Letwin—the right-wing philosopher and hostess, who has written a book on Trollope and the English gentleman—and her husband. This was the meal:

APERITIFS:
Laurent-Perrier (Cooks' Prerogative)
Gewurztraminer 1979

Barry's Smoked Salmon
Brown Bread & Butter Toast

WHITE BORDEAUX:
Sauvignon Côtes de Duras 1979
Sauvignon Côtes de Duras 1980

Daube of Beef
Fresh Green and White Tagliolini
Haricots Verts

CLARETS:
Château Siaurac Pomerol 1970
2 Bottles
Château Duhart Milon Rothschild 1970

Cheeses: Goat, Gruyère, Explorateur

PORT:
Morgan's 1960

Grapes, Pears, Nuts, Almonds

Sybille Bedford remembers "Bruce at his most vivacious that evening—I still see him sitting sideways on the sofa in his little open-necked polo shirt out-talking even the Letwins."

The meals that he arranged himself were minutely considered. Howard Hodgkin was treated to a Bruce lunch in Paris during the early Sixties. Earlier in the day Bruce had contrived to break into his friend's hotel room to borrow a book on Indian ornaments: with its help, he had managed to prove to an important Sotheby's customer that a piece of metalwork was a fake. He was sure Sotheby's would stand them a good lunch. "He took me to a very famous old restaurant in the Ile de la Cité, and we ate upstairs. He'd booked a table which had an incredible view of the Seine and he was at his *most* affected and *most* grand and he said: 'I hope you don't mind, I've ordered the meal; I never like a heavy lunch.' And he beckoned the waiter. He didn't in those days do this with complete ease, but he did it nevertheless, and I was like a little schoolboy sitting next to him. I've never forgotten the meal. We had a tiny bit of *foie gras* each. We then had a whole truffle each *en croûte* and a bottle of Champagne Nature, followed by a bowl of *fraises des bois* and a cup of coffee. And then he said: 'I hope you've had enough.' "

Staying with Bruce in Gloucestershire in the late Seventies, Francis Wyndham spent a few days dominated by his host's exacting palate. Each morning there were rigorous expulsions of food from the fridge: Wyndham would come down to see his fellow guest James Fox and his host throwing out, "before my hungry eyes," any less than perfect item. There was a lengthy drive in search of a pub, with no candidate coming up to scratch. There was "a not frightfully nice walk," in the course of which an unexpected stall selling shellfish appeared in the middle of the countryside—swooped on with excitement by Wyndham but dismissed as unsatisfactory by the two gourmets. And there was Bruce's meal.

When Fox's girlfriend of that time, Cloe Peploe, arrived with Susannah Phillips, the host was put on his mettle. Chatwin was an enthusiast for female beauty, even when he didn't desire the woman in question: Fox remembers him sitting next to Cloe running her bracelets up and down her arm, stroking her with the measured sensual admiration he might have extended to an antelope. He was responsive to the advent of these two beauties, one dark, the other fair, and announced that he would cook the dinner: "We'll have soufflé of wild strawberries." Wyndham and Fox were set, serflike, to toil in the garden picking the tiny fruit and at the end of the day had gathered a sizeable mound. The women were ravenous. The soufflé came. "It was nothing," Wyndham remembers. "It looked very pretty, it was a wonderful mauve colour, and, just like soufflé, it turned into a trickle and didn't have any taste. And there was practically nothing else." Wyndham, who on one of their expeditions had sneakily bought some Bendicks bittermints—"which I kept rather dark"—rescued the famished women by feeding them chocolates. But Chatwin behaved as if he didn't know what hunger was: "It was as if," says Wyndham, "these were two rather gross fleshy females, and we lived on this other plane."

His food plans sometimes went wrong. When he cooked a chicken with garlic for the Wilkinsons, he prepared the bird with fifteen whole bulbs of garlic. The recipe, which he had disdained to consult, called for only fifteen cloves: the chicken was chucked. Sometimes he was sabotaged. While staying in Diana Melly's Welsh tower, he discovered that she and his fellow guest Francis Wyndham had scoffed the amaretti he had been hoarding in a jar, and wasn't much amused. On another of his many visits there, he elected to cook a special dinner to cheer up his hostess, who was due to appear in court charged with possession of cannabis. He bought a lobster and a bottle of good brandy in which to cook it—and was dismayed by the suggestion that the delinquent Diana might be given his superior drink to calm her nervous sickness, while he could use her cooking brandy as a substitute in his dish: that, he said, would ruin the feast. When he left the kitchen, his hostess switched the bottles, but waited for a month before she told Bruce what she had done. "Don't think," he protested, "that I didn't realise. It was perfectly obvious from the way the lobster tasted."

The chef as guest had unpredictable blind spots. "I remember you cooking sweetcorn," Diana Melly wrote to him, reminiscing about one of his visits to her tower, "and asking me how to boil the water. Perhaps it's one of the things you can't do—judging by the tea you make." Coffee fell into the same category, she recalls. In the vegetable plot at the bottom of her garden she would hear Bruce descending from his room. "He'd come hammering down the stairs. He'd stand on the front steps and shout: 'Di, is there any coffee?' I felt he could have made *me* a cup." People were always doing things for Bruce. Diana Melly found herself sawing at the legs of a table which the author had pronounced too high for composition. Peter Eyre was turned "into a tweeny," ferrying drinks and snacks to and fro, when Chatwin decided he would like to correct the proofs of *The Viceroy of Ouidah* in Eyre's Chelsea garden. "Why are *we* doing this?" David King asked Elizabeth on another occasion, as they puffed behind a broken-down car, pushing it along while Bruce waved them on from the driver's seat.

Some hosts groused, some laughed at the small tyrannies of Bruce's arrangements. He was always looking for the perfect place in which to work, always thinking he had found it, always becoming disillusioned or alighting on somewhere more desirable. "How I envy you your eyrie in the hills," he wrote from his house in a Gloucestershire valley to Martin Wilkinson in the land bordering Wales. "This is better than the Welsh Mountains," he declared a few years later, in a letter from Italy to Francis Wyndham: "Bare hills, bright light and most of the English gone back for the winter. I cycle to Siena for groceries and speak to shopkeepers in an incoherent mixture of Spanish, Portuguese and Latin; they smile breezily and ask if I want peanuts." In a long Bruce epistle from Rajasthan, Diana Melly learnt that he had decided "to sell the flat and look for a bolt-hole, somewhere in the Mediterranean, to work in . . . I have a feeling that the fatal thing is to go for somewhere 'unspoiled'—as if one isn't a spoiler oneself—because it takes so much money and emotional effort keeping it unspoiled." In another letter, she heard from him that he was based in a friend's house, one that was "ideal for writing"—in "the most beautiful place you can imagine."

That particular most beautiful place was Kardamili in the Peloponnesus, where Chatwin, staying with the writer and war hero Patrick Leigh Fermor and his wife Joan, was offered, as he wrote his letter, a view of sea and cypress trees; behind him stretched rows of hills and mountains. A picture taken there by Elizabeth shows him striding away from the camera, past bare trees, grey stone walls, bright red anemones and the lemon-yellow blossoms of a Euphorbia bush. Here he went walking with his host, and vied with him in telling stories. He also relished a letter sent to Leigh Fermor by Daphne Fielding, the Duke of Beaufort's mother-in-law. When the body of the old Duke was partially exhumed by animal-rights campaigners, she wrote saying that she thought the young men concerned—known to Chatwin as "the Duke-diggers at Badminton"—were "very romantic" and had "wonderful cheekbones."

The Leigh Fermors were part of a sunny cultural web for Bruce. In the south of Spain there was Magouche Fielding, who had introduced him to the Leigh Fermors, and whom he had met at Teddy Millington-Drake's. He had camped out with her in a cottage on a Patmos beach; he later turned up out of the blue on her doorstep in the Moorish town of Ronda. And kept turning up. He made excursions there with his wife and with his wife's mother; he was also often alone. He sped across Spain in his Deux Chevaux with a huge surfboard strapped to the roof: "I really do want to be seventeen all over again and become a professional wind-surfer." He climbed a mountain near Ronda with one of his hostess's daughters—the Susannah Phillips of the Gloucestershire soufflé—and rushed down it when his arrival at the summit was greeted by an eclipse of the sun; in 1978, escaping from another of his escapes—"a nightmarish week in the Pyrenees, humid valleys screaming with French children"—he rented "a Neo-Classical 'pavillon' on a high, dry hillside." His visits to the Fieldings' house often coincided with lunch being put on the table, and very often with his own period of maximum vitality after he had finished a morning's work: "Are you resting?" he would sing out rhetorically.

Sometimes his burden of good news, anecdotes, information, jokes and advice was too much for the husband of the hostess, Xan Fielding, struggling to finish a book of his own. Once, his hostess, needing some time to herself, dispatched her visitor to Seville for Easter. Soon after he'd arrived in the city, she got a call from Bruce. "It's a complete hoax, this Holy Week in Seville. They're all paid, they're not penitents. And it's all eau de cologne and garlic underneath those cloaks." "But Bruce," she pointed out, "you're not supposed to be underneath the cloaks. You're supposed to be looking at them." Chatwin took off for North Africa.

In Italy he stayed with the couple he called "the flying Rezzoris." Beatrice Monti, a former art dealer and editor-at-large for Condé Nast, shared Chatwin's taste for austere objects and flamboyant behaviour. She commissioned articles from him for *House & Garden* and *Vanity Fair*. They planned to go to the Bosphorus together. On New Year's Eve, the Rezzoris would dress up in Oriental clothes, and Bruce would play his part in cashmere, silk and turban. Beatrice Monti's husband, Gregor von Rezzori, born in the Bukovina a few months before the outbreak of the First World War, was another witness to that old Europe which fascinated Chatwin. He has written fictionally and autobiographically about its recent history and about the cossettings and losses of his early life. He has done so as a confident cosmopolitan and as a pre-emptive self-deprecator; his latest book is called

Anecdotage. He and Bruce—twenty-six years younger to the day and always "so all-of-a-piece"—became friends in the Seventies through a mutual regard for the icy composure of Clint Eastwood. They also shared a zest for strange-sounding words. Von Rezzori, who had once studied mining geology, delighted Chatwin by telling him the impossible-to-pronounce names of the five places where gold could be found in the Austro-Hungarian Empire: Schemnitz, Chemnitz, Nagybanya, Ofenbanya, Vorospatak. When Chatwin became ill and was too weak to talk on the phone, von Rezzori sent these names as a last message to the friend he thought of as an extra son.

The von Rezzoris often used to put friends up in a partly restored fourteenth-century signalling-tower which stood close to the house in which they lived. Encouraged by his hostess, Bruce wrote a piece for American *House & Garden* about this tower—one of the two towers in his life—with its thick walls, Romanian cushions, Sicilian beds, Lebanese mother-of-pearl, and the pugs Desdemona and Celestina. While working there, he startled the Rezzoris' housekeeper, who had been sent to tell him that lunch was ready. She approached the tower expecting to find a solitary figure but as she crossed the threshold heard a great clamour, a great number of different voices. What she had heard was Bruce reading aloud the account he gives in *On the Black Hill* of celebrations held to mark the end of World War One. John Updike, reviewing the book for *The New Yorker,* found echoes of *Madame Bovary* in this scene; when Gregor von Rezzori read the passage, he found that one of his own memories from the Bukovina had been given a voice.

While staying in this tower, Bruce talked about his own work, not about his host's: "I took it as a sign of discretion," says von Rezzori. But he did quiz his friend about his experience of Eastern Europe. It was von Rezzori who came up

with a title for Chatwin's last book: he explained to its author that some names in German are abbreviations of He-
brew words—and in "Utz" lit on a name for the book's
Meissen collector which appears to take that into account,
and which also contracts the name of Chatwin's collector
friend, George Ortiz. Parts of his background—an Eastern
European landscape, a South German servant, a homeland
which is occupied at different times by Germans and by Russians—are also parts of Utz's background. And something of
his demeanour—sardonic and elusive, romantic but unsentimental—is discernible both in Utz and in the book's nar-
rator.

Both these friends take an authoritative interest in Chatwin's attraction to the Greek Orthodox Church. This must,
Beatrice Monti thinks, have been "very aesthetic, because
everything before reaching the heart was passing through the
eyes." Von Rezzori, himself brought up in an Orthodox country, with "all the glory and the chants," speaks of the Church
as being "much more Sotheby's than any other Church." The
golden halo and the secret hidden behind the iconostasis: these
things would have appealed to his friend. The Orthodox
Church is, Rezzori says, a "chrysanthemum"—an image
which could also be applied to Bruce Chatwin.

There was more than one aspect to Bruce's visitations. He
was looked after. And he had a ready audience for his books.
On Patmos he would read a fresh instalment of his work
aloud each morning: "Did he listen to what you said about
it?" Teddy Millington-Drake was asked. "No." In the Usk
valley he followed Diana Melly round her kitchen, large yellow pages fluttering, as he acted out a fresh excerpt. "I'm
looking forward—very much—to the next chapter," she
wrote to him, to be "read aloud while apple chutney is on
the boil."

But more than this, being away from his own address came to be a condition of his writing anything: being at home meant having writer's block. It was sometimes an additional help to be removed from the setting he was writing about. He produced much of *On the Black Hill* in Wales, but had a breakthrough with the book when he took up a place at Yaddo, the retreat near Saratoga Springs for musicians, writers and painters—where one of the artists was specialising in "vaginal iconography in sand and acrylic." He found it "extremely strange to conjure up a vision of Radnor or Brecon, hemmed in, as I am, between a racecourse and a kind of suburban pine forest." But it turned out to be easier to imagine his characters when he was an ocean away from their models and cut off from further data: "I think it's because the story stands a chance of being a circular whole, when you can't get at any more material," he once wrote, and went on cryptically: "If I am thinking, what colour are those clouds, or what are the twins up to, the story rapidly gets out of shape—becomes, instead of circular, pear-shaped."

He wrote about slavery and the viceroy of Ouidah in Ronda, on Patmos and in a London mews near Victoria Station. When working on *The Songlines* he went to Katmandu with Elizabeth, but they were driven out by her falling ill, by a black fog which settled over the town, and by their accommodation, "a sort of 'ornamental cottage' built as a royal love-nest, right behind the main shopping-street and right next, as it turned out, to the city's Number One shithouse." He moved out via Benares to Delhi, and to Rajasthan, where he indulged in some name-dropping—"I knew, from years ago, the Maharajah—who lives in a palace that dwarfs Buckingham P, but for all that is the simplest and easiest person"—and received a stroke of luck: at the simplest person's birthday party—"where all the Rajput gentry appeared in their *real* jodhpurs and multi-coloured turbans"—he met a local landowner who offered him his fort to work in. Some of the rocks and dust and restlessness of *The Songlines* were evoked in the graceful calm of these surroundings.

> The Fort, in which we have a suite of cool blue rooms, overlooks a lake which is a bird-sanctuary and the resting place for hundreds, if not thousands, of migrating duck, spoonbills, storks, herons—all waiting for good weather before striking north over the Himalayas. There is an island with a Shiva temple on it—the priests go out once a week on inflated rubber tyres—and we have a long terrace, shared with peacocks, with little pavilions where we can curl up with a book. Food arrives three times a day, on solid mahogany trays carried by a procession of astonishingly beautiful girls and their mothers, and, in the courtyard, little children play tag or hopscotch with tinkling bells sewn into their dresses.

Bruce, when not writing "like an express-train," was reading, "properly for the first time, Proust." Elizabeth Chatwin went "visiting the village ladies, learning Hindi from the Brahmin school-teacher, and I've not seen her happier or more cheerful in 20 years (the time we've been married!). I think even she is coming round to the fact that those houses"—the ones they had been inhabiting for those twenty years—"and that particular way of life, are as bad for her as for me."

He hated being shut in. When he was living in the Ozleworth valley in Gloucestershire he got, he said, so depressed from being enclosed within the hills that he used to bang his head against the wall. The damp air there was rotting his chest, the sleepy atmosphere sapping his brain. I went to this valley one weekend in the late Seventies when I was working with him on *The Viceroy of Ouidah*. He met me at the station, perched rather experimentally in his car: as a driver he was noted for determinedly cleaving to the middle of the road in case he wanted to overtake, motoring accompanied by a bleat of angry horns. He pulled up suddenly on a hill overlooking the wet dip in which his house lay—and near which his neighbour Charles Tomlinson had written so many poems in praise of the natural world—and denounced it as somewhere in which it was impossible to work: he made it sound bewitched. When Francis Wyndham walked through the valley with him, a cloud of flies settled round Bruce's head while he fulminated against the place: he strode along with the swarm engulfing him, looking to his friend like Orestes pursued by the Furies. Finally, enraged, he ran off up a hill, the flies still dancing around him, "symbolically, comically, like someone in an Ibsen play."

Chatwin wrote often about his escapes and adventures, though less often about the anxiety which prompted them. But in his second book he produced a saga of constraint and confinement—a saga in which claustrophobia is entwined with exoticism. *The Viceroy of Ouidah* is a tale of enclosed spaces and constricting conditions. Its hero, who considers "any set of four walls to be a tomb or a trap," makes his life's work the business of confining others—leaving his native Brazil to become a slave trader in the Kingdom of Dahomey in West Africa. There is a palace with few doors, a prison, a seraglio. There are men in manacles, nightmares about airless rooms, thwarted dreams of escaping from one country to another.

The plot is compressed into a small span: two continents, two centuries and a great many terrors are covered in less than 160 pages. The paragraphs are tiny—Bruce was infuriated when editors tried to run on his stabbing little sections. The sentences are short. Clenched and lapidary, every line is heavily freighted. There are rare words, arcane pieces of information—and it isn't always easy to know what is going on: "He swore to defeat the Egbas in their stronghold at Abeokata, and he told the Alafin of Oyo to 'eat parrots' eggs.' " There are soaring moments, graphic juxtapositions, Conradian visualisings. Brazilians settle in an African town: "Instead of dull pinks and ochres, the houses took on the hues of a Brazilian garden; and as the women leaned over their half-doors, they seemed to be wearing them as an extension of their dress." A young photographer has "a shaved gourd-like head, skin so black it glinted blue and the most serious approach to his profession. On the back of his sleeveless orange jumpsuit were a purple lamb and letters reading 'Foto Studio Agnew Pascal.' " It is a book in which the illuminating and the impenetrable are constantly brought up hard against each other.

It is also a book with an ambiguous hero. Francisco Manoel da Silva is a slaver with tender feelings, a willing expatriate who becomes an exile, a patriarch who was once nicknamed "The Catamite." As a young man in South America, "with partners of either sex, he performed the mechanics of love in planked rooms." *The Viceroy of Ouidah* has many glistening black male bodies and many lithe black females. Bruce was to talk—sometimes as if it were fantasy, sometimes fact—of a day at the Rio Carnival spent making love first to a girl, then to a boy.

Like all Chatwin's books, *The Viceroy of Ouidah* presents a puzzle to classifiers. He had originally set out to write a life of Francisco Feliz da Souza, a slave-trader with a Portuguese background who is described by Hugh Thomas in his book on Cuba as a "scarcely credible figure"—a description that must have inflamed Chatwin. He had made a trip to Dahomey in 1971, and made jottings in his notebooks about the king's palace, a fetish dance and the "big black phallus-like pods in the trees which have no flower." When he went back a few years later to collect material for what he now saw as a book, he got caught up in an attempted coup, was wrongly arrested as a mercenary, imprisoned and threatened: *"Il faut vous tuer. Massacrer même."* He never wanted to go back to the country and, considering his research too insubstantial for a biography, "decided to change the names of the principal characters—and went on to write a work of the imagination."

This history has left a strange legacy. Some but not all editions of *The Viceroy of Ouidah* contain a preface—added after Bruce had written the book—which explains that the story has a basis in fact. The book was generally reviewed as a novel, but when Chatwin's third book, *On the Black Hill*, came out, it won the Whitbread Prize for the Best First Novel—effectively recategorising its predecessor as non-fiction.

Other influences had a part in shaping the book—which was originally to be called "Skin for Skin." The South American expert Malcolm Deas told Chatwin about a Colombian woman who—lacking a piano on her hacienda—had played arpeggios on a piece of wood painted to look like a keyboard. Chatwin adapted the incident—embellishing it with some wormholes and dust—and slipped it seamlessly into his tropical narrative. For help in telling the story of his slaver's wanderings, he turned to the tale of an ancient exile: the gory animation of the *Aeneid*'s third book—dense with grisly encounters, prodigious sights and sudden miseries—lent its flavour to *The Viceroy of Ouidah*.

But the main influences on the book came from France, to whose literature and language Bruce was always susceptible. Edmund White, the American novelist and biographer of Genet, used to dine with him from time to time in Paris, where White lives, and was often embarrassed by the carrying clarity of the Chatwin voice, with its abrupt, punctuating laugh, exclaiming its stories amid the murmuring French. In an effort to deflect him, White would switch into French, at which Bruce, without drawing breath, would himself change languages: as he did so, ever the mimic, his voice would drop to a murmur. The accents of French literature stole with equal ease into his books. Francis Wyndham has seen some parallels between Chatwin's writing life and that of Bruce's admired Flaubert. Both left six books with striking variations of subject-matter and approach. Both favoured an impartial style. Both wrote a version of pastoral: *On the Black Hill* is Chatwin's "Un Coeur simple." Both also wrote extravagantly: "La Légende de Saint Julien l'Hospitalier," in which the legendary hero atones for killing his parents by clasping a leper in his arms, is, Wyndham points out, "very Brucey"; he was also a great fan of the weltering *Salammbô*. Towards the end of his life Chatwin said he wanted to write a triptych based on Flaubert's *Trois Contes*, with one of the stories to be set in Ancient Ireland.

In *The Viceroy of Ouidah* the influence is particularly marked. "Hérodias," Flaubert's account of the events leading up to the beheading of John the Baptist, is close to the book in its re-imagining of historical events, its colonial setting, its mixture of opulence and extreme cruelty, its narrative trimmed to the point of obscurity, its skinny paragraphs— often only a sentence long. *The Viceroy of Ouidah* also contains, as "Un Coeur simple" contains, a woman who, abandoned by her lover when young, lives to extreme old age in a piety of her own devising: both Flaubert's Félicité and Chatwin's Mama Wewe turn their rooms into shrines, making use of peculiar bits and pieces as well as conventional holy objects—Mama Wewe's shrine includes some of the items which Chatwin put inside the "God Box" he made after his first visit to Africa. Both women have a dying vision in which one of their relics comes to life.

To help him describe, from a distance and without a moral

commentary, the suffocating enclosure and terrors of the slaver's world, Chatwin looked at a work which viewed a claustrophobic Byzantium through cool French eyes. Racine's tragedy *Bajazet*, which is glancingly mentioned on the second page of *The Viceroy of Ouidah*, had been recommended to Chatwin by Francis Wyndham. Set in a royal harem of the seventeenth century, it was, in the twentieth, perhaps the least performed of Racine's plays. It became a Chatwin obsession. Drawn to the combination of austerity and voluptuousness in the play, he wanted to arrange an English production and sketched costumes, with many hats, for the event. He echoes some of its features—the seraglio, the sealed-off palace—in *The Viceroy of Ouidah* and adapts one of its names: Roxane becomes Mae Roxa. But what really interested him was the sense of constriction: whenever he spoke about *Bajazet* he talked with horror about the confined space in which the characters were stuck together.

The Viceroy of Ouidah is the least immediately beguiling, though not the least accomplished of Chatwin's books. It is the most jewelled and the most horror-filled: there are knifings, brandings of flesh, poisonings, cholera, beatings, pus and dysentery. It is the work which most exemplifies Francis Wyndham's observation that "artless spontaneity was among the qualities he least desired the result to express." All this has proved too much even for such a fervent admirer of Chatwin's work as Sybille Bedford, who thinks it contains "too many leprous details" and "too much wallowing in abstruse knowledge." Paul Theroux remembers Bruce sending a proof of the book out to friends, who annotated it: "My remarks were anodyne, but some other snippets of marginalia were shrieks of derision: 'Ha! Ha!' or 'Rubbish' or 'Impossible.' "

The book was nearly too much for Bruce, too. The cruelty of his material oppressed him. He left his desk each day

washed out, often having found it difficult to produce anything. *In Patagonia* had spilt out of him, full of vagaries and
curlicues, byways, fresh starts and false starts; he hadn't found
it difficult to expand a point or add a story—and he hadn't
found it difficult to cut. *The Viceroy of Ouidah* was squeezed
out sentence by polished sentence: nothing was slapped
down; nothing was provisional. Bruce, who didn't have any
resistance to showing work in progress, sent parts of the book
to Cape well in advance of finishing it. These met with a
mixed response. An early note from Tom Maschler, in response to the first 107 pages, talked, with a publisher's tone
of encouragement, about the need to extend "the character
parts" of the book, which "at its best (which is to say the section on Eugenia) goes way beyond *In Patagonia*." Six months
later, in the summer of 1978, I had a completed manuscript
and was filing memoranda about its anxious author which
ranged from the tender to the bossy. "I said I thought he
should have a rest from the slavers for a week or two." My
comments stressed the need to unravel obscurities, and to
make the story more cohesive and more flowing: there were
conversations and revisions; the opening of the book was ad-
justed, and some explanatory material about Ouidah and the
Da Silva family added; an attempt was made to bring the historical and the contemporary sections of the book into a
clearer relation to each other. Nevertheless, in the high summer of 1978 there were still congested patches, and still concern about the book at Jonathan Cape.

I went to see Bruce at his Albany room to discuss these
patches. It was the middle of a sunny, warm day, and London
was noisy, crushed with traffic. Albany stood aloof from all
that, like a big, cool ship, and Bruce's room, perched high up,
was sealed off from any town noise or smell. I reached the
end of my sermon on his book and half-apologetically
looked up at Bruce, who was sitting on his grey bed against

the white wall. He matched his surroundings; he looked drained. I thought of this moment when I read Paul Theroux's comments on Bruce and the subject of writer's block: "I often felt that he was not really bemoaning it at all, but rather boasting about the subtlety of his special gift, the implication being that it was so finely tuned it occasionally emitted a high-pitched squeal and seemed to go dead." I never thought of Bruce as habitually suffering from block— rather the reverse—and he was free with advice on the subject to his friends: "Don't get white knuckles about it," he used to instruct James Fox. But he was certainly blocked when he was writing *The Viceroy of Ouidah*. Bruce was full of pantomimes, but there was no affectation or exaggeration on this occasion; he was miserable. I also remembered the grimace he made when he caught my eye, as if to indicate that we'd both been discovered taking part in some disreputable prank and would just have to stick together until we'd been punished. Not that the finished book was disreputable: the feeling we shared had to do with the sense of strain involved in the enterprise, with a scabrous subject-matter—and with trying to please a worried publisher.

❧ 8

ON THE MAGAZINE

Bruce Chatwin became an author in his thirties. During his twenties he had pursued and abandoned two professional courses: he had succeeded at Sotheby's and escaped from his success; he had left his archaeological studies at Edinburgh unfinished—interviewed for a French radio programme, he described himself as an *archéologue raté*. He had also travelled widely in Europe, Africa and Asia, often raising the money for his trips by selling objects. By the time he was thirty the enthusiasms and experiences for which he came to be read—the visual excitement, the historical curiosity, the relish for abroad, the fascination with contradictions and with byways—were already features of his life. And, after years of keeping private notebooks, he had started to write for publication, submitting his synopsis about nomads to Cape in 1970. He was turning into a writer. But the books that he was to write were radically affected by three years in the early Seventies. These were the years which he spent working, in a semi-detached way, on the *Sunday Times* Magazine.

From its inception, as the first of the Sunday colour-supplements, under the editorship of Mark Boxer, the Magazine had been a mixture of the commercial and the high-principled, the investigative and the celebratory. The first issue in 1962 had starred Mary Quant and James Bond;

there was soon to be coverage of wars and coups. There were the fashion photographs of Brian Duffy, Terence Donovan and David Bailey—young men from the East End attuned to the mood of Sixties Swinging London, interpreters, in Francis Wyndham's words, of the "toughness and chic peculiar to their time"; their antic vivacity ("David Bailey makes love daily") was captured in Antonioni's film of a hallucinatory London, *Blow Up*. There were Eve Arnold's photo-reportage features. And there were Don McCullin's pictures of hard times at home and wars abroad: when McCullin went to Vietnam he was given an unprecedented spread of thirteen pages for his photographs.

The Magazine was open to sniping from outside: its claims to seriousness were thought inappropriate, its frivolities distasteful, the advertisements too many and too much. Objections were made to its juxtapositions—of the slimming and the starving, the war-torn and the jet-setting. And there were also objections from inside the *Sunday Times*. The newspaper and the Magazine frequently took different positions: most strikingly when they supported different sides in the Biafran War—the Magazine was a strong defender of the Biafran cause. James Fox, one of the close friends Chatwin made on the Magazine, remembers the division between its journalists and those on the newspaper: "When you pressed the button to the fourth floor, eyeballs would roll towards the roof, sneers were barely concealed. 'Trendy' was the rude word in those days; also 'radical chic'; a hard man from the newsdesk once described us to me—in the lift—as 'jammy buggers.' There was even something suspect and effete about a 'colour' magazine, as if it suggested hallucinogenics, or Afghan robes—or perhaps Edna Everage's view of Spain: 'colour and movement.' Reality was in black and white."

Chatwin would have been sympathetic to the colourful contradictions of the Magazine, its swerves in subject-matter and in tone. Paradox is one of his subjects: he was seen by his contemporary Angela Carter as being "a combination of high camp and high thinking—a Fabian in a frock." His pieces of journalism—some of the best of which were written for the *Sunday Times* Magazine—are rich in unexpected conjunctions: the private collection of art in a Communist country, the woman who lives alone in the Peruvian desert but welcomes publicity—"I am Elizabeth Taylor in front of the camera." Under his pen such contrasts are most often wry, genial, humorous, but he appreciated the more pointed satirical use to which they could be put. He and Valerie Wade, who edited the Magazine's "Design for Living" section, developed a passion for Jean Vigo's film *A Propos de Nice*, a short black-and-white documentary made in 1930 in which pictures of the rich at play in the seaside town—deckchair-lolling, dog-walking, tennis-playing—are followed, wordlessly and to considerable dark effect, by cramped scenes from the city's back streets. After a trip to America, Chatwin came up with the idea of making a film called *A Propos de Miami*.

It was Valerie Wade who first suggested that there might be a place for Chatwin on the Magazine. It was Francis Wyndham—at different times Show Business Editor and Senior Editor—who effected it. Chatwin had taken a sheaf of his photographs—of desert land and brightly-coloured African doorways and walls—to the Magazine's arts adviser David Sylvester, who was impressed and enthusiastic, though none of the pictures was to appear in the Magazine. When Sylvester resigned from his advisory position, Wyndham thought of Chatwin for the job. His approach came when Chatwin was at his lowest. He had no regular income and, mired in the nomad manuscript on which he had been working for the past three years, was on the point of giving it up as hopeless. Gloomy in his Gloucestershire kitchen, he answered the phone as soon as it rang and immediately agreed to come up to London. The job became his over a drink with Francis Wyndham and Magnus Linklater, the Magazine's new editor, in the Blue Lion, opposite the *Sunday Times* building in the Gray's Inn Road. In the course of doing it, he found new subjects to write about and his own way of writing about them. He also made several close friendships.

One of his first editorial projects was devised by a new friend. David King, working as a designer on the Magazine, came up with the notion of a pictorial series called "One Million Years of Art": a sequence of photographs of works of art arranged chronologically, with brief explanatory captions but with no evaluating commentary. Chatwin, with the art critic Edward Lucie-Smith as a consultant, chose and captioned 1,000 illustrations which move freely between continents and cultures, ignore most of the acknowledged masterpieces of Western painting—and serve as a vivid guide to his own aesthetic. The very first picture—in an issue which featured fierce chiaroscuro photographs by Don McCullin of people sleeping rough on the streets of London— was of stone tools from the Olduvai Gorge in Tanzania, dating from about two million years B.C. The one thousandth and last picture had been painted in 1972 by a Chinese People's Collective: it showed a busy operating theatre and was called "Acupuncture Anaesthesia." Between these were a fifteenth-century ceremonial seat from Haiti— "possibly," the optimistic Chatwinesque caption reads, "the chair on which Columbus sat"—Raeburn's portrait of the Minister of the Kirk skating and Andy Warhol's picture of boxes of Del Monte peach halves. The rows of tiny images— about the same size as Donald Evans's admired lines of postage-stamp watercolours—gave Chatwin an opportunity to show that objects made to serve a purpose could be as graceful and appealing as works of fine art. He included a Japanese tea-ceremony jar whose creamy-pink colour is decorated only with a few brown twig-like strokes, a wooden Iroquois club, with a little face, dotted with eyes and mouth, bent over at the top, and a group of Shaker furniture—two stiff-backed chairs, one on rockers, and a cast-iron stove with a long black pipe. He was also able to create the sort of conjunctions he enjoyed, putting together startlingly different artefacts from the same period: Landseer's picture of a dog and a puppy, entitled "Dignity and Impudence," is followed by a fetish figure from Fang, Gabon.

Chatwin's visual obsessions were given full rein in the series. There are several feathered items—a headdress, a helmet and his own Peruvian wall-hanging—and a burst of Russian avant-garde art. He casts a glance at his own history in the selection of a watercolour by the painter of his honeymoon region, John Marin. And he makes some jokes. One glistening picture, which looks as if it represents two interlocked bunches of silver bananas, turns out to show fish spread out for sale in a Turkish market: no photographer is named, but the picture is described as "contemporary." A striking pattern of red, green and yellow oblongs is, in fact, a photograph of painted shanty-town doors in Mauritania—one of those photographs by Chatwin that the *Sunday Times* had failed to publish.

This was one of the few occasions on which Chatwin acted primarily as art adviser; despite this, at least one of his enthusiasms was later translated into print. His discussions with Bruce Bernard about the sixteenth-century Dutch painter Hercules Seghers—a mysterious obsessive, whose mountainous landscapes, coiled like brain-tissue, were ignored during his lifetime—led to Bernard's commissioning a substantial piece on the subject by Lawrence Gowing. Chatwin's role on the Magazine soon altered. He suggested ideas for pieces to Francis Wyndham—among them, an article about the couturier Madeleine Vionnet. Chatwin knew she was a good subject but couldn't think of anyone to write about her. Wyndham told him he must do it himself—and in doing so pushed him into a new phase of his life.

Madame Vionnet, who maintained that she had been the first dressmaker to dispense with corsets, was old and French, influential but neglected. The clothes she designed were simple but sumptuous; her Paris apartment had an ornamental Belle Epoque exterior but a spare, sleek Art-Deco interior, with lacquer and chromium and aluminium—"as clean-cut and unsentimental as Mme. Vionnet herself." She was fierce and lofty—chasing the short and portly away from her salon—but lived modestly. She had a passion for her work and an acid turn of phrase. Chatwin produced an article—oblique and digressive, admiring but amused—which could have served as a model for his future profiles. A rush of journalism followed.

The Magazine was buoyant with ability and with money; Don McCullin thinks of his time there as spent "trapped in a submarine" of talent. Magnus Linklater, the editor during what he considers this "period of maximum arrogance and maximum independence," had been told by his predecessor Godfrey Smith: "There's about eighty thousand pounds' worth of over-matter: on the whole you should keep it to sixty or seventy thousand, but don't let it fall below forty." Writers and photographers were free to pursue their ideas without much budgetary constraint or editorial interference. Don McCullin went to Paraguay with Norman Lewis and to Cuba with Edna O'Brien; he went to Bangladesh and to Biafra. Chatwin brought stories from Peru, from Russia and from India.

His first assignment with Eve Arnold took him to Verrières-les-Buissons, to interview André Malraux: the aging adventurer talked fluently but was very frail. He trembled so much that Arnold couldn't take any pictures until he steadied his hand on his chin. For their last story together they went to India to follow Mrs. Gandhi on her campaign trail: "I can only give you my little finger to shake," she said, "because there's something the matter with the others." Sunil Sethi, the Indian journalist disguised in Chatwin's piece as "Rajiv," remembers the arrival at a filthy restaurant in the blazing heat—111 degrees in the shade—of a ramshackle Ambassador car: out of it "popped this very funny sight of a very pink Englishman and what seemed to me a very distinguished, diminutive, silver-haired lady with her hair bound up in coils . . . they were obviously about to expire that very second." Sethi, who became friendly with Chatwin, gave up his bed to the admired photographer: "Your pictures of Joan Crawford are absolutely fabulous!"

Chatwin got on well with Eve Arnold, and he got on well with Don McCullin, who is cautious about the kind of writer who refers to "my photographer"—as if he was his batman. The two men had first met by chance when McCullin had gone on a job to the Marquess of Dufferin and Ava's house in Holland Park. As he reached the door, it flew open to show Chatwin standing there—"like Miss World." He looked, McCullin remembers, as if he had "gone into a shop and said: 'give me the best smile, the best eyes and the best barnet.'"

There was a high-society dimension to several of the stories they covered. When McCullin went to do a feature with Nicholas Tomalin on fox-hunting in the West of England, Chatwin, because of a connection with the Duke of Beaufort, went along to ease their path, but, embarrassed by being caught between two sets of friends, he kept gingerly apart from both. McCullin spotted him hiding in the long grass, "like a highly-trained member of the Viet Cong." On another occasion they went together to the South of France, and then to Algeria to examine the tension between the

French and the North African inhabitants of Marseilles—a story which sprang from the murder of a French bus-driver by an Algerian. The result of this visit was one of Chatwin's most searching essays. "The Very Sad Story of Salah Bougrine" surveys the harsh history of the Algerian *fellahs*—the small farmers—and the condition of the French North Africans of that time, looks at the atrocities carried out during the Algerian War of Independence and considers the contribution of the immigrants to the French economy. It is one of Chatwin's most prescient articles. It is also—without any loss of sharpness—one of his most obviously compassionate. Some of the strongest passages describe the war-desolated Algiers that the immigrants have left and the ramshackle *bidonvilles* in which they had settled in Marseilles.

Their own experience of the city was different. As soon as they arrived in Marseilles Chatwin announced that they were invited to dinner at the house of the mayor's estranged wife. McCullin found it a "socially testing" evening. As they sat looking out over the sea having coffee, one of their fellow guests snapped open her handbag and produced a small glittering object, flourishing it as if it were a miniature gun. It was a great block of jewellery which she had had crushed together—"like a chevvy"—into a huge key-ring. Immediately one of the other women delved into her bag, and waved a similar shining lump. Chatwin, sitting with crossed legs, observed the scene with rolling eyes. McCullin, not speaking the language and uncomfortable with all this carry-on, was eager to get to work and to Algeria, but when they arrived he met considerable hostility among those whose photographs he wanted to take. He asked his companion what his subjects were saying as he pointed his camera at them. Chatwin translated: "Do stop taking photographs. We are no longer the slaves of France."

Most of Chatwin's ideas for stories came from outside England, but when, in the last year of his life, he made a selection of his articles from the *Sunday Times* and elsewhere, he put only two into the section called "Travel." The book includes some squibs and genuflections to grandees, as well as some of his strongest essays: these, like the Algerian story, focus on an individual in order to unravel a swathe of cultural history. None of the articles is especially well-served by the title "What Am I Doing Here," which suggests a book bulging with descriptions of foreign voyages. The words are a quotation from Rimbaud—it is what he asked himself in Ethiopia—and were pronounced by Bruce with emphatic self-ridicule, and a stress on the "am." On the cover of his book they are bewilderingly unpunctuated. This has led some readers to suspect a typographical error; others, Terence Stamp among them, have thought that Bruce was intending in this book to tell us the meaning of it all. What happened was this. Ian Craig, head of the design department at Jonathan Cape, was laying out the possibilities for the cover of *What Am I Doing Here* in 1988. None of his lay-outs looked quite right and eventually he offered his conclusion to Tom Maschler: "It looks shitty with the question-mark." Maschler agreed, and the alternatives were presented to the always design-alert Chatwin, who declared that the question-mark wasn't needed. Off it came.

What Am I Doing Here was a best-seller and a good book. But in terms of practical arrangements Bruce was never an editor's dream. Magnus Linklater, who admired and published his pieces, used to experience a "slight sinking of the heart" whenever a Bruce trip was proposed: the cost and unpredictability of his expeditions, on which Chatwin wouldn't phone in or take much account of instructions, meant that there was "a slightly nightmare quality about dealing with him"—until the traveller returned to tell his stories over lunch at the Kolossi Restaurant or the Quality Chop House—

Progressive Working-Class Caterer. Not everyone liked his work. "Isn't it awful? They hated it," Francis Wyndham told Chatwin, who was emerging from one of those *Sunday Times* lifts wanting to hear how his piece on Mrs. Gandhi had gone down with colleagues. The article—personal, impressionistic, by turns entranced and appalled—had been considered insufficiently hard-nosed, but was eventually published, much cut. Hunter Davies succeeded Linklater as editor of the Magazine and proved not to be a Chatwin fan: "all purple prose and self-indulgence, I thought." Davies's brief from the paper's editor, Harold Evans, was "to pack it tight, keep the budget down, and be consumer useful, so we began a new section called Lifespan and cut back on the big poncy foreign spreads by people like B. Chatwin."

It was Francis Wyndham who was Chatwin's main source of support on the Magazine, and Bruce never forgot this. "I spent my solitary lunch," he wrote to Wyndham from Siena in 1977, "thinking of the enormous amount I owe to you." It was, he often said, Wyndham who taught him how to prune and how to pad his articles. And it was Wyndham who, by suggesting that he go beyond his brief as art adviser, was responsible for their existence. Chatwin found his flair on the Magazine: there is a huge difference between the crispness and economy of his journalism and the strained theorising of his earlier work on nomads. He also developed a way of structuring his prose which never left him: all his books contain sections which can be read as discrete essays.

There were others who had reason to be grateful to Wyndham. On the Magazine he encouraged James Fox, David King and Don McCullin. As an editor at André Deutsch, he had been instrumental in the publication of V. S. Naipaul's first books, and in rediscovering the works of the then forgotten Jean Rhys. What was particularly striking about his advocacy of Bruce Chatwin, and the friendship

that developed from this, was that in temperament and inclination the two men seemed to be opposites.

Wyndham dreads travelling: "My theory," he explains,
when considering the well-worn proposition that someone
as perpetually on the move as Chatwin must have been running away, "is that the travellers are escaping and that the
people like me are hiding." He likes to loll: his novel *The
Other Garden*, for which he won the Whitbread First Novel
Award in his sixties, is a book set in the Second World War
which is elegiac about inaction. He thinks of himself as visually deficient and chronically literary: as someone who when
the rhododendrons are in bloom will amble round Savile
Gardens reading the labels on the trees. Chatwin had little
feeling for the popular culture of his own time: George
Melly has still not got over the fact that he, who knew so
many things, had never heard of the Muppets. Wyndham,
some fifteen years older, floats on an encyclopedic memory
for the popular songs and musicals and film stars of the past—
Alice Faye, Connee Boswell, Ruth Etting, Helen Morgan.
On the Magazine, he and the Fashion Editor Meriel Mc-
Cooey, with whom he shared an office, were noted for their
duets from Hollywood musicals, and for their daily six
o'clock—or 5:30—purchases of a half-bottle of Teacher's for
"pre-drinks drinks"; eventually the two of them, deemed to
have a bad influence on each other, were separated—"like
children in a school."

The novelist Ada Leverson, nicknamed "The Sphinx" by
her friend Oscar Wilde, was Wyndham's grandmother, and he
has written warmly about her "dedicated frivolity" and her
"celebration of inconsequence." He has something of these
attributes—and is something of a Sphinx to his own friends.
Richard Wollheim and Colin MacInnes were once overheard
at a party on a balcony talking about Wyndham: "There we
were," MacInnes said, "like two Chinese civil servants in the

snow, talking about the Emperor." When Bruce first met Wyndham he thought him "the *most* glamorous person I'd ever seen"—"glamour" was unalloyed praise from Bruce.

"No one would ever mess with Francis," says McCullin, recalling the chilly look he gave anyone who perched on his desk, the sweep of his little finger as he brushed away ash from its surface—but referring also to his writing and editorial talents. In the heyday of the Magazine Wyndham produced a stream of profiles and interviews—comic, strange and melancholy, and shaped as short stories. In them he often left the obvious thing unsaid, dispensing with physical description and concentrating on not just the matter but the manner of his subject's delivery: the most telling remarks were often rather dippy asides. When the Kray twins—who had been in the habit of dropping in at the Magazine, and whom Wyndham went on to visit in prison—approached him to write their biography, they explained that they wanted the book to be "true—like Harold Robbins." He made light of the skill involved in all this. The cookery writer Arabella Boxer consulted the expert when she was about to undertake her first interview: should she take a tape-recorder, or notes, or both? He advised: "I should just take two purple hearts and see what happens." Wyndham himself was helped by possessing a clear and capacious memory.

Chatwin and Wyndham, both great talkers who had definite ideas about what didn't need to be said in their work, brought distinctly different talents to the *Sunday Times* Magazine. Chatwin was an imaginative visualiser. Wyndham was more intimate—an ingenious chronicler of embarrassment and tender feeling. They were appreciators of each other's work: Wyndham describes the painterly quality of Chatwin's style as being "like the things that moved him visually: a mixture of over-the-top and very cut-down," and says he did hardly anything to Chatwin's pieces on the Magazine, only occasionally cutting a bit of preciousness. Bruce felt he did much more than that, and made Wyndham one of the dedicatees of his third book.

Chatwin's disengagement from the *Sunday Times* has since his death become misted by surmise. In 1974 the Magazine was preparing a series of illustrated articles under the general heading "Great American Families"—a series which three years later was published as a book. Among the contributors were Gore Vidal on the Adamses, V. S. Pritchett on the Vanderbilts and Peter Conrad on the Roosevelts. On the eve of his departure with David King to research the first articles in New York, Wyndham talked about the project to Bruce Chatwin, who was to write a lively piece on the Guggenheims. The night that Wyndham arrived in New York he went to a party given by John Richardson, and talked to his host about Chatwin. Richardson had hated the Chatwin of his Sotheby's days, whom he thought a "narcissistic troublemaker" and an "evil messenger" from Richardson's former lover, the art historian Douglas Cooper—messages which presumably emanated from their estrangement. But meeting Chatwin later, he had begun to like him, and was generously disposed to Wyndham's news that he had taken to writing, and was writing well. As they talked, the door opened and a bevy of particularly chic New Yorkers swept in. In the middle of them was Chatwin.

He turned out to have taken the next plane out of London after Wyndham's, and to be perching in the empty apartment of his parents-in-law, enjoying the New Yorkness of its long corridor, its canopy and doormen. Wyndham and King lunched with him, and later arranged to have a drink with him at the Chelsea Hotel. It was there that Bruce—in shorts and rucksack—told them, as if he had suddenly got the idea, that he was going to go to Patagonia, and pushed off. Some hours later, looking from a taxi in another part of town, King exclaimed: "There's Chatwin." Wyndham looked out, and saw "this figure striding down Broadway as if he was literally walking to Patagonia."

These appearances and shootings-off could have been accounted for: Bruce had flown out of England without warning because he had just heard from Elizabeth in America that her ailing father had died; he had wanted to follow the trail of Butch Cassidy and the Sundance Kid for the Magazine; he was free to come and go from the Magazine as he pleased, being on a retainer, not a salary, and he had always made full use of this freedom. But no such accounts were forthcoming. Bruce was as short on explanations in life as he was in his books. A letter to Wyndham, sent from Lima in December 1974, shows the flair he had for weaving together a number of hints—cryptic references to the *Sunday Times*, a tantalising mention of a Turkish story, which never materialised, a nod towards what became his first book:

> I have done what I threatened. I suddenly got fed up with NY and ran away to South America. I have been staying with a cousin in Lima for the past week and am going tonight to Buenos Aires. I intend to spend Christmas in the middle of Patagonia. I am doing a story there for myself, something I have always wanted to write up. I do not, for obvious reasons, want to be associated with the paper in Argentina, but if something crops up I'll let you or Magnus know. I'm working on something that could be marvellous but I'll have to do it in my own way.
>
> The third part of the Guggenheim saga is already complete in note form and will take only a day or two to write, but we will have to compress the rest together. Later on I'll be looking at the Guggenheim mines in Central Chile because my cousin's husband runs a mine near Chuquicamata.
>
> Can you tell Magnus that Ahmet Ertegun is defi-

nitely on, but I want to wait until the spring and go
with him to Turkey (at his expense) and watch the king
of rock music, who firmly intends to be President of
Turkey, in action.

I'll give you an address in Buenos Aires through
which I can be contacted, but I don't want to receive
any official S.T. correspondence in the Argentine.

When he described his writing life for the *New York Times
Book Review*, and when I interviewed him a few years before
he died, Bruce said he had sent a telegram to the office:
"Gone to Patagonia." No one can produce evidence that he
did so. Magnus Linklater clearly remembers a "sudden revelation" that Bruce was leaving for South America: "Chatwina's
off again" was his reaction. A telegram fits with Linklater's
sense of the episode and was "an extravagant gesture of the
kind one had come to expect from Bruce," but he doesn't recall actually getting one. Francis Wyndham doesn't remember
seeing it either. Nothing can be proved either way, but when
Nicholas Murray pointed out in his study of Chatwin that the
telegram couldn't be confirmed, he found himself unwillingly
conscripted in an attack on his subject, which encompassed
not only Chatwin's "myths" but also his admirers—"bores of
uncertain sexuality" and "polo-necked thinkers of Notting
Hill." Telegrammed or not, Chatwin's departure to Patagonia
didn't put an end to his relationship with the *Sunday Times*: he
went on receiving a retainer of £2,000 until it was stopped by
Hunter Davies; his pieces on Maria Reiche in Peru, on the
Guggenheims, and on Mrs. Gandhi appeared after his departure to Patagonia. He did, however, regard this as the beginning of his life as a writer of books.

❧ 9

TWINS

"It always irritated me to be called a travel writer. So I decided to write something about people who never went out." Chatwin fell into an interesting confusion in talking about his third book, speaking as if it were the subject rather than the writer who puts the travel into travel writing. He did so in attempting to account for one of the swerves in his literary output. The five books that he published during his lifetime form a series of contrasts, some of them calculated. *In Patagonia*, cool and elliptical, was followed by the extravagant and hectic *The Viceroy of Ouidah*. *Utz* is small in size, carefully focused and sparely written: it was preceded by *The Songlines*, which is long, speculative and loosely-organised. At the mid-point of his writing life, Chatwin set out for the first time to write a piece of fiction. He produced the most lyrical of his books, and the only one to be set in the British Isles.

On the Black Hill is the story of two farmers from the Welsh borders, identical twin brothers who live their long lives together in pastoral seclusion. These brothers are peculiar, anomalous—and anointed with a touch of telepathic magic. They are unmarried, unmoving, and almost entirely unaffected by technological change. The few encounters they have with world events and urban manners are such as to drive them further into an isolation whose harshness is of their own devising: they are brutally treated by patriots and the military at the time of the First World War; they later suffer an alarming brush with some short-skirted females. Their relations with their nearest neighbours are frequently sour.

This is a novel in which things come in twos: there is a pattern of pairs and of contrasts. There are two Jones brothers, two homesteads—called "The Vision" and "The Rock"— and two favourite walks. A clock in the squire's house is decorated with the figures of the Heavenly Twins, Castor and Pollux. There are two countries—Wales and England; two religions—Church and Chapel; two Ways—the Broad and the Narrow. There is this world and the next. Chatwin at first thought of calling his novel "The Vision and the Rock," indicating that this most domestic of his books is also at times other-worldly. His epigraph is from Jeremy Taylor, the seventeenth-century divine whose work had always appealed to him, and who, in speaking of the limitations of Earthly life, makes Heaven sound like abroad: "Since we stay not here, being people but of a dayes abode, and our age is like that of a flie, and contemporary with a gourd, we must look some where else for an abiding city, a place in another countrey to fix our house in . . ."

The allure and achievement of *On the Black Hill* is the creation of a region and a landscape which is at once local and visionary, real and imagined. Invention and documentation are mixed, as in all Chatwin's books. At the centre are a number of characters who never existed and a sequence of events that never occurred, but the book also contains historical episodes, incidents from Bruce's childhood and descriptions of existing buildings and actual terrain. He combined and rearranged anecdotes he was told and facts he discovered; he mingled different aspects of people he had met, and he used real names for his imaginary places—between Hay and Llanthony on the Welsh borders, there is still a farmhouse called

"The Vision." Cape extracted from Bruce a letter assuring them that this was "not a *roman-à-clef*," but they nevertheless referred the text to their libel lawyer.

Chatwin had first visited the Welsh borders as a child with his father and brother; he stayed there as a schoolboy from Marlborough; he went back later with an ex-girlfriend, Gloria Birkett, and his future wife, Elizabeth. The landmarks of his novel are drawn from different areas of the borders, in which there is more than one "Black Hill"—Chatwin said that the story could be set "anywhere between South Shropshire and Monmouthshire"—and the book bears the traces of several friendships. He stayed for long periods in Diana Melly's house at Scethrog, near Brecon: a stout-walled Medieval structure built to repel roving bands of outlaws, and now besieged by writers, sheep and fishermen. From the small window in the top room where much of *On the Black Hill* was written—the most monastic of the rooms—Chatwin could see meadows, the loops of the Usk river, some wooded and some grassy hills. From here he undertook expeditions with Diana Melly which were rehearsals for incidents in his book. They went to Pembrokeshire, to St. David's, where the twins are sent for a seaside holiday; they crawled around standing-stones, imagining how these would appear to a child; they flew over the Welsh countryside in a four-seater plane, as the twins do on their eightieth birthday. Inside the keep, benign territorial battles were waged. According to his hostess, Bruce ruled: he selected his fellow guests—he liked Wyndham, on whose opinion he relied, to be there—and spread his work over three floors. Bruce saw things differently: "Diana's claim that I have colonised the whole house is quite without foundation," he wrote to Wyndham. "She is the puppet-mistress who moves me around."

On the Black Hill is dedicated to Francis Wyndham and Diana Melly in recognition of the importance to the book of this tower and these friends. But they were not Bruce's only links to the border country. He stayed in the cottage of his publisher, Tom Maschler, in the Black Mountains, just above the monastery in which the poet and painter David Jones had stayed. Further north, at Clunton in Shropshire, he wrote some of his novel—surrounded by photocopies of the *Hereford Times* and large-scale Ordnance Survey maps—in a block of stables belonging to Martin Wilkinson. Here he came back from a walk exclaiming: "I've found my title"—he had seen a "Black Hill" marked on a Forestry Commission sign. And here, in a pub with his host, he looked up as a young farmhand came in steaming from his work in the fields and observed: "What an *odalisque*." Bruce's italics.

In Radnorshire he visited Louisa and Alexis de la Falaise, bicycling to their farm through the Black Mountains from Abergavenny. They told him about a local family with whom they were friendly, who lived, as Chatwin's family at "The Rock" lives, in tinker fashion, with a pack of dogs as fierce as hawks. They took him to a school Nativity play in which their two children were making what turned out to be one of many public appearances: translated to New York via Fontainebleau and Paris, Daniel de la Falaise became an actor and an escort of the latter-day Madonna; Lucie, an angel in the play, a Saint Laurent model. Chatwin used the play—and its stage curtains made out of Army blankets—in his novel. The family also introduced Chatwin to Mary Hayward, the local district nurse since the Fifties, who took him to a farmhouse above Painscastle lived in by two bachelors in their forties and their spinster sisters. He was shown the bedroom of their late parents, with its high feather mattress and on the wash-stand a large ewer and basin. Nurse Hayward remembers that in the kitchen he "crossed the room to look at a picture on the wall. I think it was probably one of those representing the Broad and Narrow Ways that I had seen on so many farmhouse walls."

In the public library at Hereford he went through bound volumes of the *Hereford Times* stretching back to the First World War. He scooped up incidental details for his novel from the Situations Vacant columns: "Wanted: kind person to nurse baby girl, six months old." From reports of the 1918 peace celebrations he retrieved information about cloud-bursts and a dramatic reversal of fortune: "A soldier, named Thomas, invalided home from Salonika, who had been deaf and dumb for some time, recovered his speech when he saw the hoisting of the flag." He was particularly pleased to find the story of a corrupt Hay solicitor, Herbert Rowse Armstrong, who was hanged in 1922 for the murder of his wife—and popped him into *On the Black Hill* as Mr. Arkwright. He consulted old account books belonging to Simon Harpur, a farmer living near Diana Melly, for details of agricultural prices. From A. J. P. Taylor's *English History* and Julian Bell's *We Did Not Fight* he extracted material about the treatment of conscientious objectors. He also read "the memoirs of a Methodist minister who was hounded out of Wales because he got drunk once—*The Life and Opinions of Robert Roberts, Wandering Scholar*. It's my book of the year."

The idea for the central characters of the novel came from Penelope Betjeman, who had a house in the foothills of the Black Mountains. She introduced Chatwin to two bachelor brothers—"the young men," as she always referred to them—who lived together on a neighbouring farm, and told him a story about them which took his fancy: "Some time before the War their mother, seeing them to show no signs of interest in the opposite sex, had sent them to the Fair at Hay-on-Wye to meet some young ladies. They came back with crestfallen faces, never having seen girls in short skirts before. This put them off for ever."

When Chatwin was first researching his book he stayed often in Penelope Betjeman's house, at what she called "Kulu-on-Wye in the Hereford Himalaya." For the last twenty years of her life she travelled extensively in India—leading treks, examining temple architecture and investigating Hindu ritual—and her arrangements on the Welsh borders were planned to replicate the simplicity of her life there. Details of her spartan accommodation were relayed enthusiastically to her family: "Also a NEW CHEMICAL LAVATORY HAS BEEN INVENTED IN EIRE COSTING £100 . . . We have built a lovely little room for it which I shall paint puce." Her writing-paper was headed "NO TELEPHONE THANK GOD"; her water came from a spring in the garden. "Every moment of recreation off a horse's back I have always considered wasted," she claimed, and Bruce was an enthusiastic passenger in her pony and cart. As a return for her hospitality, he hewed wood for her stove: James Fox once found him there, hard at work in the middle of the forest, "glistening, like something out of *Seven Brides for Seven Brothers*."

Penelope Betjeman appears briefly in *On the Black Hill* as an exuberant visitor to the twins, a visitor who exclaims at the top of her voice—"Gosh! Cinnamon toast!"—and who spends some time every year bicycling alone around India. She is "a short and very courageous woman with laugh wrinkles at the edge of her slaty eyes, and silver hair cut in a fringe." In life she was small, round, jolly and a devout Catholic convert: Evelyn Waugh drew on her qualities when he was creating the character of the Emperor Constantine's mother in his novel *Helena*. When she saw Chatwin after a long absence she would burst out laughing with joy—and he came to perform a genie-like role in her life. He happened to be staying with her when, trying to boot her terrier out of the door, she slipped, broke her wrist and had to be taken to hospital. He was lunching with her in her snowbound house when she became delirious from the onset of malaria. And in 1986 he chanced to be travelling in the Mussouri Hills when he read of her death in the *Times of India*. She had been trekking through the Sutlej Valley, had got off her pony on a steep track above a temple she had just visited, sat down on a rock and died. Chatwin, who had many times discussed travelling in India with her but never done so, arrived in time to help scatter her ashes with flowers into the Beas River at the foot of the valley.

The Welsh border region is an area of high skies and low churches, of old farming families, of solitaries and colourful colonisers: since the Sixties the hills have been scattered with alternative-lifers—aromatherapists and reflexologists and astrologers, with long locks and beaded velvet bags and children named after birds and precious stones. The more itinerant of these incomers have not always been welcomed: printed notices declaring "No Hippies" have been distributed through local towns; rumours have been rampant, including one that involved defecation in the corner of a public house—"they used it *deliberate*." Some of this suspicion is registered in *On the Black Hill*, although the novel's chief hippie and the farming brothers become friends, with improbable rapidity. This tent-dweller, who is given the mystical name of Theo, has some things in common with Bruce Chatwin: he believes that "all men were meant to be wanderers"; he quotes from the Chinese poet Li Po; he is attracted to far-flung places and to rare words. He reads, as did Chatwin, the lesson in a local chapel: "I know the stones of new Jerusalem," Theo explains to the minister who asks him to read from the Book of Revelation, and, in one of the more indulgent passages of the book, lists "without misplacing a syllable . . . the jasper and jacinth, the chrysoprase and chalcedony" of the holy city. In doing so, he echoes another vision of purity and precious stones, created by the intensely autobiographical Fin-de-Siècle novelist Frederick Rolfe—alias Baron Corvo. In his novel *Hadrian VII*, Rolfe set his impoverished hero-turned-Pope to wander among gems more swooningly described but no more rare or eternal than Chatwin's: "He bathed in the beauty of sea-blue beryls, corundums, catseyes, and chalcedonyx. A vast rose-alexandrolith mysteriously changed from myrtle-green to purple as He turned it." In 1904, the year that *Hadrian VII* was published, Rolfe bathed in the River Usk and stayed with friends outside Abergavenny.

The sequestered spots of the area have long been documented and extolled. And dreaded. "Alas!" wails the letter-writing heroine of Jane Austen's *Love and Friendship*, "how am I to avoid these evils I shall never be exposed to? What probability is there of my ever tasting the Dissipation of London, the Luxuries of Bath or the stinking fish of Southampton? I who am doomed to waste my Days of Youth and Beauty in an humble Cottage in the Vale of Uske." Austen is likely to have formed her leery view of the valley in reaction to the praises heaped on its picturesque qualities by William Gilpin in 1782. Gilpin—for whom an "irregular" landscape was a scene of romance—had found the area "a very romantic place, abounding with broken grounds, torrents, dismantled towers, and ruins of every kind," and free of "any regular and unpleasing shapes." Nevertheless, some readers have found its features resistible. Dr. Johnson disdained the principality; "Welsh rivers" were really brooks. Two hundred years after him, Teddy Millington-Drake, one of the most fastidiously cosmopolitan of Chatwin's friends, explained his reservations about *On the Black Hill*: "I'm just not terribly interested in people in Wales somehow."

There have always been those who *are* interested. Francis Kilvert was curate to the vicar of Clyro—near Hay-on-Wye—from 1865 to 1872; Chatwin stayed near his parsonage while the film of *On the Black Hill* was being made. Kilvert chronicled in his diary a weather-laden landscape that is recognisable from Chatwin's novel: "dark hopeless rain,"

"tender showery lights," "the brilliant blue of the Beacons."
He wrote about places that were known to Chatwin: "a few
days ago a man named Evans kicked his wife to death at
Rhulen. He kicked her bosom black and her breast morti-
fied"; the name Rhulen is used in *On the Black Hill*, although
Chatwin said that the description of the town could be that
of Knighton or Kington or Clun or Hay-on-Wye. He reported an inquest on the barmaid of the Blue Boar, Hay, who
had drowned herself. A later barmaid at Hay's Blue Boar
watched Chatwin's "theatrical way" in the bar and considered that if he "had been born in the twelfth century he
would have been a wizard."

There are plenty of would-be wizards in the area, and
much local lore. Chatwin was interested in a lake legend—
that of the lady of Llyn y Fan Fach, a reputed member of the
Fairy Folk, who rose from her watery home to marry a local
farmer. "There are strange things about the Black Mountain,
but I have travelled the hills at all hours, night and day, and
never saw anything bad," an old soothsayer told Kilvert.
Chatwin's novel speaks of mighty weather, hard times and
clear spirits. Sentiment is not a prominent feature of his
work, but *On the Black Hill* shows a feeling for equality: despite his weakness for duchesses, Bruce here reserves his
severest censure for the privileged and speaks up for the weak
and unworldly against their bullies.

He sometimes overpaints his case. He goes a blemish too
far with a windbag brigadier, who is given both a purple face
and an inability to say his "r's." And he allows too many rus-
tic touches in describing Meg, his retiring, admired child of
nature—a case not of fabrication but of drawing too enthusiastically from life. Her real-life model—a middle-aged
woman with whom Diana Melly observed his "flirty" manner—slept on a dishevelled heap of old mattresses on the
floor by a fire; over the flames hung a black kettle which was

sometimes used to boil a potato; a cow lived alongside the room. She spoke, sometimes with some difficulty, in a high, sing-song voice. When she went outside, birds stood on her head. Chatwin chopped logs for her, and organised advice from solicitors when her tenancy was threatened. He regarded her as "a heroine of our time." His description of her in his notebook—in an unravelling sweater, with jodhpurs over a new pair of men's trousers—could have fitted unaltered into *On the Black Hill*: "a truly Shakespearean entrance with two birch branches over her shoulder."

The region is rich in recluses. Chatwin took a keen interest in Kilvert's "Solitary of Llanbedr," a vicar and Master of Arts who wore a dress coat, carried a tall hat, and lived in a hut heaped with Biblical commentaries. He dosed himself with camomile pills for an internal inflammation and spent his time devising two systems of shorthand which he used to write his sermons. Kilvert "sat in amazement taking mental notes of the strangest interior I ever saw." Chatwin— whose schoolboy fascination with hermits was never extinguished—was to find and delight in, though not to write about, his own religious solitary in Wales: a hermit priest who lived in a terraced house with a back garden cut into the rock and managed single-handed a Greek Orthodox monastery, whose font was in the garden shed.

Literary connections and echoes reach far further back than Austen and Kilvert: Chatwin's are not the only celebrated twins to have been seen in the region of the Black Mountains. John Aubrey devoted one of his *Brief Lives* to the Vaughan twins, identical poetic brothers, from Llansantffraed in the Usk valley: "Their grandmother was an Aubrey: their father a coxcombe and no honester than he should be— he cosened me of 50s. once." Thomas Vaughan, the more acclaimed of the pair during his lifetime, was an alchemist, satirised by his contemporary Samuel Butler in his "Character of a Hermetic Philosopher"; according to the historian Anthony Wood, he died while experimenting with mercury, some of which "by chance getting up into his nose marched him off."

The poet Henry Vaughan, described as proud and moody by Aubrey, outlived his twin by thirty years, and his fame has eclipsed Thomas's for centuries. He is buried in Llansant-ffraed churchyard, two-and-a-half miles from Diana Melly's tower at Scethrog: a large flat stone shows the family coat of arms with three strong-featured round faces. Bruce Chatwin visited this grave, and was intrigued by the fact that in the seventeenth century a relative of Vaughan's mother had lived in the tower. His Welsh novel shares a geography with Vaughan's verse, and something of its temperament.

Henry Vaughan, the great poet of light, is studied as a visionary; his words are sung as a religious consolation. He is also a lyrical ambassador for his native land. He called himself a "Silurist"—a reference to the ancient British tribe who once inhabited Brecon; he also became known as "The Swan of Usk." Breconshire—with its "cold damps" and shades, its "windswept mountains" and "broad valleys"—is apparent throughout his verse; its contours are present even when the poet's eye is most determinedly set on a world beyond this one. His poems draw on a wooded and watery landscape, with grey and clear but rapidly changing skies. There were in the seventeenth century, as there are now, great stacks of clouds, and unexpected breaks in the clouds. There are woods and moorlands and bright patches of water. The hills are swept by the shadows of big clouds and by surprising shafts of sunlight; whole mountains disappear in mists, and are suddenly revealed—it can seem as if there must be entire cities concealed up there. The Black Mountains are full of light.

This is a landscape formed for a drama of visions and revelations. Vaughan—here referring to the Pharisee Nico-

demus, to whom Christ explained his doctrines at night—
made it into a place whose illuminations and occlusions were
a pattern for spiritual insight:

> *Through that pure Virgin-shrine,*
> *That sacred veil drawn o'er thy glorious noon*
> *That men might look and live as glow-worms shine,*
> *And face the moon:*
> *Wise Nicodemus saw such light*
> *As made him know his God by night . . .*
>
> *God's silent searching flight:*
> *When my Lord's head is filled with dew, and all*
> *His locks are wet with the clear drops of night;*
> *His still, soft call;*
> *His knocking time; the soul's dumb watch,*
> *When Spirits their fair kindred catch.*

He made a poetry of shadows and clearings and sudden radi-
ances, of seeing in the dark, of white days and dazzlings and
darknesses—and of "a dazzling darkness." He also produced
one poem that might have been invoked by Chatwin to
express his creed of restlessness. According to Vaughan—for
whom the word "irregular" had yet to acquire its later
picturesque sense—Man

> *hath no root, nor to one place is tied,*
> *But ever restless and irregular*
> *About this earth doth run and ride,*
> *He knows he hath a home, but scarce knows where,*
> *He says it is so far*
> *That he hath quite forgot how to go there.*

Meanwhile, his twin Thomas was also writing poetry in
praise of "the crystal Usk" and prose which identifies light as
the source of life.

The cases of the Vaughans and of Chatwin present a correspondence between a real set of twins and an imaginary one. Both sets look both to England and to Wales (the Vaughans are thought to have been bilingual) in a landscape whose geography encouraged a mystical as well as a practical view of life. The correspondence includes an absorption on Bruce's part with light, in both the spiritual and the meteorological sense, with inner and outer weather. The light which floods Henry Vaughan's poems shines on the first page of *On the Black Hill*, in the engraving of Holman Hunt's "Light of the World" which hangs in the brothers' bedroom. The verses from Matthew's Gospel, illustrated in the picture of "The Broad and Narrow Way"—which the twins of *On the Black Hill* remember as a part of their early boyhood— were connected in Henry Vaughan's thoughts, too, with the days of his youth. Evoking in his poem "Childhood" the innocence of his boyish plans—those "white designs which children drive"—he wrote:

> *Oh for thy centre and mid-day!*
> *For sure that is the* narrow way.

Chatwin's view of the border country was coloured by a memory of his own childhood and the end of wartime austerity: "By 1949 the hard times were over and one evening my father proudly drove home from work in a new car. Next day he took my brother and me for a spin. On the edge of an escarpment he stopped, pointed to a range of grey hills in the west and then said, 'Let's go on into Wales.' We slept the night in the car, in Radnorshire, to the sound of a mountain stream. At sunrise there was a heavy dew, and the sheep were all around us. I suppose the result of this trip is the novel I've recently published." The contours of this memory sometimes shifted: he was later to recall the occasion of the trip as being "to fetch our old car, a Lanchester, which had been sitting in my great uncle's barn since before the war." But the essential ingredients—his father, austerity, war and the Welsh mountains—remained the same.

The childhood experiences of the *Black Hill* twins frequently turn out to be the childhood experiences of Bruce Chatwin. The painter with whom the twins stay at the seaside as boys is a version of one of his own great-aunts. As infants, the twins are given a teddy bear and a felt Humpty-Dumpty: they burn the teddy and push the other toy, which they have christened "the Dump," into a stream, explaining to their anxious mother that "we never liked the Dump." The boy Chatwin "lost teddy bears without a murmur"—though he was devoted to a wooden camel he called Laura and to the "glorious pink mouth" of a conch shell known to him as Mona. He, too, had a felt Humpty-Dumpty, which he one day left on a railway platform. As his stricken mother rushed back to retrieve the cherished item her son piped up: "I never liked the blasted Dump."

The first time the twins see snow they hide from it, explaining to their mother: "God's spitting." This enshrines a moment remembered by Bruce's mother. As a tot, he passed onto her his observations on snow: "Is that God spitting? It looks like frozen spit to me." It was a memory he may also have put to use on another occasion. In one of his letters to Diana Melly from Yaddo, written when he had amassed nearly three hundred pages of his Welsh novel, Chatwin enclosed a "tentative version" of a poem by the fourteenth-century Welsh poet, Dafydd ap Gwilym, whose grave "we must go to see." He had been looking at early Celtic nature poetry while he was trying to establish a cyclical seasonal framework for his novel. Dafydd wrote skilfully as a comic drinker, suitor and soaring poet of nature, and was capable of some wonderful effects:

> *A fine gull on the tideflow,*
> *All one white with moon or snow.*

"The White Poem," whose title alone would have given Chatwin pleasure, is mournful, beautiful and bitter. It opens:

> *I cannot sleep,*
> *I do not stir by day.*
> *Sadness has come upon me,*
> *The world has gone.*

It moves from one favourite Chatwin image—the earth is covered with a "cloak of white feathers"—to another, to the recluses who fascinated him:

> *I will not wear a floury Miller's apron, or a hood.*
> *I will not venture out in a coat of white fur.*
> *Every year, around New Year, we live like hermits.*
> *He has whitewashed the dark earth.*

It goes on:

> *Drifts are on the heather*
> *Blowing this way and that.*
> *The piles of chaff wear ermine over their bellies.*
> *White dust covers the footpaths.*
> *He has covered the paths where we sang our songs.*

> *I ask, Who is it that spits on us in the white season?*

Words of the child Chatwin are given to Benjamin and Lewis Jones, and the brothers also resemble their creator. Benjamin is, as Chatwin was, a baker of cakes and a student of the Classics who has difficulty with the Odes of Horace. Like Chatwin, Lewis Jones dreams of travel and adventure. John Updike has observed that "their twinship is in fact a homosexual marriage," with a yielding and a more vigorous partner, and a shared, though chaste marital bed: "For forty-two years," the book's opening sentence explains, "Lewis and Benjamin Jones slept side by side, in their parents' bed." One of Chatwin's early titles for the novel was "Mr. and Mr. Jones."

Chatwin said that what he had first thought of as being a short story turned into a novel when he found himself writing the sentence: "The brothers were identical twins." He began to read about twins, and was advised—by a French friend married to an identical twin—to look at Michel Tournier's *Météores*, published in England as *Gemini*. Various Tournier themes—Cain and Abel, Robinson Crusoe—coincided with his own interests, and Bruce had, he told Francis Wyndham, promised himself "to have a big go" at Tournier. Nevertheless, each time he started on one of his books, he was defeated: "either my French isn't up to it, or I start feeling that there's something unbearably portentous about the writing; that he's an 'important' literary personage, and is concerned to let you know it." He got halfway through *Gemini*, and then moved on to look at some psychoanalytic literature, where he took pleasure in finding himself in a web of twin-like correspondences, and reported to Wyndham:

> The only book that really impressed me was by a Professor Zazzo, written, I think, in the Forties. Last January, I went to lunch with the translator of *The Viceroy* in Paris, and there, on his desk, was *Météores*. "Funny," I said, "I'm writing a book about twins." "Funny," he said, "my wife is a psychiatrist who works with the leading expert on twins, one Professor Zazzo." We rang for an appointment. The Professor was in his eighties. Utterly charming! . . . I wanted to make sure my story held together. "But Monsieur," he replied. "I have 1200 case-histories on twins, and if I had your talents, I would be Balzac." He then put me straight on a num-

ber of points, and mentioned Tournier. It seemed that Tournier had also been obsessed by his book, and had checked his plot with Zazzo, as I did mine.

Gemini features a pair of identical twins who have sex with each other, and there are those—notably Edmund White— who think of a preoccupation with twins as distinguishing a vein of fiction by homosexuals or about homosexual experience. A pair of identical twins excites the protagonist of Thomas Mann's *Felix Krull*; in Mann's variation on *Die Walküre*, "The Blood of the Walsungs," a male and female twin make love on a bearskin rug. Genet was fascinated by twins. Patrick White's *The Solid Mandala* shows a pair of reclusive male twins from the Sydney suburbs whose relationship has the appearance of a marriage. Chatwin's twins are notably sexually abstinent but he once told Edmund White that he was sure that sixty per cent of identical twins were lovers—he did not live long enough to hear reports by American doctors of foetuses kissing and fighting each other in the womb. White, who remembers most of Chatwin's tales as being gayer when told than when published, cherished an oral rendering of the novel in which the two men "were madly in love with each other and had lots of sex." This was a version that Bruce was more likely to expound to the famously homosexual White than to some others, and one which stood little chance of getting onto the page, where the celibacy of Chatwin's brothers is broken only when one of them succumbs momentarily to the lure of the female. Bruce shuddered at the idea of describing "what Michael Ignatieff calls the hydraulics of sex."

The story told in *On the Black Hill* is not the story of Bruce's sexual life, but is a monument to his dilemmas. He was of two minds. In the notebook he kept while preparing to write the novel he recorded: "Lunch with Elizabeth.

Poignant. Sad. We discussed our lives in the past tense." His homosexual friendships—including one with Edmund White—had been mostly ephemeral, but at the time of the book's publication were changing. He had a protracted affair with an Australian described by one friend as the male equivalent of the glamorous blonde on a man's arm, and was reported to have enthused by postcard about making love to him in a tent, while outside a lion roared. He separated from his wife for a time, but hated the idea of divorce: having come to a judicial arrangement with Elizabeth, he immediately began to see more of her. He declared that he found something "awful" in the idea of two men living together. But a year or two after the publication, in 1982, of *On the Black Hill,* he had considered buying a cottage in Wales—a cottage in the hills with no road leading up to it—and living there with the dress designer Jasper Conran. Conran was the other man, the first being Teddy Millington-Drake, whom at the end of his life Bruce said he had loved.

❧ 10

NOMADS

Nomadism was the biggest of Bruce Chatwin's big themes. It was more than a blazing topic about which to write: it was an obsessional interest which was also a creed, a way of making sense of—and of enhancing—his archaeological inquiries, his geographical investigations, his own history and neurosis. His first, unpublished, book was about nomads. Nomads were the subject of several of his essays. They were the impetus for *On the Black Hill*, which was conceived as an anti-nomad book, a book about people who never left their house. But it wasn't until he wrote *The Songlines*, which appeared in 1987, two years before his death, that he managed to publish an extended discussion of the preoccupations about which he so often spoke and which many of his friends experienced as an uneasy ghost patrolling his work and conversation. Travelling with him around Australia while he was collecting material for the book, Salman Rushdie began "to think of Bruce's unwritten book as the burden he's been carrying all his writing life. Once he's done this, I think, he'll be free, he'll be able to take flight." There was a sadness for Rushdie in the sense he had that in *Utz* "Bruce was indeed beginning that new light-spirited phase of flight. *Utz* is all we have of what had become possible for him once his Australian odyssey helped him to express the ideas which he'd carried about for so many years."

The Songlines is both animated and oppressed by these ideas. Chatwin found in the Aboriginal myth of Creation an incandescent image, an image which was wide-ranging in its suggestiveness and which acted as a vehicle for concerns of his own. His exposition of the myth is graphic. In the Dreamtime, the Aboriginal equivalent of the period covered by the first two chapters of Genesis—a time, or non-time, in which everything was first conceived and created—the mineral forms, animal species and varied vegetation of Australia were summoned into existence by song. Legendary beings known as the Ancestors formed themselves from clay and began to roam over the continent. As they roamed, they sang out "the name of everything that crossed their path—birds, animals, plants, rocks, waterholes": they sang the land into being. In doing so, they left invisible trails of words and musical notes—"a spaghetti of Iliads and Odysseys, writhing this way and that," in which features of the landscape are hymned as sacred sites and which are constantly re-created in Aboriginal ritual and song. "The whole of Australia can be read as a musical score."

This account of the myth is stirring and elegant. It is also partial. Chatwin's emphasis on song—"songlines" are more commonly known in Australia as "dreaming tracks"—diminishes the other legendary actions which brought the world to life, and simplifies the variety of ways in which Aborigines re-enact this creation. Aboriginal ceremonial activity is treated as more uniform than it is. The intricacies of totem and taboo are smudged.

In Chatwin's rendering the legend provides a version of the writer bringing his world to life—and of a human being re-creating his own history. It is a legend in which walking is celebrated, as is the desert landscape, and in which it is suggested that it is more natural to move than it is to settle. These were articles of faith for Chatwin. He was an enthusiast for bleached terrain—for scrub and scree and thorn bushes. He was also an advocate of travel on foot, to the alarm of some more sedentary acquaintances: "We're here for most of July," he wrote to Michael Davie, who was living some five miles away from the Chatwins' house in Oxford-shire, "so as we're in walking distance . . ." And he prized journeys which broached new ground. He is said to have arrived one evening with a BBC cameraman at a beautiful, secret place somewhere in the wild. The cameraman said how desolating he found it not being able to share the sight with his nearest and dearest. "Oh do you think so?" asked his companion, airbrushing out the cameraman from that par-ticular photograph as he went on to explain that for him the thrill of being in such isolated regions was that he alone was seeing them.

"He travelled all those woebegone places," sorrowed the American writer Elizabeth Hardwick. He seldom did so alone. He went to Afghanistan first with Robert Erskine, his companion on several Oriental excursions, and later with his schoolfriend David Nash, who remembers Bruce spinning a story about an old admiral who had perished in the Hindu Kush while looking for a particular kind of cow-parsley that grew only there. He visited the country again with Peter Levi and with Elizabeth: all of them collected unusual stones; Bruce cooked a dinner using three different kinds of apricots; Elizabeth rescued a quail that was being tortured by children and carried the balding bird with her on her journey. A ten-der passage in Bruce's notebook describes this rescue, and captures one of their marital exchanges: " 'How are you?' I call to Elizabeth as we crash over the rocky road. 'The bird is drinking,' she calls back." With Elizabeth, too, he went to Nepal, Pakistan, Norway, Germany, Spain, Tunisia. With Kasmin, he went to Haiti and Botswana; to Benin, where he met a descendant of the Viceroy of Ouidah, and read Huysmans's handbook to Fin-de-Siècle aestheticism, *A rebours*; to Namibia, where they stayed in a toolshed beside a garage in the middle of dunes. The Australian writer Murray Bail was with him in India, amused at his huge amount of luggage— "like travelling with Greta Garbo"—and at the posh pyjamas into which he climbed on night-time train journeys.

The trips he made while collecting material for *The Songlines* had a convivial flavour. He hated Australia on his first visit: "Australia is hell," read one postcard to his Italian publisher, Roberto Calasso; "I can't bear it—it's so *old*. I want to be in some new mountains," he exclaimed to Elizabeth. But he changed his mind. He drove through Central Australia with Salman Rushdie in a four-wheel-drive Toyota. He went to the Adelaide Festival, and found it "a little like going to a clinic for a week, in that there were always young, encouraging, nurse-like figures at one's elbow, with gentle words to say it was time to do this or that."

At the Festival Rushdie was eager to introduce Chatwin to another friend, Angela Carter. Both Carter and Chatwin were reluctant to meet at first, each suspicious of the other's different way of going on. But when they did so, Bruce set out to charm. "We must celebrate," he said as they shook hands. "We're going to have some excellent wine. I'm going to get it." He then disappeared for half an hour, to come back, with the air of a man who had hiked to a particularly exclusive cellar, bearing two chilled and delicious bottles. On that occasion his charm worked, but he wasn't always successful. During a literary debate held in the Festival's big open marquee, Rushdie had been distracted by the figure of a young woman hovering at the edge of his vision. She had short blonde hair and was wearing khaki shorts. She was, he thought, possibly the most beautiful woman he had ever seen, and she looked exactly like Chatwin. At lunch afterwards he told Bruce about the beauty, and then spotted her

nearby. Chatwin looked, and agreed that, against his expectations, she was in fact the most beautiful woman in the
world: "And I'm going to ask her to join us for lunch."
Carter and Rushdie looked on as Bruce approached his twin,
beaming and cajoling. The two khaki-clad, golden-haired
figures nodded and becked at each other for a minute or so,
then Bruce's expression changed, and he turned back to his
companions looking abashed. "She says," he explained, "she's
not interested in writers. She's only here for the sunshine."

Chatwin went on to impress one acquaintance in Adelaide
with his account of English social divisions: in Singapore
some years after the Festival Jonathan Hope was doing business with a Chinese Malaysian who told him he had learnt all
about the iniquities of the class system from "the writer
Bruce." In Sydney he stayed with the film-maker Benny
Gannon: he developed a strenuous beach life, became a specialist in goat's yogurt fruitshakes, and achieved some status as
a social trophy in the eastern suburbs of the city. In Byron
Bay, in the rain forest, he woke up the model Penelope Tree
at dawn to tell her his ideas, took delight in the antics of a
gigantic sea turtle, and had one spell of despairing speech-
lessness when the weather was so wet and squally that the sky
couldn't be seen: sitting in a deckchair on the roof among the
fog, Bruce infected a whole household with his depression.
When he visited Maisie Drysdale, widow of the painter Russell Drysdale, in her big bungalow in the Sydney suburbs, she
discovered him guiding fellow guests around her home:
"Isn't it just like a Russian dacha?" "No," his hostess protested. "It's an Australian house, dear heart."

He became an admirer of Frederick Williams's minimalist
Australian landscapes, of the grey abstracts of Ian Fair-
weather, and of Tom Roberts's hectic, zigzagging picture
"The Breakaway," with its stockman, its rising dust and
wheeling dogs. He was, too, an admirer of Australian

women: "Why also am I moved, almost to tears, by the women, and indifferent to the men? Except, I may add, to the drunk truckie at a pub famous for its redneck attitudes, who, when taunted and abused for having an Aboriginal wife, tried to explain to his tormentors the immense elaboration of Aboriginal society and when completely lost for words, shouted, 'I tell you, it's so com . . . fuckin' . . . plex!' " An earlier woman who interested him was the turn-of-the-century fantasist Daisy Bates, who lived for thirty years in the South Australian deserts, wrote a book called *The Passing of the Aborigines*, and produced elaborate, contradictory accounts of her own life. Amid all his enthusiasms he couldn't resist the boasts which amused friends but sometimes gave him a bad name. When Murray Bail took him to his country's Blue Mountains—a region of dramatic heights and gorges—hoping to amaze him with the magnificence of the landscape, Chatwin cast his eye round and hesitated only a moment before trumping the view: "This time next week I shall be in the foothills of Mount Everest."

Chatwin was an inventive and adventurous traveller; he wasn't a pioneer. His most effective broaching of new ground was in his descriptions of expeditions—in making other people see places for the first time. *The Songlines* benefits from the vigour of these descriptions: of the priest who lives in a corrugated-iron hermitage and speaks of "my brother the Wallaby"; of expanses of spinifex and dust and red rock; of the Aborigines' interpretation of their land in paintings—richly coloured, cursively patterned, dappled, stippled, intricate, opaque. The book is also arranged with some ingenuity to project Chatwin's personal mythology. This story about journeys is in the form of a journey. This tale of songlines encloses what some friends have thought of as Bruce's own songline—a selection of items from his notebooks which opens a path through his own history and beliefs.

But, despite its boldness and excitements, *The Songlines*

creaks in trying to make its large statements. Chatwin at one point considered writing the book as a single letter addressed to Roberto Calasso: he was then intending a short volume of some one hundred and twenty pages encapsulating his nomad thoughts, with a title in the form of "A Letter from . . ." containing an obscure Australian place-name. He also thought of casting the entire book as a dialogue between two men in Alice Springs, sitting under a tree. He discussed this notion with Salman Rushdie, and said that he was think-ing of calling the book "Arkady": he was planning to write a large novel on a Russian theme and may well have plucked the name from Turgenev's *Fathers and Sons*. In the published version of *The Songlines* the Arkady figure who engages in Songlines talk with a Bruce figure is a character of lofty con-versations, moral earnestness and few possessions—a big walker and talker who lives in a neat white room with a harp-sichord and Indonesian cloths. He was immediately recog-nised by more than one reader as a man of Russian descent called Tolly Sawenko, though Chatwin was later to say that the character was "of course" Salman Rushdie. But Rushdie doesn't recognise a word of what the Arkady figure is given to say in the book, and suggests, more plausibly, that "Bruce is Arkady as well as the character he calls Bruce. He is both sides of the dialogue." Not for the first time.

Arkady—too transparently a useful device to be persua-sive—is one unsatisfactory stratagem for advancing Bruce's arguments. The notebooks are another. Two-thirds of the way through *The Songlines* Chatwin halts his debates, his sketches of landscape and people, his pictures of life on the wing, and reproduces pages from these notebooks written in a first person less equivocal than the one who takes part in the dialogue. At this point the narrative of the book comes apart and is never put together again in an entirely satisfac-tory way.

Chatwin's notebooks contain a heap of material, fascinating in itself and as background information for anyone interested in his writing methods. They are lodged—along with the rest of his manuscripts—in the Modern Western Manuscripts Section of the Bodleian Library, where there are forty grey cardboard boxes of his work: eight of these are given over to *In Patagonia*; others contain bundles of index cards and swatches of financial correspondence. Boxes 31 to 35 contain the notebooks: eighty-five altogether, of the moleskin kind featured in *The Songlines* and of other kinds. All these documents are embargoed to readers until 2010, and the notebooks in particular excited a certain amount of fevered discussion after Chatwin's death. The author's stationery preferences—he graduated from Parker and Schaeffer pens to a Mont Blanc, liked to sharpen his pencils with a knife, not a pencil-sharpener, and produced his first drafts on foolscap green-lined American yellow legal pads—have attracted both awe and irritation. His small black books, with their squared pages, punitive elastic bands and mysteriously-derived "moleskin" covers, were bought in the rue de l'Ancienne Comédie in Paris. Why not at Ryman's? asked one London sceptic. These notebooks have also been the subject of dark musings: they were, it was reported, written in code and likely to be intimate, revelatory and sexually explicit; Redmond O'Hanlon declared that they were "André Gide with all the bits put in."

In fact, Chatwin hardly wrote a confessional line in his life. The notebooks are an unstructured accumulation: records of conversations, reading-lists, descriptions of landscapes and people, quotations from books, chronicles of colours, line-drawings of doorways and arches, huge speculative statements, tiny anecdotes. They indicate how Chatwin trimmed and tucked and compressed his sentences before they got into print: they also show how little attention was sometimes necessary. They contain paragraphs with more flab than he would have allowed in a finished piece of work. But they also contain paragraphs which gain in verve because they have not been tooled over. They are lively fragments, musings, beginnings of ideas. But in *The Songlines* quotations from these notebooks are used not only to reveal obsessions and preoccupations, but to advance arguments. There was always a thin line between Bruce being brilliant and Bruce being batty, and some of these passages show him at his wildest. In them he proposes, in one of his easy swoops from the personal to the theoretical, that human beings are sanest and happiest when they are on the move. He claims that patterns of dominance and hierarchical structures come with settlement; that the birthplace and true home of the human race is the savannah; that man's repertoire of fighting skills arose not in order to conquer other tribes but to protect him against a particular non-human predator, a giant cat who specialised in eating primates. His most speculative excursions are delivered with signs of strain. Those passages where the master of ellipses starts to explicate are scattered with baggy expressions— "some deep level of the psyche"—and evasive formulations—"it can be argued," "I have sometimes thought it possible to advance a theory," "it would seem there exists." His larger statements—continent-spanning, epoch-hopping —have the ring of conversations held at midnight.

With Bruce it was always midnight. His whirling eloquence was a source of irritation to those who were immune to his charm, and could have a basilisk effect: "He came into the room in his gym shoes, flopped down on the floor, and held forth." What he gave was a performance, but a peculiarly unguarded one, like that of a child. When, during a television feature on his work, he was challenged in the middle of one of his conjectural torrents—predicting that an age of asceticism was on its way—he provided an unusual, embarrassing and revealing televisual moment. "Maybe you've got me," he responded to his interviewer, Melvyn Bragg—causing Bragg to protest that the exchange was not designed to get him.

There were also those for whom he was insufficiently whirling. John Michell, a guru of the hippie world in which Chatwin found a corner, thinks that Chatwin left it too late to write his nomad book, and that he was "far too deferential to literary people," scared of being didactic and too ready to include what Michell considers gossip—"pointless anecdotes about driving a bulldozer." Michell and Chatwin were friends, and temperamental opposites. John Michell, who has written about magic mushrooms, flying saucers and, most recently, the authorship of Shakespeare's plays, is a mild-mannered Merlin—Notting Hill Gate's ruminative wizard. Chatwin, with his crispness and crackle and Brooks Brothers shirts, was never much of a flower child. What they shared was an interest in ancient systems of belief.

When he first met Chatwin in the mid-Sixties Michell was living in Bath, a city hated by Chatwin—who didn't like sleepy hollows—and memorably described by a Seventies inhabitant, Angela Carter, as having "rather more than its fair share of occultists, Neoplatonists, yogis, theosophists, little old ladies who have spirit conversations with Red Indian squaws, religious maniacs, senile dements, natural-lifers, macrobiotics, people who make perfumed candles, kite-flyers, do you believe in fairies?" In her days on the hippie trail Henrietta Moraes visited John Michell there:

> When I arrived he made me welcome and then said that he was going to spend a couple of days with his brother. "If you could bind a few of these pamphlets for me while I am away," he said, "I should never forget it." He waved towards a table, on which lay a pile of papers. I picked one up. It was entitled "Jesus Christ, The Great Cock."

Michell was collecting material for his book *The View over Atlantis*, which describes a world covered in largely ignored but visible patterns, patterns which are astronomically-influenced, geometrically-determined and religiously significant. Huge zodiacal figures—their lineaments sketched by the curve of rivers and hills, and completed by man-made ditches and roads—have been detected on the countryside near Glastonbury. Inscribed on the Peruvian desert are the "triangles, rectangles, spirals, meanders, whip-like zig-zags and superimposed trapezes" chronicled by Bruce Chatwin in an essay. Bruce was caustic about the supernatural significance ascribed to these Pampas designs, but wrote a not entirely sceptical piece about the "dragon paths" which are said to cross the land of China, affecting its atmosphere. Michell interprets such configurations, including Aboriginal dreaming-tracks, as signs that prehistoric geomancers have been at work, divining and controlling a fertilising cosmic force.

Modern archaeological excavation is dismissed by Michell as given over to the pursuit of "treasure hunting and grave robbery." What he admires are the intuitions of individual seers. John Aubrey is valued for recognising the prehistoric stone circles at Avebury, just as the villagers were beginning to break them up to build new houses. William Stukeley is praised for having seen a sacred order in the disposition of earthworks and stone structures throughout Britain; at Avebury, he made out a great serpent which snaked across the countryside through a circle to form the symbol of alchemical fusion. Both Aubrey and Stukeley brushed Chatwin's life—Michell thinks that Stuart Piggott used his book on Stukeley to "make academic fun." Both of them—like Michell and like Chatwin—were dreamers, delvers, dowsers, connoisseurs of the remote, patrons of coincidence and correspondence, magical anthropologists.

Michell thinks that Chatwin left some information out of *The Songlines* for fear of being thought a crank. He also remembers the food enthusiast declaring himself opposed to a balanced diet throughout the year: diet should, Chatwin once proclaimed, reflect a seasonal cycle of glut and scarcity. This is in tune with Michell's precept: that everything is always in flux and moving. As proof, he mentions annual festivals which, in celebrating different aspects of human nature, concentrate on extremes: "They're always to do with sex or drinking or abstinence or purity"; there has, he points out, "never been a Festival of Common Sense." Had there been one, Michell and Chatwin were unlikely to have been revellers there.

They did undertake several expeditions together. They went to West Cornwall to look at megalithic stones. They went to Wales, where they saw a solicitor called Mr. Williams who was also interested in megalithic alignments. And one February they went with Christopher Gibbs to the Orkneys. There they looked at the mounds and megaliths of Stenness, explored the burial passages at Maes Howe and had a picnic on the site of the Neolithic village of Skara Brae. They went to Hoy to see Melsetter, one of the few houses designed by the nineteenth-century Arts and Crafts architect W. R. Lethaby. Gibbs remembers that "Bruce and I drooled over the little avenues of stunted thorns and the wooden drainpipes, the singing Morris glass in the tiny chapel and the plaster friezes of Orcadian wild flowers. John thought the house like the gloomiest prep school." They walked for miles through the length of the day to the tip of one island where, at the very end of a long road, they saw a telephone box: they went in and called a taxi, which wound its way down to them through the hills. On that trip John Michell was reading *De Abstinentia*, by the Neoplatonist Porphyry, and interested Chatwin in what it had to say about animal food. Chatwin was reading Porphyry's teacher, Plotinus.

Bruce liked to talk about nobs and about nomads, to write

about big ideas and about individuals. He was less forthcoming about politics: social and economic considerations rarely feature in his accounts. When in 1970 he heard of a suggestion by the NSPCC that children who were pent up for long periods in high-rise flats might run some risk of retarded mental development, he flew to an explanation which disregarded financial and educational deprivations in favour of one featuring his own psychology: "Travel does not merely broaden the mind. It makes the mind. Our early explorations are the raw materials of our intelligence . . . Children need paths to explore, to take bearings on the earth in which they live, as a navigator takes bearings on familiar landmarks. If we excavate the memories of childhood, we remember the paths first, things and people second—paths down the garden, the way to school, the way round the house, corridors through the bracken or long grass. Tracking the paths of animals was the first and most important element in the education of early man."

His wife thinks of him as being "hopeless politically" because he was swayed by the opinions of people he liked. Francis Wyndham remembers that when Bruce came back from South Africa and regaled his left-leaning colleagues on the *Sunday Times* with genial reports about ambivalently liberal whites, "we just had to sit on him." After the Falklands War, however, he gained a mild reputation for political prophecy: the closing passages of *In Patagonia*, published five years earlier, had described a youth from the Islands, sporting notable teeth and a sealskin hat, who declares: " 'Bout time the Argentines took us over . . . We're so bloody inbred." He was shrewd about the gathering strength of Muslims in Eastern Europe, which became one of his compulsive subjects. And in Australia his reliance on gut feelings about political figures didn't always serve him badly: "Last night I got back to Sydney and we sat up watching Bob Hawke become the new Prime Minister. Seriously, although one can't say so, I think they'll regret it: not because he's LEFT or Republican etc, but because he has the meanest mouth imaginable and terribly shifty eyes."

He thought of himself as celebrating Aboriginal activity in *The Songlines*: "At a dinner in Sydney, a very intelligent man picked a quarrel with me; said he never met Aborigines; implied that Aborigines were irrelevant to the Australian situation. I then found voice and said that Aborigines, or their destruction, were as important as the Penal Colony in the Australian consciousness." But some Australian commentators and anthropologists have objected to the book as projecting a semi-colonial view of the white man as hero, relying too much on whites' accounts of Aboriginal culture, and undervaluing the work done by those involved in the land rights movement.

Chatwin had no taste for debating questions of sexual politics. When Peter Eyre allowed the vogue word "sexuality" to drop from his mouth Bruce hooted with derision: " 'Sexuality'—my *dear*!" When the writer Richard Sennett arranged a meeting between Chatwin and Michel Foucault, the French philosopher who wrote a several-volumed *History of Sexuality*, the encounter wasn't a success: the two men "took one look at each and decided no." And when Bruce contracted the AIDS virus he did not talk in public about it.

The Songlines ends with a picture of three dying Aboriginals, stretched on bedsteads in the open air. They are skeletal, almost hairless and calm: "They knew where they were going, smiling at death in the shade of a ghost-gum." Chatwin was ill when he began the book; when he finished it he thought he was dying. The notebooks' preoccupation with a predatory beast, and with darkness and the struggle for survival, reflects this; some of its rough edges and muddles in argument are due to the rush to get everything down, and the lack of time for revision. Angela Carter, who was born the same year and within a week of Bruce Chatwin, and who died three years after him at the age of fifty-one, responded to this element when she reviewed *The Songlines*: "The true romance of this always enchanting, sometimes infuriating book is . . . the one between an Englishman and the wilderness. The journey of the one within the other leads to the only happy ending the traveller can honestly aspire to, a happy death."

In 1982 Chatwin, leafing through a copy of *Time* magazine which had an article about him in it, came across a piece which talked about "the gay plague." He told his wife later that he had immediately thought that it applied to him, but he wasn't diagnosed as HIV positive until four years later— after he had begun to be seriously ill. In November 1985 he had gone to China, where he had developed a fungal infection. The following summer, he felt able, it would appear, to say that he had finished *The Songlines*. He dropped off a copy of the manuscript with his agent, Deborah Rogers, announcing that he was off to Switzerland, taking "just a sketchpad— no books." From there he rang his American editor, Elisabeth Sifton, explaining that he was very ill and was being treated by a doctor who knew about rare Chinese diseases. He asked if she could come and work on the manuscript. She offered to bring some music and arrived with some Brahms and some Chopin mazurkas. A letter he wrote to Shirley Hazzard in that year gives some sense of the state of mind in which he worked with Sifton on *The Songlines*:

> 1986 I'm glad to see the back of. Last winter, when we
> went to Yunnan, I must have picked up, by inhaling it
> in the dust, a fungus which first attacks the lungs, then
> gets into the bloodstream, then lodges itself in the bone
> marrow, where it prevents the making of red blood cor-

puscles. There are ten cases of this particular blight on record: all Chinese peasants (from Western China, where we were), all fatal. All last summer I was being treated for ever worsening attacks of asthma, and it was suggested I go into the clean mountain air of Switzerland in the hope of a cure. When, on my first morning in Zurich, I could hardly walk across the hotel bedroom there was obviously something seriously wrong. The amazing thing was that, the day before leaving England, I handed in my Australian opus (I hadn't really noticed I was ill) and then the whirlwind struck. The Swiss doctors, though excellent, failed to find the cause. I was brought back to Oxford, to a crack team of young specialists who are expert in tropical or exotic ailments. They did not, admittedly, think I'd last the night. After five days, of wild, behind-the-scenes activity, they nailed what kind of Penicillium it was: I might add that the only other case, apart from the peasants, was that found in the corpse of a killer-whale cast on the shores of Arabia. So when, in the fog of my delirium, the chief doctor asked me, "Have you been consorting with Chinese peasants or killer-whales?" I was able to whisper feebly, "Peasants."

In Zurich Elisabeth Sifton had planned to go through the typescript with him, page by page and line by line, working as she had worked with him on *On the Black Hill,* but Chatwin was too ill. Sifton took a typewriter to his room each morning, before he went to the clinic round the corner for tests: Chatwin talked feverishly; Sifton took down his ideas. They usually had lunch at a nearby vegetarian restaurant; Chatwin, whose strength came and went, was too weak to eat out in the evenings. He spoke of sick animals who slink away when they are sick and don't want to be fussed over; he said that he had told no one where he was. He made telephone calls to some friends in Britain announcing that he was dying.

The manuscript was much too long, and both Chatwin and Sifton were concerned about how the extracts from the notebooks should be used. Sifton suggested that one way of resolving their relation to the text might be "to make more of it, not less": the extracts, at one point placed at the back of the book in the manner of an appendix, were brought forward, introduced and explained. Chatwin spent much of his guttering energy in talking about the sources for *The Songlines*, in which any line could trigger a torrent of reminiscence. He didn't have the strength to consider moving any large passages or changing the structure of the book. When Sifton went back to New York—Elizabeth Chatwin being on her way to Switzerland, her husband having finally submitted to being looked after—she left him with a manuscript marked with her suggested cuts and alterations. Chatwin took some of these. He was later to say that he thought the book a failure and that he should have revised it.

Bruce had his own way of both concealing and declaring what was wrong with him. He didn't like people challenging him about his illness, but summoned some close friends to tell them that he had AIDS. More publicly, he talked about a malady caused by Chinese eggs, a malady which did exist: he had developed a fungus thought to have been caused either by eating a black egg in Lijiang, or by a visit to the Hong Kong bird market. He also spoke about a disorder caused by bats in caves, and about arranging an expedition to Africa to find a stable form of the HIV virus—the Aga Khan was to be approached for funding. He said he wanted to write a book called "Sons of Thunder," which was to be about the search for the AIDS virus. He meant to involve doctors from the Radcliffe Infirmary in Oxford, to include a historical survey of virology—together with some observations drawn from his study of archaeology—and to expand the topic into an examination of healers. He spoke about setting up a research unit into the virus in Oxford, and at times of being made a don himself: when, in the summer of 1988, he wrote a letter to the *London Review of Books* about an article on AIDS by John Ryle, he wrote as if from this unit—at once denying and proclaiming his own interest:

AIDS PANIC

In a review of three American books, *And the Band Played On, Crisis: Heterosexual Behaviour in the Age of Aids* and *The Forbidden Zone*, Mr. John Ryle (*LRB*, 19 May) begins: "There is no good news about Aids. With a total of 85,000 cases reported at the beginning of this year the World Health Organisation estimate of the true figure is nearer 150,000. Their global estimate for HIV infection is between five and ten million. Most HIV-positive individuals have no symptoms and don't know they are infected: but the majority of them— possibly all of them—will eventually develop Aids and die; in the meantime, of course, they may infect any- one they have sex with and any children they bear." This is hogwash. The word "Aids" is one of the cru- ellest and silliest neologisms of our time. "Aid" means help, succour, comfort—yet with a hissing sibilant tacked onto the end it becomes a nightmare. It should never be used in front of patients. HIV (Human Immuno-Deficiency Virus) is a perfectly easy name to live with. "Aids" causes panic and despair and has prob- ably done something to facilitate the spread of the dis- ease. In France, not even M. Le Pen could do much with *le Sida*. He had a go, but was made to look completely ridiculous. HIV is not some gay Götter- dämmerung: it is another African virus, a very danger- ous one, presenting the greatest challenge to medicine since tuberculosis, but one for which a cure will be found. Any virus, be it chicken-pox, mumps or HIV, will create a kind of mirror image of itself known as an "antibody" which will in time stabilise the infected person. That should be the pattern. But HIV is a very slippery customer. There is no positive evidence of antibodies at work, only negative evidence that a great many infected people are alive. In one case in the US an infected person suddenly became HIV negative. We should, in fact, take Mr. Ryle's own figures. There have been 800,000 infected persons in the United States, of whom 80,000 have died. That means nine survivors to one death. This can mean only one thing: that some mechanism, pharmaceutical or otherwise, is keeping them alive.

One point cannot be emphasised too strongly. An infected person must never use anyone else's toothbrush or electric razor. We all have gingivitis from time to time.

What is most horrifying about Mr. Ryle's article is the callous cruelty with which he condemns hundreds of thousands of people to death. If a young man who has just been told that he is HIV positive got hold of the article, the chances are he might commit suicide. There have been many such cases.

Bruce Chatwin
Oxford Team for Research into Infectious
Tropical Diseases, Oxford University

This letter, with its grief and its swerving logic, went through more than one version: the first pages he sent were too distraught and too difficult to follow. When the letter appeared, it was taken by some readers to be Bruce's first public, if ambivalent acknowledgment of what was wrong with him.

THE END

In the last years of his life, Bruce, intermittently feverish and sometimes high on the drugs he was being pre-scribed, appeared as hyper-Bruce, an exaggerated, speeded-up version of his already emphatic self. He was given to excited speeches, to big, generous gestures, to ambitious plans for the people surrounding him and for the outside world. His fluency and intensity were hypnotic, and it wasn't always easy to know when he was deluded. His eyes grew bulbous as his face shrank; he was fragile but aflame. His ob-sessions were the obsessions, heightened and more grandilo-quent, that he had had all his life. But he became, if anything, sweeter in character, more gentle, more likely to praise and to help people. He was full of ideas about what to do next.

He had always had plenty of projects, many of them never fulfilled, some of them offered as jokes or self-parody. He had had an idea for a one-act ballet to be called "The Knife-Grinder"—which he liked to mime by striking a statuesque posture in front of a mangle and rippling his muscles; the bal-let was, naturally, to be performed at the Met. He had meant to walk the boundary of East and West Berlin, and was tempted by the idea of a series of pieces about boundaries. He started to make plans for researching a novel about the in-habitants of a South African dorp. He became interested in writing a play, and, hoping for rules to guide him around the physical constraints of the theatre, went for guidance to the director Richard Eyre, to whom he spoke with fervour about the Marsh Arabs.

He had also had a scheme for an opera. He talked to Peter Eyre about collaborating on a libretto, but both men had reservations about opera in English. Chatwin's plan met the objection. He proposed an opera about Florence Gould, the *grande dame* from San Francisco who, before her second marriage to the son of an American railroad magnate, had been a leading soprano at the Opéra Comique in Paris. During the Second World War Gould had worked as a volunteer nurse in Paris: in a blouse designed for her by Lanvin, she dispensed *foie gras* and champagne to her patients. At her massive villa in Cannes she built up a collection of porcelain and Impressionist paintings. At the age of eighty she travelled, festooned in diamonds and sapphires, on the back of an elephant to the temples of Angkor. But it was the salon over which Gould presided in wartime Paris that Chatwin saw as the nub of the piece he had destined for the English National Opera. Every Thursday, first at the Hôtel Bristol, and subsequently at her apartment in the Avenue Malakoff, fine wines and scarce real coffee were served to guests who included Jean Cocteau, the critic Paul Léautaud (who took left-overs home for his pet monkey) and German propaganda officers. It was a multilingual salon which could, as Peter Eyre saw Chatwin's intention, furnish "an opera in English in which there was going to be hardly a word of English spoken."

For years he had had it in mind to write a large Russian novel, and towards the end of his life this began to take a definite shape. The book was to feature "four decadent cultures"—the USA, the USSR, France and Britain—with a main character from each country; there was to be a lot in it about the Orthodox Church. An American woman was to be the most degenerate figure—she was to be pictured rush-

ing around buying up everything—and a Russian man, determined from an early age to raise sufficient money to go to
Paris and paint, was to be the most elevated. The heroine—
evacuated as a child from wartime Paris, where her mother
remained, perhaps collaborating with the Germans—was to
have grown up in the United States, in an East Coast Estab-
lishment family living up the Hudson, where many of Elizabeth Chatwin's family live; she was eventually to marry the
Russian painter. Bruce had decided that she was to be called
"Lydia Livingstone," a name which suggested both the Slavic
and the Western elements in the novel—and that the book
was to be named after her. This was a name taken—as were
other aspects of the book—straight from life. Bruce had
heard a friend talking about an Australian woman called
Lydia Livingstone and had sent her a postcard saying that he
intended to "borrow" her name. He was subsequently to
meet and make friends with her, prizing her for her "great
sense of the idiotic." He asked Diana Melly to accompany
him on a long train journey which was to occur in the novel.
For the mother of his heroine he had intended to draw on a
French acquaintance of his who had married a German officer, and on Louise de Vilmorin, the aristocrat with an equivocal wartime record who for the last three years of her life
was the companion of André Malraux.

Bruce was familiar with the geography that was to feature
in the book. When I went to the Soviet Union in 1987 he
rattled off a crisp list of instructions about what to see—
Chekhov's house, the Rublev icons, Rodchenko's studio—
but insisted that a visit to Komsomolskaya Square in Moscow
was the best introduction to the country. Here, trains from
St. Petersburg, from Kazan, from Yaroslavl come in to three
stations, bringing the faces of the north and of Central Asia
to the metropolis, and giving the observer an idea of the vast-
ness, diversity and precarious unity of the USSR. He urged

me to find out whether the heated open-air swimming-pool behind the Pushkin Museum still functioned, and, if so, at what times of the year: he wanted to use it in a story. He had also once wanted to write about the German community which settled in Russia at the time of Catherine the Great.

He had been talking about Russian émigrés in Paris when *On the Black Hill* was published, and had become fascinated by a Russian Orthodox church he had come upon in the city. A year or so before he died he carried his investigation further, turning up at a conference in Paris organised by PEN to discuss émigré Russian writers, and asking to be introduced to Russian Jesuits: he said he wanted to study Russian with them in Paris.

There were plenty of unscheduled arrivals, long and excited conversations, surprising rendezvous in these last years. He appeared at a barn dance in Wiltshire in a wheelchair, his eyes gleaming beneath a bush hat. He whizzed round London in this chair, looking for friends to take him in: he had a way of making cab-drivers do what he wanted—"a mixture of charm and command," according to Kasmin: but some people found his wildness and frailty alarming and wouldn't put him up. Grey Gowrie, recalling for *Spectator* readers a string of AIDS charity galas, remembered seeing him after one such event: "I was hailed on the pavement by the late Bruce Chatwin. Bruce, in a wheelchair and also, apparently, in denial, insisted he come along to the ensuing dinner. The guests received him with so-so grace; the hostess behaved perfectly. He was treated as a slight spectre at the feast, and indeed looked like one. Yet he was magically entertaining." The denial was intermittent: insisting at one benefit that an extra place should be made for him in Kasmin's box, Bruce explained, "I'm one of them"—meaning one of the victims.

He rang me one day at my office and asked if I could join him—immediately—for coffee in his room at the Ritz. I couldn't, but did attend a picnic at the Rebecca Hossack Gallery in Windmill Street, off the Tottenham Court Road. Bruce was in his wheelchair; his thin legs dangled and as Elizabeth propelled him over the threshold, one of his shoes fell off; when I pushed it back on, it sat like a boat round his skinny ankle. The gallery, which has specialised in bringing Aboriginal art to London, was showing large, fondant-coloured canvases: Bruce praised them, and talked of buying several. On the pavement outside was a wooden garden table on which Elizabeth set up lunch—bread and pâté and greengages which she cut into small pieces for Bruce with a Swiss Army knife. Bruce stayed in the open air for only a short time: as soon as the tepid August sun came out from behind the clouds, he felt it beating on his head—his hair was thin and lank.

He was full of his schemes. Some days before the picnic he had rung from hospital to say that he—or was it Hugh?—had found out about a plastic which was easily manufactured and could be shipped to India and the East and be used to make decent dwellings. Driving round London with his brother, who took care of him when Elizabeth was away, he had spotted an executive from Jonathan Cape and had hauled the man into the back of the tiny Citroën to regale him with a chapter-by-chapter account of the Chatwin brothers' publishing plans: "We are going to write a book about *oil*."

He wanted all his friends to get married, and arranged them neatly in pairs. The weddings were to take place on Christmas Day in the church at Ewelme, the Oxfordshire village where Geoffrey Chaucer's son and granddaughter are buried. The sudden pairing of two characters at the end of *The Songlines* is as peremptory and ecstatic as Bruce's matchmaking was in life. When Diana Melly's daughter Candy gave birth to her daughter in 1986, Bruce said he had known the exact time of the delivery: at precisely the same moment, his stomach, which had been swollen with wind, had suddenly deflated.

He also told me to spend £500 of his money on a painting for myself, and to spend the same on a picture for Francis Wyndham—an offer which I didn't pursue. Bruce had always been a generous present-giver. He gave George and Diana Melly an etching by Max Klinger, the German precursor of Surrealism—one in his fetishistic series "Adventures of a Glove." He gave me a beautiful big white pottery bowl, decorated with splashes of blue and green and red and yellow. He gave Yvette Day, the Mellys' housekeeper in Wales, soaps from France and a jam pan. When he was ill, he wanted to give presents to everyone all the time. Francis Wyndham was presented with a first edition of Flaubert's *Trois Contes*, stamped with Bruce's name in Mandarin. Kevin Volans, who stayed for some time at Homer End, composing a string quartet and helping to look after Bruce, was given an upright piano and a sixteenth-century Japanese lacquer box. Christopher Gibbs was given a turquoise Egyptian gaming-piece, one of Bruce's talismans. After Bruce's death Salman Rushdie received another of these talismans, which used to be kept in a box tucked under the bed in Bruce's workroom at Homer End. Rushdie's gift was a polished grey stone, veined with natural blue-grey markings which give the appearance of an economically sketched Chinese landscape. The stone has been cut into an octagonal shape to frame the picture; there is a piece of Chinese calligraphy on the top, and on the back, in Bruce's handwriting: "Mountain village in misty wood."

When Bruce went to Switzerland to hand over a gift to George Ortiz he came back with a plan to make his own collection of objects to leave to Elizabeth. Collecting, which he had so often raged about and written against, became another obsessive pastime: "The Chatwin Collection" was one of his

most passionate pursuits in the last year of his life. The items
he acquired for it were the sort of objects which had always
interested him. He went on hectic shopping sprees. Pushed
through Bond Street by Kevin Volans, his valuable purchases
swinging in plastic bags on the wheelchair as they progressed
through pouring rain, Bruce paused in each gallery only long
enough to pronounce, "I'll have that, that and that." Volans
remembers him buying a piece of the Red Fort with an in-
laid flower pattern, prehistoric ceremonial adzes and a piece
of calligraphy in praise of Allah which was somehow connected to Tamburlaine. Anything he brought back to Homer
End was very carefully positioned: Christopher Gibbs rushed
up and down the stairs with a Celtic head, in an attempt to
get the sun to shine on the right profile. Bruce also said that
he intended to open an extension to the National Gallery,
which he would fill with coracles and with clothes. He
bought a slew of designer outfits—Fortuny dresses, Balenci-
aga costumes, a Chanel jacket like a piece of armour—which
he wanted to give to Jasper Conran. He told taxi-drivers he
was rich, and announced to store-owners: "I'm going to be
one of your major customers." What he spent bore little relation to the money he had. He explained to George Melly:
"God is filling up my bank account all the time." "That's all
right, then," said Melly, while Elizabeth and Bruce's friends
busied themselves with cancelling cheques and returning
objects to dealers.

He moved into London hotels for brief stays. At the Por-
tobello, in Notting Hill Gate, Francis Wyndham found
"what could only be called a merchant" at Bruce's bedside,
delving into a pouch from which jewels came tumbling out
and got lost in the blankets; Robert Erskine also visited him
there when Bruce's eye had begun to play him false, and he
was exclaiming with wonder over undistinguished objects.
At the Ritz—"I must say it's frightfully reasonable," he an-

nounced as he made out his cheque—Kevin Volans tried to restrain some of Bruce's excursions from his room, at one point advising: "*No* pee bottles in the Ritz dining-room." Unfazed, Bruce came up with a solution: "We'll take my shawl." He entertained there like—as he put it—some comtesse, firing off telephone calls, summoning art dealers with goods for him to examine. When Jonathan Hope visited him he was presented with a parting gift. "It's an Aboriginal subincision knife," said Bruce, as he lay on the bed, with his wife massaging his wasted legs—and held out a small round object with sharpened edges. He had found it in the Bush and correctly identified it as an instrument designed to be used in an Aboriginal initiation rite in which the underside of the urethra is slit open. Then he held it up to the light. "It's obviously made from some sort of desert opal," he said: "It's a wonderful colour, almost the colour of chartreuse." A few weeks later the Director of the Australian National Gallery arrived at Hope's house to look at some Indonesian textiles. He picked up the opal from the table, and in his turn held it up to the light: "Hmmm. Amazing what the Abos can do with a bit of an old beer bottle."

In the middle of these tumults Bruce Chatwin produced his most intricately-structured book. *Utz*, the tale of a collector of Meissen porcelain in Communist Prague, brought together a number of his long-standing and more recent interests. For years he had been intrigued by the situation of the private art-collector in a Marxist state: it was something he had touched on when discussing, in his *Sunday Times* article of 1973, the avant-garde works of art assembled in the Soviet Union by George Costakis. In *The Songlines* he had described one creation myth. *Utz* contains another, in the story of the golem, the Jewish legend of the clay figure which is brought to life by cabbalistic ritual and recitation. This legend is connected in *Utz* with the making of ceramic sculpture, and the collector with his porcelain figurines has something in common with the author bossing around his creatures; he has also been identified with the figure of a promiscuous homosexual amassing conquests.

Chatwin was writing *Utz* while talking about and preparing for his big Russian novel, and the evocation of Eastern Europe—at once dingy and dignified—is one of the best things in the book. This story about miniatures is itself a miniature—short and elliptical, sometimes to the point of archness. It contains scarcely any physical description of Prague, but the austerity and the calm of the city is strongly registered. As a train carries Utz across the Czechoslovakian border into Germany, he watches a greedy girl peel an orange, and sees the juice drip "over the monster's fingers." The smell of the rind which fills the compartment seems to be the smell of the West.

At the centre of the novel is a study of the compulsive collector. Utz and his collection of porcelain are surrounded by present and historical variations on their theme: Utz's friend Dr. Orlik who collects flies; the Emperor Rudolf, who—among other exotica—collected the nails from Noah's Ark; Frederick William of Prussia, who collected giants; Bruce Chatwin, who collected collectors. "The collector" was another of Bruce's big categories: the opposite of the nomad; the person who—he declared every now and then—it was important to stop being. As so often in Chatwin's writing, the vivacity is not in the big idea, but in its offshoots and tangents, in what his schoolmasters identified as his fondness for "the byways of historical accident." Bruce was not keen on Meissen porcelain and Utz's figurines are not described as lustrously as he used to describe the objects in the Chatwin Collection. The excitement of Utz's collecting is in the lengths to which he goes to procure his objects: his tricks and subterfuges, the smuggling across frontiers, the wrangling in a Swiss vault, the accommodations he makes with the Czech authorities. *Utz* is the story of a secret life.

The story had a basis in fact, and in Bruce's own history. Within months of his arrival at Sotheby's, a young woman had joined the firm. Kate Foster started by working on the front counter, the public face of Sotheby's, dealing with general inquiries about catalogues and sales, and steering towards the appropriate experts people who arrived with paintings or objects to be appraised; it was at this counter that George and Diana Melly, bringing in a Surrealist painting to be valued, first caught sight of a grey-suited, disdainful-looking Bruce—a Brucey of whom Chatwin was later ashamed—dismissing someone's treasure. Within a year, Miss Foster had been offered a position in the Works of Art Department, which covered everything from enamels, old sculpture and glass to paperweights and Japanese sword furniture. In an upstairs passage, with porcelain stored overhead and underfoot, she first typed up catalogue copy written by her seniors, and later wrote her own entries. She washed dozens of pieces of porcelain. She found a subject for a book in the elaborate scent bottles made by the famous eighteenth-century Chelsea factory. And she decided that since so much literature about porcelain is in German, she must learn the language. In 1966 she was granted two months' paid leave, and spent a little time with a Viennese family, relatives of Wittgenstein, before travelling to Dresden. She went to Dresden by way of Prague, where she had an introduction to a great collector of porcelain. This was the man whom Bruce Chatwin wrote about as "Utz."

The elusive figure at the centre of Chatwin's novel accords well with Kate Foster's memory of the man she met some thirty years ago—whom she described to Chatwin, and whom Chatwin sought out when he went to Prague not long after her visit. Much is made in *Utz* of the character's "immediately forgettable" features: his face is "waxy," he may or may not have had a moustache. He is like an object waiting to be moulded, a model of Czech pliability and evasiveness in the face of Soviet force. This indistinctness was not invention: Kate Foster thinks of the appearance of her collector as "nondescript." He was wiry and cynical, with a light dry voice and a sharp eye, not particularly charming but intellectually energetic. The broad contours of the novel also corresponded to his life as she remembers it: the existence of the collection and its unexplained disappearance; the details of particularly florid porcelain pieces; the collector's tussle with the Czech authorities; his marriage to his housekeeper; the restaurant frequented by the Party faithful.

Some alterations were made to disguise and protect "Utz's" son, who was living in Prague and who might have known about the fate of the collection, and the dealer who met "Utz" in the West, who introduced him to Kate Foster—and who was in real life neither male nor American. Other changes made a point in the novel. In describing Utz's apartment, Chatwin injected a note of dandy surprise, setting the porcelain—the elaborate tureens and teapots, the harlequins, the flirting courtiers, the monkey musicians—in a room containing only a few pieces of modern furniture. The room Kate Foster saw was crepuscular, congested, untidy, and furnished with old, heavy pieces covered with tasselled rugs.

The collection itself Chatwin made much less eclectic. Kate Foster remembers a varied assembly of early tableware, silver-mounted serpentine tankards and bowls, some wonderful German glass and some eccentric baubles of glass and stone. When she left, she was presented with a ceremonial axe-head, carved with crossed hammers and with the figures of Saxon silver miners, including one tiny troll-like person pushing a truck; the memento echoed the figures of miners with crossed swords or hammers on their hats produced by

the Meissen factory. Chatwin also introduced a few spectac-
ular objects. In the Prague flat visited by Kate Foster there
would hardly have been room for the large white porcelain
sculptures of animals modelled for the Japanese Palace in
Dresden: the most compact of these creatures is some two
feet long; the rhinos are enormous. The harlequin flourishing a tankard as he sits on a tree trunk is taken from a rare
model sold at Sotheby's when Chatwin was there; his hat,
yellow in the book, was blue in life. There was not a great
number of Meissen figurines: Kate Foster remembers this
as "much more a cabinet of curiosities than a porcelain collection." In Chatwin's hands, it became less diverse, more
obsessive—and much less like something he himself would
have cared for. The fussy pieces he describes—pieces which
Francis Wyndham has described as having a "deranged
daintiness"—were the opposite of the sort of things he liked.

Utz is a sequence of secrets, surprises and mysteries—most
of them unsolved. There are the secrets of porcelain manu-
facture, the secret of the golem, the mystery of what happens
to Utz's collection. And there are the surprises of the collector's sexual life. The dressing-gown hanging in Utz's flat is
revealed as a frothy concoction of roses and plumes and
peach-coloured silk; his bedroom is satin, pink, frilled and
flounced. These discoveries, which cast the collector in a
transvestite role, are treated with a comic recoil: when, some
four years before writing the scene, Bruce was introduced to
a man friend of Miranda Rothschild's who liked to dress as a
woman, he "freaked-out," and wasn't able to be "girly" with
the six-footer. It turns out that the feminine touches in Utz's
flat are the work of his housekeeper, Marta. It also turns out
that Marta—a country girl and one of Chatwin's nature
sprites—is married to her employer. Kate Foster, who met
the model for Marta, is sure that when the collector made her
his second wife he did so in order to stay in an apartment

judged by the authorities to be too large for a single man. Chatwin's account in *Utz* is different: he paints the picture of a marriage of convenience, but ends—in one of the several twists in this tiny novel—by suggesting that it was really a romance.

Bruce's own marriage intrigued people, with its independent expeditions and its separations. "What an amazing marriage it is," said his father-in-law, not much amusing Bruce: "One goes in one door and the other goes out the other." There were friends who didn't meet Elizabeth, and those, like Paul Theroux, who enjoyed the mystery of her role in Bruce's life:

> Everyone knew Bruce was married—we had met his wife, Elizabeth. But what sort of marriage was this? "A *mariage blanc,*" a friend once said to me, pursing his lips. Bruce was in his way devoted to his wife, but the very fact of Bruce having a wife was so improbable that no one quite believed it.
>
> One night at dinner, just before he left the table, I heard Bruce distinctly speak of his plans for the near future and say, "I'm going to meet my wife in Tibet." Afterwards, one of the people present said, "Did he say his wife was dead?" and another replied, "No. He said his wife's in bed."

There were those who thought he disregarded Elizabeth's feelings, and others who caught glimpses of a settled intimacy. When Michael Ignatieff watched them in the South of France they reminded him of Russian eccentrics, of the kind that he and Bruce liked to discuss: under a mulberry tree Elizabeth combed her husband's hair; Bruce sat there accepting his grooming "like an old baboon." The uncharacteristic dash of sentiment at the end of *Utz* is a tribute to the pleasure and commitment of an unconventional arrangement.

By the time the novel was published in September 1988 Bruce was physically dependent on Elizabeth who, between his spells in hospital, was nursing him with only intermittent professional assistance. The switchback of his illness was very pronounced in the last year of his life: while putting the finishing touches to *Utz* in January he was mobile and energetic. He had rung me when he had completed the first draft of the book and asked me if I would edit it. I had left Jonathan Cape some years before, after working on *The Viceroy of Ouidah*; Elisabeth Sifton, who had edited *On the Black Hill* and *The Songlines*, had gone to a different publishing house in New York; Bruce wanted some continuity.

He arranged for a copy of the manuscript that had been read by Michael Ignatieff to be sent to me. The two men had spent hours talking about the novels they were planning—both featuring Russia, and emigration from Russia. Bruce was very fascinated by the contrasts in Ignatieff's background—Slavic, Canadian, patrician, liberal—and the heterosexual Ignatieff has spoken of "a strong portion of the erotic" in their friendship, a portion which was evident in several of Bruce's platonic male friendships in his last years. Shortly before Bruce died Ignatieff received a jiffy bag containing Bruce's copy of the Russian Jewish writer Isaac Babel's *Red Cavalry*; on his writing-desk Ignatieff still has a picture of Chatwin.

"I don't agree with *everything* he says," Bruce observed about Ignatieff's annotations on *Utz*, "but with most of it I do." He was writing in a spin of activity. He and Elizabeth were "off to Guadeloupe, no less, for a couple of weeks' swimming. It's one of the cheapest places to fly to, because it's a part of metropolitan France and the fares are subsidised. We're booked to fly back on the 25th, but may, depending on various imponderables, go down to the South of France. I left the car in a garage for repairs on October 15, saying I'd be back the next day—and now look!" A month later, having been unable to go to the South of France to edit the manuscript there, a journey for which Bruce had offered to pay, I went down to Homer End.

The adjustments made to the manuscript of *Utz* were tiny: a question of trimming and tucking. Some adjectives were lost, some sentences reduced or turned around, but there was no large-scale cutting or moving of material. The manuscript was not, as *In Patagonia* had been, overabundant to the point of bagginess, nor was it in need, as *The Viceroy of Ouidah* had been, of opening up. Though full of mysteries, it was always locally clear; its components neatly hinged together. Bruce was not, in any case, capable of making any strategic changes. On the one occasion when I did suggest moving the position of a story in the book—a move which would have involved some rewriting—he said that he couldn't face it. But he worked prodigiously hard on the pages. One cold bright morning we sat for hours without a break in the sitting-room, each with a copy of the manuscript, reading over each sentence; as I paused before making a point, Bruce anticipated my quibble with a triumphant beam: "Beat you." Halfway through lunch—spaghetti and bacon in the kitchen—he suddenly went completely blue in the face. He got a blanket to wrap round himself and, huddled up, looked about ten years old: "I'm a child of the tropics," he wailed.

A couple of days later he said he had a cold. When I went down to Homer End the following weekend he was more noticeably afflicted. "My stomach is like a calabash," he proclaimed, drumming rather proudly on his swollen middle. He also talked more plaintively, in the manner of a forlorn infant, about his ailments. He had a cough and his feet were numb; when we went for a walk with Elizabeth at the back of the house he moved stiffly, like a tin man, negotiating brambles with difficulty and needing help from his wife in climbing over a fence. At supper time he asked for milk, and

Elizabeth bent over him, trying to tempt him to eat by of-
fering pears in chocolate sauce.

When I visited him two months later at the end of April,
he was in bed, thin and subdued but volatile. He wanted to
show me a photograph and got up to look for it: as he
moved, his pyjama trousers slipped off his tiny back and bottom. He couldn't find the picture, and began to cry. Elizabeth was summoned from the kitchen to help, and they both
rustled through various boxes stuffed full of papers—one of
them, assembled during Bruce's illness, was labelled "Nice
Letters." "It'll turn up," Elizabeth consoled. "You always say
that," Bruce sobbed. He then suddenly became calm and
said: "It doesn't matter."

Kevin Volans was there on that occasion, and Bruce played
a tape of his music, excited by its buzzings, tappings and
rustlings—which he thought of as "the sounds of thorn-
scrub Africa." He listened to a diversity of music while he
was bed-ridden. He asked the young mezzo-soprano Tisi
Dutton, the daughter of his Australian friend Nin Dutton, to
come to Homer End to sing for him: remembering Bruce at
this time as "always scheming to bring people together," she
thinks he also wanted Volans to hear her voice; she sang some
Brahms, some Schubert and some Fauré. Francis Wyndham
and James Fox made him a tape which included music from
Mali and "Parlez-moi d'amour," sung—as it is sung in *Utz*—
by Lucienne Boyer. He enthused about the songs of Cole
Porter, and about Poulenc's mischievous, mellifluous Clar-
inet Sonata.

His taste in contemporary music has been characterised by
the composer Michael Berkeley as "ubiquitous and fastidious." He liked Giles Swayne's big choral work, *Cry*. He was
fascinated by Peter Maxwell Davies's *A Mirror of Whitening
Light*, a piece written for the London Sinfonietta whose title
and intention—to celebrate the Northern light of Hoy in the

Orkneys as it meets the water—might suggest a Henry Vaughan poem. *A Mirror of Whitening Light* is turbulent and densely-textured, the opposite of Volans's stripped-down style. But both composers have a strong visual tendency—Volans nearly became a painter rather than a musician—which attracted Chatwin. It is a tendency apparent in the imaginative narrative titles that Volans gives his works: "Cover him with grass," "Kneeling Dance," "She who sleeps with a small blanket." Bruce enjoyed supplying Volans with further titles: he suggested that a work might be named after a pair of bright pink earrings in the shape of fuchsias which I once wore when visiting him.

Volans, who studied with Stockhausen in Cologne and has also been influenced by Zulu guitar music, brings together the music of Europe and Africa. One of his string quartets contains "windows" of natural noises—cowbells, cicadas, birdsong—recorded in Africa; another is based on the sounds of Basotho people at work—splitting logs, singing, road-building, shouting. A number of his compositions have a walking rhythm, and it was his idea that he might base a theatre piece on *The Songlines* which led to his first meeting with Chatwin. He had sent Bruce a letter with a tape of his music; Bruce had rung him in Belfast, where Volans was composer-in-residence at Queen's University, and invited him to Homer End. The day after his arrival, both men having decided that *The Songlines* was insufficiently dramatic for theatrical treatment, Chatwin suggested another subject: the death of Rimbaud. This was to lead to the making of a short opera, which can be seen to embody an oblique portrait of Bruce Chatwin in his last few months.

There are quotations by and about Rimbaud in Chatwin's notebooks, and he had previously wanted to write a play on the poet's death. But he was too weak to undertake the libretto for Volans. He got round the difficulty by enlisting the pen of Roger Clarke, who had shortly before sent Bruce some of his poems and visited him in hospital. As Volans and Clarke greeted each other, Bruce beamed from his wheelchair: "This is a *momentous* occasion."

The opera which resulted from their collaboration was entitled by Chatwin "The Man with Footsoles of Wind"—a translation of Verlaine's description of Rimbaud—but was first performed, at the Almeida Theatre in Islington, North London, as *The Man Who Strides the Wind*. Volans and Clarke devised a piece in two parts: the first shows Rimbaud ill in bed at his mother's farmhouse, and later in a Marseilles hospital, where he dies; in the second act, he is travelling through the Ethiopian desert with his servant and companion Djami. Volans aimed in his music to show a distinction between the two parts of the opera: the European episode was complicated and "neurotic"; in the African section he had in mind Chatwin's description of *The Songlines* as "an imaginary conversation on an imaginary journey"; he also had in mind an African textile, with "completely different patterns juxtaposed suddenly and dramatically." Clarke's libretto drew on conversations with Chatwin and quotations from his notebooks, on Rimbaud's last piece of work, *Une Saison en enfer*, and on Hesiod and the Bible.

Chatwin is evident in certain of the opera's central preoccupations and visual ideas. He was fascinated by the picture of Rimbaud, returning to France from Africa, having suffered from syphilis, now dying of a tumour, lying in his mother's living-room in a tent of Ethiopian hangings. The opera opens with this picture. He was intrigued by the notion of Djami, Rimbaud's servant and companion, poring over his master's manuscripts at night: this image went into the second act. He had always been interested in Rimbaud's last letter, dictated to his sister the day before he died. The letter—in which Rimbaud seems in delirium to think himself back in his days of African trading but which also conveys a suggestion of ghostlier ferries—formed the climax of the opera's first act, which ended with its words: "So send me the list of fares from Aphinar to Suez. I am completely paralysed: therefore I wish to be embarked early. Tell me at what time I must be carried on board."

Throughout, there are episodes which echo Chatwin's life; the opera becomes his last songline. When the notoriously severe Madame Rimbaud comes to her son's bedside she is experienced by him as a malign force. When Bruce was dying he was fearful of an unidentified woman: "Keep her away from me," he groaned—but no one knew who she was. He was convinced that Rimbaud's sister, thinking the poet raging with fever, had failed to take down a poem he tried to dictate to her as he lay dying. Bruce was to appeal to Volans in his last months: "They think I'm mad: you must get me out. I'm not mad at all, I'm just thinking too fast for them. They can't keep up."

He was fascinated by Rimbaud's abrupt renunciation of poetry at the age of twenty, and expounded a theory to explain it. According to Bruce, Rimbaud—after his teenage years with Verlaine, absinthe and hashish—was on the verge of a nervous breakdown. He had denied having a homosexual affair with Verlaine, by whom he had been shot and wounded; he had completed his long, last, hectic piece of work, and begun a dizzying round of travels, first in Europe and subsequently through Egypt, Aden, Abyssinia and the Somalian desert. His travels, thought Bruce, were a way of walking away from madness and back to health: he himself believed that if he could regain the use of his legs and walk again he could be cured.

"*Je devins un opéra fabuleux*," Rimbaud proclaims in *Une Saison en enfer*. This work—with its wildernesses, red glades, its drums and its burnings—was crucial to Bruce's idea of Rimbaud, and to the opera about him. He read *Une Saison en enfer* as a statement of intent, a "songline" in which Rimbaud turned his back on absinthe and imagined his future travels in Africa. It is also a catalogue of the physical disorders consequent on Rimbaud's condition. Some of these were shared by Bruce:

> *Ah! les poumons brûlent, les tempes grondent! la nuit roule*
> *dans mes yeux . . .*
> *La peau de ma tête se dessèche . . .*
> *Les hallucinations sont innombrables . . .*
> *Je suis maître en fantasmagories.*

Eventually Bruce announced that *he* would have to sing the part of Rimbaud.

Bruce Chatwin died, as Arthur Rimbaud had died, in the South of France. He had been staying with Elizabeth for the last weeks of 1988 in Shirley Conran's house near Grasse: when his bed was wheeled onto the terrace, he wore, his hostess remembers, "a little hat like you give to premature babies." Kevin Volans was also staying there, and on Saturday 14 January George and Diana Melly arrived with Francis Wyndham for the weekend. Elizabeth had been hoping that they would be able to accompany her and Bruce back to London. A bed was found for Bruce in the Lighthouse, the hospice in Ladbroke Grove for people with AIDS, but it wasn't clear that an airline would agree to fly him. In any case, he was becoming too weak to travel.

He spoke very little that weekend, and when food was put into his mouth it just lay on his tongue. He said: "You're hurting me," when someone touched him; he said he was frightened of a face that kept appearing to him; his eyes were open even when he was asleep; he had spells of groaning. A doctor came from Grasse to examine him; a homoeopathic practitioner from Devon was also in attendance. Elizabeth had gathered bunches of jasmine, and an orchid was placed in Bruce's room. His friends took it in turns to sit with him to relieve Elizabeth.

On Sunday morning he was taken, sleeping peacefully, out onto the terrace to lie in the sun. An anxious amount of food was prepared in the course of that Sunday. Elizabeth cooked fish pie for the vegetarians, stew for the meat-eaters, soup and a coddled egg for Bruce. Shirley Conran made cabbage and bacon, fennel salad and potatoes Lyonnaise; she also ordered dishes to be sent up from the local restaurant. A Christmas pudding, put on to steam, boiled dry and burnt the saucepan.

In the small hours of Monday morning Bruce got worse: lying beside him in bed, Elizabeth heard the sound of his breathing change, and telephoned for an ambulance; at half-past three he was carried on a stretcher down the long flight of steps leading from the house. He spent his time in hospital in a coma. He died on Wednesday 18 January 1989.

During his months of moving in and out of hospital in England, Bruce had kept with him a prayer by David Jones. In plain lettering on a piece of white vellum this said: "SANCTE MICHÄEL ARCHANGELE DEFENDE NOS IN PROELIO UT NON PEREAMUS IN TREMENDO IUDICIO"—"May the blessed Archangel Michael defend us in battle lest we perish in the terrible judgment." It had hung in all the places he had lived in since Albany; now it hung over his hospital beds. He had also been receiving instruction from the Greek Orthodox priest in Oxford. He sometimes said he wanted to become a monk, and he was desperate to revisit the Orthodox monastery on Mount Athos; he spoke in fever of regaining his health as a silent black cat within the white walls of a monastery. Elizabeth arranged for a Greek Orthodox priest to conduct his funeral in the South of France.

She also organised an Orthodox service of commemoration in the Greek Cathedral of Saint Sophia, in West London's Moscow Road. At 2:30 on 14 February the building—high-domed and dark—was full. There were many writers among the congregation, but this was a religious service, not a literary homage. Black-robed, long-bearded priests paced the church swinging censers and talking of lost sheep, eternal rest and the end of pain. There was no encomium, no evocation of the man who had died. No one got up to praise his gift for finding stories and for condensing these stories into startling images. No one spoke about his talent for making people look at things. No one said how much his conversation lifted the spirits of his friends. And no one warned that the praise he was lucky enough to get during his lifetime would be paid for later in years of journalistic cutting-down-to-size. You might say that Bruce was absent from his service, rather as Flaubert said that the artist should be absent from his work. And yet that absence seemed to fill the church with his qualities.

Bruce Chatwin would have enjoyed the formal and hermetic nature of the occasion. Some, like Martin Amis, saw the ritual as Bruce's "last joke on his friends and loved ones: his heterodox theism had finally homed in on a religion that no one he knew could understand or respond to." Some thought its theatricality—the robes and the censers—camp. Some found it beautiful. It was a mysterious day—as Bruce was mysterious, and capriciously elusive. It was paradoxical, bringing together austerity and a metropolitan bustle. And it produced its own stories—its comic coincidences and uncertain identities.

Peter Eyre, acting as an usher, had come to the cathedral in the middle of rehearsing *King Lear* at the Old Vic: he was playing Edgar and had dressed in clothes which would allow him to roll around as Poor Tom, Edgar's other self, before going smartly to the service: he wore black exercise pants, a black jacket and a black sweatshirt, all from Issey Miyake; a tip of white T-shirt peeped out at the back of his neck, and he had a beard. In these clothes he discovered another alias. As he started to give out programmes, he was approached about the possibility of converting to the Orthodox Church, asked about an Orthodox bishop, consulted as an expert. The actor had become a priest.

An hour and a half before the service began, Radio 4 had given the news of the fatwa pronounced on Salman Rushdie by Ayatollah Khomeini. Rushdie, friendly with Chatwin since their peregrinations in Australia, turned up at the service. As he made his way out at the end, journalists were making their way in, peering into any tanned face in search of the Rushdie features: Tom Maschler was under particular scrutiny. Paul Theroux was to offer Rushdie some advice: "Keep your head down, Salman, or next week we'll be back here for you." Martin Amis pointed out that the fatwa was a serious matter. A few months before, Bruce, acting as intermediary in a quarrel between Rushdie and a friend, had warned that he wasn't hopeful of an easy resolution of the quarrel. "We're up against the Muslim inability to forgive," he explained.

Bruce Chatwin had wanted to write an English opera in which no words of English were spoken. In Saint Sophia's he became part of one. The English ears of the congregation could recognise among the foreign pleas only one familiar repeated word: "Bruce."

ACKNOWLEDGMENTS

I am grateful to the following people: Martin Amis, Gabriele Annan, Noel Annan, Colin Anson, Eve Arnold, Murray Bail, Barbara Bailey, Sybille Bedford, Michael Berkeley, Bruce Bernard, Gloria Birkett, Georges Borchardt, Roberto Calasso, Carmen Callil, Michael Cannon, Diana di Carcaci, Pascal Cariss, Gertrude Chanler, the late Charles Chatwin, Elizabeth Chatwin, Hugh Chatwin, the late Margharita Chatwin, Anne Chisholm, Shirley Conran, Michael Crick, Robyn Davidson, Michael Davie, Hunter Davies, Yvette Day, Nell Dunn, Tisi Dutton, Stephen Edwards, Barbara Epstein, Robert Erskine, Peter Eyre, Richard Eyre, Alexis, Daniel, Louisa and Lucie de la Falaise, Magouche Fielding, Kate Foster, James Fox, Dan Frank, Dan Franklin, Benny Gannon, John Garratt, Christopher Gibbs, Sarah Giles, Sue Goodhew, Matthew Graves, Vanessa Green, Ian Hamilton, Elizabeth Hardwick, Simon Harpur, Mary Hayward, Shirley Hazzard, Derek Hill, Tim Hilton, Christopher Hitchens, Howard Hodgkin, Alan Hollinghurst, Jonathan Hope, Robert Hughes, Michael Ignatieff, Liz Jobey, Diane Johnson, Kasmin, David King, Francis King, C. R. King-Farlow, Magnus Linklater, Marcus Linell, Celia Lowenstein, Candida Lycett-Green, Lydia Livingstone, Katherine MacLean, Don McCullin, Tom Maschler, Sonny Mehta, Diana Melly, George Melly, John Michell, David Miller, June Miller, Karl Miller, the late Teddy Millington-Drake, Beatrice Monti, Nicholas Murray, David Nash, Felicity Nicholson, Redmond O'Hanlon, Sarah Papineau, the late Stuart Piggott, Nicholas Rankin, Gregor von Rezzori, John Richardson, Elizabeth Riddell, David Rieff, Deborah Rogers, Hannah Rothschild, Miranda Rothschild, Salman Rushdie, John Ryle, Caroline Sandwich, Richard Sennett, Elisabeth Sifton, Sunil Sethi, Susan Sontag, Terence Stamp, the late Francis Steegmuller, Michel Strauss, Jeremy Swift, Emma Tennant, Jennie Tierney, Claire Tomalin, Maggie Traugott, Penelope Tree, Patrick Trevor-Roper, Petronella Vaarzon-Morel, Hugo Vickers, Kevin Volans, Valerie Wade, Shelley Wanger, Marina Warner, Cary Welch, Edmund White, Martin Wilkinson, Stella Wilkinson, Francis Wyndham.

Extracts from Bruce Chatwin's unpublished material are reproduced by kind permission of Elizabeth Chatwin. Extracts from Hugo Vickers's unpublished diary are reproduced by kind permission of the author. My account of *L'Homme aux Semelles de Vent (The Man Who Strides the Wind)* draws on published writings on the subject.

A NOTE ON THE TYPE

This book was set in a version of the well-known Monotype face Bembo. This letter was cut for the celebrated Venetian printer Aldus Manutius by Francesco Griffo, and was first used in Pietro Cardinal Bembo's *De Aetna* of 1495.

The companion italic is an adaptation of the chancery script type designed by the calligrapher and printer Lodovico degli Arrighi.

FOR THE BEST IN PAPERBACKS, LOOK FOR THE

In every corner of the world, on every subject under the sun, Penguin represents quality and variety—the very best in publishing today.

For complete information about books available from Penguin—including Puffins, Penguin Classics, and Arkana—and how to order them, write to us at the appropriate address below. Please note that for copyright reasons the selection of books varies from country to country.

In the United Kingdom: Please write to *Dept. JC, Penguin Books Ltd, FREEPOST, West Drayton, Middlesex UB7 0BR.*

If you have any difficulty in obtaining a title, please send your order with the correct money, plus ten percent for postage and packaging, to *P.O. Box No. 11, West Drayton, Middlesex UB7 0BR*

In the United States: Please write to *Consumer Sales, Penguin USA, P.O. Box 999, Dept. 17109, Bergenfield, New Jersey 07621-0120.* VISA and MasterCard holders call 1-800-253-6476 to order all Penguin titles

In Canada: Please write to *Penguin Books Canada Ltd, 10 Alcorn Avenue, Suite 300, Toronto, Ontario M4V 3B2*

In Australia: Please write to *Penguin Books Australia Ltd, P.O. Box 257, Ringwood, Victoria 3134*

In New Zealand: Please write to *Penguin Books (NZ) Ltd, Private Bag 102902, North Shore Mail Centre, Auckland 10*

In India: Please write to *Penguin Books India Pvt Ltd, 706 Eros Apartments, 56 Nehru Place, New Delhi 110 019*

In the Netherlands: Please write to *Penguin Books Netherlands bv, Postbus 3507, NL-1001 AH Amsterdam*

In Germany: Please write to *Penguin Books Deutschland GmbH, Metzlerstrasse 26, 60594 Frankfurt am Main*

In Spain: Please write to *Penguin Books S.A., Bravo Murillo 19, 1° B, 28015 Madrid*

In Italy: Please write to *Penguin Italia s.r.l., Via Felice Casati 20, I-20124 Milano*

In France: Please write to *Penguin France S.A., 17 rue Lejeune, F-31000 Toulouse*

In Japan: Please write to *Penguin Books Japan, Ishikiribashi Building, 2-5-4, Suido, Bunkyo-ku, Tokyo 112*

In Greece: Please write to *Penguin Hellas Ltd, Dimocritou 3, GR-106 71 Athens*

In South Africa: Please write to *Longman Penguin Southern Africa (Pty) Ltd, Private Bag X08, Bertsham 2013*